D1085419

Also available

Pick of Punch
The Punch Book of Cricket
The Punch Book of Golf
The Punch Book of Utterly British Humour
The Punch Cartoon Album: 150 Years of Classic Cartoons
Punch Lines: 150 Years of Humorous Writing in Punch

PUNCH ON EUROPE

'Oh no! I've got a birthmark!'

Edited by
Amanda-Jane Doran

Foreword by
Miles Kington

HarperCollins*Publishers*

HarperCollins*Publishers*
77–85 Fulham Palace Road
Hammersmith, London W6 8JB

Published by HarperCollins*Publishers* 1992
9 8 7 6 5 4 3 2 1

A catalogue record for this book is
available from the British Library

ISBN 0 00 224061 0

Set in Plantin by
Rowland Phototypesetting Ltd
Bury St Edmunds, Suffolk

Printed in Great Britain by
HarperCollinsManufacturing Glasgow

CONTENTS

LIST OF CONTRIBUTORS

FOREWORD

by Miles Kington

To be honest, I don't think the British are ever going to feel really European. The fact of the matter is that most of them don't even feel *British* yet – they feel English, Welsh, Scottish or Irish. I can't remember ever having heard a sports crowd shouting 'Come on, Britain!' So the European finishing post, that mark beyond which we will all get prizes for feeling European, is even further away. And as evidence I would like to ask for Exhibit A to be produced: this book. The very fact that a British publisher can cheerfully offer a humorous book about Europe suggests that he thinks of Europe as somewhere else, and Europeans as someone else. Can you imagine a French publisher producing a book of cartoons about Europe? Or an Italian humorous book about being European? I don't think it would strike them as being worth joking about – it's just a fact of life.

Mark you, we British feel that we *ought* to feel European. We go through twinning ceremonies with French villages and German towns (I have heard it said that Basingstoke is twinned with a huge roundabout near Darmstadt), and we have programmes on TV and radio called 'Eurofile' and 'Hello Europe', and we worry constantly about being banned from European football, and we try very hard to take an interest in what's happening over there, but it *is* an effort. It's an effort even getting there, all that queuing to get on ships and planes and things, whereas if you live in Italy or Spain you can just slip across a border. We don't *know* what it's like to slip across a border. When I was on holiday in Provence in 1990, the year the World Cup was being held in Italy, I was taken aback by a notice in the local town square: 'Bus trip to the World Cup next Saturday! Brazil v Costa Rica in Turin! Gents, see the game – girls, go for a shopping spree!' I was British enough to find the concept of slipping across the border to see a bit of World Cup pretty hard to grasp.

The silly thing is that nothing is ever quite as British as it seems. *Punch*, you might think, was as British as you could get, but look at the old subtitle: '*Punch*, or the *London Charivari*'. *Charivari* was the name of a French magazine, which the first editors of *Punch* were trying to emulate, so it must have been well-known to English readers in 1841. Mr Punch himself was directly descended from Italian ancestors, and however hard they tried for 150 years to domesticate the old man with the big nose, paunch and randy eye, there was always something odd and foreign about him. We have never objected to European things over here in Britain, as long as we were given the chance to adopt them and pretend they were really British all along. There could be nothing more British than Madame Tussaud's, that palace of passing wax fame, and I don't suppose it occurs to more than one Briton in a million that it is a French import. (If it did, he would find it ironic that at any time of the day or night there seem to be 1,000 French students queuing to get in.)

I have seen this process at work in the near past, at a boules tournament in Bath, where the British contestants knew that they were playing a French game but *felt* that they should play it in a British way. Several of the best teams were entered by French restaurants in Bath, and they had all played the game from birth, but we all felt there was something a bit too French about the way they shouted, and sank to their knees to launch their boules, and exclaimed in horror or ecstasy. As the French teams were knocked out one by one, and the final turned out to be between a Chinese restaurant and an English café, we felt rather that the natural order of things had been restored. That a Chinese team should do so well seemed not at all odd, because briefly the Chinese were our allies against the French.

Alliances come and go. At the moment the best reason for feeling European is the threat of the big neighbour across the pond, the USA, without whom we would all feel much less European. But during the 150 years covered by this book things have changed constantly within European borders. Germany has made several more or less successful attempts to invade France and on most, though not all, occasions, we have come to help rescue France. Just before *Punch* started, of course, France had invaded Germany and we were helping the Germans to get rid of Napoleon . . . And as I write this in mid-1992, things are still not peaceful. Every day, in Queen's Square, Bath, squads of foreigners are practising to beat the English. They are the French kitchen staff of Le Beaujolais Restaurant, thirsting for revenge for last year's boules disaster. I will try to get the result printed here, if there is another edition of this book.

Meanwhile, also as I write this, England are about to play Sweden in the European Football Cup, knowing that the side that wins will go through. A sportswriter in the papers says that after the ferocious displays by the English fans and the boring display by the English footballers, everyone out there is hoping that Sweden will win and knock England out. In other words, the English *are* a force for European unity, even if it is against us. It is nice to know that we *do* have a role in Europe.

1

THE DARK CONTINENT

Mrs Thatcher's
EUROPE
OPEN FOR BUSINESS
Map
DON'T TAKE ANY NONSENSE. IF THEY WON'T ORDER, THREATEN TO START EXPORTING JEHOVAH'S WITNESSES
THE WATCH TOWER
It's brick-proof and sound-proof, just what you need for the return of the British football fans!
ANGLO DOUBLE GLAZING
IF THE CHUNNEL ISN'T FINISHED, START DIGGING YOUR OWN
Naturally we wouldn't call them condoms, we'd export them to you as 'Willy Warmers'!
BRITISH RUBBER CO
It's cheap and there's an endless supply of it!
H of C HOT AIR
A must for everyone in the Common Market - you can even find Luxemburg with it!
BRITISH OPTICS
With a few Irish brickies we'd have this lot rebuilt in no time!
DENMARK
Glasgow
IRELAND
Manchester
GREAT BRITAIN
London
NETHERLANDS
Hamburg
BRIT PEST CONTROL
REMEMBER, THE GERMANS LIKE TRADITIONAL METHODS
BELGIUM
Brussels
Bonn
WEST GERMANY
Munich
With British boots wine-pressing needn't be labour-intensive!
Brest
Paris
FRANCE
AND DON'T FORGET THAT PINOCCHIO IS AN OLD ITALIAN STORY
Milan
Nice
Bordeaux
Florence
And of course copies of Hansard can also be used to build dams in Venice, etc, etc...
IDEAL FOR TEXTILE SALES BUT BE CAREFUL WITH YOUR SAMPLES
BEWARE OF SHARKS
ITALY
It's a kind of financial aphrodisiac, it makes you want to take over every business in sight!
GUINNESS
Naples
PORTUGAL
Barcelona
We haven't got a Terry Venables in stock, but what about this amazing Third Division manager?
BARCELONA F.C.
Lisbon
SPAIN
Malaga
SICILY
CONCRETE BOOTS WOULD GO DOWN WELL HERE

Alan Coren

ALL YOU NEED TO KNOW ABOUT EUROPE

Germany

The People

Germans are split into two broad categories: those with tall spikes on their hats, and those with briefcases. Up until 1945, the country's history was made by those with spikes. After 1945, it was made by those with briefcases. In common with the rest of Europe, its history is therefore now known as economics. Ethnically, the Germans are Teutonic, but prefer not to talk about it any more. This ethnos was originally triform, being made up of Vandals, Gepidae, and Goths, all of whom emigrated south from Sweden in about 500 BC; why they emigrated is not exactly clear, but many scholars believe it was because they saw the way Sweden was going, i.e. neutral. Physically, Germans are tall and blond, though not as tall and blond as they sometimes think, especially when they are short, dark Austrians with a sense of destiny. When they sing, the Germans link arms and rock sideways; it is best described as horizontal marching.

The Land

The country, or *Lebensraum*, is extremely beautiful and situated in the very centre of Europe, thus lending itself to expansion in any direction, a temptation first succumbed to in the fifth century AD when Germany embraced most of Spain, and regularly indulged in since. It is interesting to note that this summer there will be three million Germans in Spain, thus outnumbering the first excursion by almost a hundred to one.

The History

For almost two thousand years, Germany was split into separate states that fought one another. In the nineteenth century, they combined and began fighting everyone else. They are currently split up again and once more fighting one another. If they combine, the result is anybody's guess. Having lost the last war, they are currently enjoying a *Wirtschaftswunder*, which can be briefly translated as 'The best way to own a Mercedes is to build one.' That is about all there is to German history, since no one has ever known what was going on, and if this is the case, then the Truth cannot be said to exist. Germany has, as you can see, provided many of the world's greatest philosophers.

France

The People

The French are our closest neighbours, and we are therefore bound to them by bonds of jealousy, suspicion, competition, and envy. They haven't brought the shears back, either. They are short, blue-vested people who carry their own onions when cycling abroad, and have a yard which is 3.37 inches longer than other people's. Their vanity does not stop there: they believe themselves to be great lovers, an easy trap to fall into when you're permanently drunk, and the natural heirs to Europe. It has been explained to them that there is a difference between natural heirs and legitimate heirs, but they cannot appreciate subtle distinctions, probably because French has the smallest vocabulary of any language in Europe.

The Land

France is the largest country in Europe, a great boon for drunks, who need room to fall, and consists of an enormous number of bars linked by an intricate system of serpentine cobbles. Exactly why France is so cobbled

'Who, I wonder, has right of way in this part of Europe? The Germans or the French?'

has never been fully explained, though most authorities favour the view that the French like to be constantly reminded of the feel of grapes underfoot. The houses are all shuttered to exclude light, as a precaution against hangovers, and filled with large lumpy beds in which the French spend 83.7 per cent of their time recovering from sex or booze or both. The lumpiness is due, of course, to the presence of undeclared income under the mattresses.

The History

French history, or 'gloire', starts with Charlemagne, and ends with Charlemagne. Anything subsequent was in the hands of bizarre paranoiacs who thought they were God (Louis XIV) or thought they were Charlemagne (Napoleon) or thought they were God and Louis XIV and Charlemagne and Napoleon (de Gaulle). Like most other European nations, the French have fought everyone, but unlike the rest have always claimed that both victories and defeats came after opposition to overwhelming odds. This is probably because they always saw two of everything.

Belgium

The People

Belgium is the most densely populated country in Europe, and is at the same time fiercely divided on the subjects of language and religion. This means that it is impossible to move anywhere in the country, which is packed with mobs standing chin to chin and screaming incomprehensible things at one another in the certain knowledge that God is on their side, whoever He is. That there has not been more bloodshed is entirely because there isn't room to swing a fist. Consequently, what the Belgian authorities most fear is contraception: if it ever catches on, and the population thins to the point where rifles may be comfortably unslung from shoulders, the entire nation might disappear overnight.

The Land

The land is entirely invisible, except in the small hours of the morning, being for the rest of the time completely underfoot. It is therefore no surprise to learn that Belgium's largest industries are coal and mineral mining, as underground is the only place where there is room to work. Plans have been suggested for reclaiming land from the sea, on the Dutch pattern, but were always shelved as soon as it was realised that there was neither room for the water that would have to be removed from the sea, nor alternatively, any spare land to spread to extend the coastline outwards.

The History

Belgium has always suffered horribly at the hands of occupying forces, which, given the overcrowding, is only to be expected. The bayoneting of babies by Prussians, for example, was never intentional; it was simply that it was impossible to walk about with fixed bayonets in such confined spaces without finding something stuck on the end of them.

Netherlands

The People

As one might expect of a race that evolved underwater and subsisted entirely upon cheese, the Dutch are somewhat single-minded, conservative, resilient, and thoughtful. Indeed, the sea informs their entire culture: the bicycle, the ubiquitous Dutch vehicle, was designed to facilitate underwater travel, offering least resistance to waves and weed, the clog was introduced to weigh down the feet and prevent drifting, and the meerschaum pipe, with its characteristic lid, was designed expressly to exclude fish and the larger plankton. And those who would accuse the Dutch of overeating would do well to reflect on the notorious frangibility of dykes: it's no joke being isolated atop a flooded windmill with nothing to eat but passing tulips. You have to get it while you can.

The Land

Strictly speaking, the land does not exist: it is merely dehydrated sea, and concern was originally expressed when the EEC was first mooted that the Six might suddenly turn into the Five after a bad night. Many informed observers believe that this fear is all that lies behind the acceptance of Britain's membership, i.e. we are a sort of First Reserve in case Rain Stops Holland. Nevertheless, it is interesting country, sweeping up from the coastal plain into the central massif, a two-foot high ridge of attractive silt with fabulous views of the sky, and down again to the valleys, inches below. Apart from cheese and tulips, the main product of the country is advocaat, a drink made from lawyers.

The History

Incensed by poor jokes about the Low Countries, the Dutch, having emerged from the sea, became an extremely belligerent people, taking on Spain, France, England, and Austria in quick succession, a characteristic that has almost entirely disappeared from the modern Dutch temperament. It is now found only among expatriate Dutchmen, like Orangemen and Afrikaaners.

Luxembourg

The People

There are nine people in Luxembourg, and they are kept pretty busy making stamps. It is not the smallest country in Europe: there are only eight people in Monaco, five in Andorra, and Herr J. F. Klausner in Liechtenstein, so as the fourth non-smallest country in Europe, it enjoys a rather unique position. The people are of middle height, with the small, deft fingers of master-perforators, and all look rather alike, except for their Uncle Maurice who lost an ear on the Somme. They are a rather arrogant people (they refer to World War I as the Battle of Maurice's Ear) but not unartistic: *My Day At The Zoo*, by the country's infant prodigy, ran into nine copies and won the Prix Maurice for 1969.

The Land

On a clear day, from the terrace of the Salon de Philatélie, you can't see Luxembourg at all. This is because a tree is in the way. Beyond the tree lies Belgium. The centre of the country is, however, very high, mainly because of the chimney on it, and slopes down to a great expanse of water, as they haven't got around to having the bathroom overflow pipe fixed. The climate is temperate (remember that 90 per cent of Luxembourg is indoors) and the local Flora is varied and interesting, especially on her favourite topic, the 1908 five-cent blue triangular.

The History

Old Luxembourg (now the coal-cellar of the modern country) was founded in the twelfth century by King John of Bohemia, who wanted somewhere to keep the lawn-mower. It escaped most of the wars and pestilences that swept Europe in the subsequent eight centuries, often because the people were out when they called, and is therefore one of the most stable political and economic elements in the EEC: its trade-balance is always favourable (imports come in at the back gate and leave by the front door as exports). Luxembourg is also the oldest ally of Stanley Gibbons Ltd., although it is probably most famous as the birthplace of Horace Batchelor.

Italy

The People

The median Italian, according to the latest figures of the Coren Intelligence Unit, is a cowardly baritone who consumes 78.3 kilometres of carbohydrates a month and drives about in a car slightly smaller than he is, looking for a divorce. He is governed by a stable conservative government, called the Mafia, who operate an efficient police force, called the Mafia, which is the official arm of the judiciary, called the Mafia. The Italians are a cultivated folk, and will often walk miles to sell a tourist a copy of the Sistine Chapel ceiling made entirely from sea-shells. They invented the mandoline, a kind of boudoir banjo shaped like a woman's bottom, not surprisingly.

The Land

Italy is boot-shaped, for reasons lost in the mists of geology. The South is essentially agricultural, and administered by local land authorities, called the Mafia; the North is industrial, and run by tightly interlocked corporations, called the Mafia. The largest Italian city is New York, and is linked to the mainland by a highly specialised and efficient communications system, called the Mafia.

The History

Italy was originally called Rome, which came to hold power over Europe by moving into new areas every week or so and threatening to lean on them if they did not fork out tithe (L. *protectio*). It was run by a series of Caesars (Eduardus Gaius Robinsonius, Georgius Raftus, Paulus Munius, etc.) who held sway until the Renaissance, when Leonardo invented the tank and the aeroplane, and thus ushered in modern Italy (in World War II, the Italians, ever brilliant, possessed the only tank with a reverse gear). In the 1920s, the Caesars reasserted themselves in their two main linear branches, the Caponi and the

Mussolini, whose symbol was the fasces, which signified 'United We Stand,' but they didn't.

1974

Sean O'Sullivan

EUROPE

The Dark Continent

West Germans are . . .

DEATH MERCHANTS: West German business's dedication to the ethic 'Greed is good' and the Government's ability to look the other way deserve a special 'Angel of Death' award. What follows is a brief list of countries that West Germany has generously provided with arms:
Libya: a poison gas plant, ballistic missile technology, in-flight refuelling capability.
Iraq: poison gas, nuclear weapons technology/ supplies.
Egypt: nuclear weapons technology/supplies.
Israel: submarine technology.
South Africa: nuclear weapons technology/ supplies, blueprints for submarines.
Argentina: nuclear weapons technology/supplies, ballistic missile technology.
Brazil: nuclear weapons technology/supplies, chemicals for refining cocaine.
Colombia: chemicals for refining cocaine.
Pakistan: nuclear weapons technology/ supplies.
India: nuclear weapons technology/supplies.

SURPRISINGLY USELESS POLICEMEN: According to *The Scotsman*, 13 October 1989, the Keystone Cop-like bumbling of the West German police force (freeing Marwan 'I'm working for the Jordanians, honest' Khreesat) resulted in the terrorist attack on the Pan Am 747 that exploded over Lockerbie.

The French are . . .

TERRORISTS: French secret service agents were caught red-handed after blowing up the Greenpeace ship *Rainbow Warrior*. But no one in the Government suffered any disciplinary action except the two agents who were caught. Even then the punishment wasn't exactly severe. Instead of spending ten years in a New Zealand jail, they spent three years in temporary exile on a French military base in the Pacific. Despite New Zealand's protests, the best France had to offer was to ask one of the guilty to return voluntarily to his Pacific exile 'in the interest of French honour'.

RACIST: The French so dislike foreigners in their country that the Government recently offered any foreigners aged 45 and older £2,500 a year (plus travel expenses) until aged 60 to return home. And that was from the Liberals. The right wing just wanted 'forcible repatriation'.

INCOMPETENT: While the Government want all the foreigners out, they are none too concerned with a group which most of France would consider even more undesirable: criminals. Last year, two out of three sentenced to jail never served their terms because of police inertia and red tape. Escaping French justice is apparently as simple as giving a bogus address.

UNWASHED: A scientific study has proved that the French, in general, smell bad. Whereas Britons buy an average of eight bars of soap a year (the US buy 11) the French only buy 3.5. Only half the population uses deodorants. They only buy 1.5 tubes of toothpaste and one toothbrush per person per year. Not surprisingly, one in four never brush their teeth at all. It also seems that the French don't change their underwear: men get through just four pairs of underpants per year; women average five pairs of knickers and 1.5 brassières.

CARBUNCLES: The new round of French techno-architecture (I. M. Pei's glass pyramid at the Louvre, the new techno-Arc de

Triomphe, and the new Opéra) lends credence to Prince Charles's attacks on modern architecture.

NAFF: Three words: Jean-Michel Jarré.

The Spanish are . . .

DEADLY: Spain is very keen on laying death-traps for its tourists: a 50-mile road near Marbella on the Costa Del Sol ('The Highway of Death') has claimed more than 400 tourists in the past six years. The resort of Benidorm had no hospital for a long stretch during 1985. A report in *Holiday Watch* said that over half the holiday hotels they inspected in Spain were potential fire death-traps.

FILTHY: Six years ago, the World Health Organisation condemned nearly 40 per cent of the beaches along the Spanish coast for not meeting sanitary requirements.

POISONOUS: Two years ago poisoned Spanish cooking oil, being peddled by 38 oil merchants, killed 584 and affected more than 20,000, which prompted Reuters last May to comment: 'The illness was seen as the most glaring evidence of the low level of public health standards and inspection after nearly four decades of authoritarian rule.' Only two of the 38 defendants were convicted.

DRUG MERCHANTS: According to a recent TV report, Spain has become the drug warehouse for Europe, due to its Colombian connections. A drug lord, interviewed on the programme, explained that Europe was an untapped market for cocaine, and Spain was the ideal country from which to launch a marketing campaign.

MURDERERS: The Spanish Government has been accused of having links with a Death Squad, headquartered within its borders, that has executed at least 25 Basque refugees on French soil.

CORRUPT: On the financial front, deficient Spanish planning laws have led to widespread fraud on holiday property deals. The situation is currently being investigated by the European Parliament.

The Portuguese are . . .

JUST like the Spanish.

ILL-EQUIPPED: Five years ago there was a public outcry over the lack of hospital facilities, especially in resort areas. The hospitals were short on staff, supplies, and equipment, and ambulances often wasted precious time going from hospital to hospital to find one that would admit their patient.

'I think I've got xenophobia.'

POLLUTED: Four years ago Portugal's Ministry of Health was forced to close nine of its beaches because they had 'levels of pollution far exceeding EEC regulations'.

The Greeks are . . .

DISEASED: Medical treatment is so bad that in 1985 over 1,500 Greeks came to Britain seeking help. Large numbers also fled to West Germany and the United States.

INSECURE: Athens airport regularly tops the American Airline Pilots Association's list of the ten most dangerous airports.

INTOLERANT: Despite letting in the likes of Abu Nidal and countless other loonies with bombs from the Middle East, they won't allow in the annoying yet harmless Hari Krishnas.

FATTIST: And in further bizarre Grecian discrimination, they won't allow people who are '70 per cent heavier than average' to have drivers' licences.

BAD DRIVERS: Common Market statistics show that Greece has by far the worst traffic accident rate in the EC despite having the fewest cars.

The Belgians are . . .

JUST like the French.

XENOPHOBIC: The Belgians too are eager to bribe unwanted immigrants to go home. They are prepared to offer aliens up to £5,000 to scram, but not only must you leave Belgium, you must leave Europe.

TACTLESS: Souvenir shops on Belgian battlefields are selling live ammunition to tourists as mementos.

The Italians are . . .

WIRED: Last year it was revealed that the use of cocaine was common practice in the Italian Parliament to try to 'relieve the tedium and stress of political in-fighting'. One MP was quoted as saying, 'Yes, the cocaine certainly flows in the Senate.'

KINKY: This is perhaps what attracted Ilona Staller, a well-known star of pornographic films, to run for Parliament. Her campaign mainly consisted of stripping at a moment's notice for any cameras or potential voters. As the voters were Italian, she naturally won.

PERVERSE: A men's lifestyle magazine recently surveyed its readers to find the woman they'd most like to bed. Mrs Thatcher won.

DISREPUTABLE: The Fascists are still on the scene.

CRIMINAL: So is the Mafia.

INDECISIVE: Considering the above it is small wonder that Italy has had 49 governments since the end of World War II.

SLIMY: As a result of polluted waterways and dumping in the Adriatic, massive amounts of brown, nauseous algae – or 'sea-slime' – have virtually closed many seaside Italian tourist towns. In July, Pete Morris, the British pollution expert who last year dealt with the Alaskan oil spill, was called in. Locals are pessimistic, no doubt in the light of Morris's clean-up success in Alaska.

SICK: The World Health Organisation reported that Italy has the fastest-rising rate of AIDS cases in the world.

CRACKING UP: 'All over Italy cracks are appearing in domes and masonry; towers and palaces creak as the ancient foundations shift,' said *The Times* last March. That month a 900-year-old bell tower collapsed, and experts are predicting that the leaning tower of Pisa will soon topple.

SHIFTY: In a public opinion survey conducted in 1981, Italians ranked as 'the most distrustful and the least trusted members of the European Community'.

The Dutch are . . .

YOBS: Their soccer hooligans are now the worst in Europe: during a game on 22 October 1989, irate fans from Feyenoord of Rotterdam threw home-made fragmentation bombs into the stands of the fans of Ajax of Amsterdam.

DOPEHEADS: Many drugs which are illegal elsewhere are legal there. It is apparently not enough that these chemicals are legal; one company in fact has a home delivery service. Their name . . . Blow Home Couriers.

SEX-CRAZED: Where there are drugs and violence there must be seedy, insalubrious sex. Hard-core pornography was made legal in 1984. And though it was not made into law, the Government very seriously considered lowering the age of sexual consent to 12.

COWARDS: The head of the Dutch Police union advised his men to 'pack up and run' in the event of a terrorist attack because he felt that they were not sufficiently trained to deal with that sort of threat . . .

The Danes are . . .

JUST like the Dutch.

LOOPY: Denmark's national health service made prostitutes available to the 8,000 mentally and physically handicapped patients in its hospitals to 'help patients satisfy their sexual urges'.

SUICIDAL: You would think that the freedom Denmark affords its citizens would make them happy . . . but Denmark has one of the world's highest suicide rates.

TERMINALLY SILLY: Last year the Danish Air Force sent out a contract to build secret aircraft hangars (designed to hide NATO aircraft from Warsaw Pact attack) to an East German transport company . . .

And what of THE BRITISH? Well, according to the rest of Europe, they're . . . death merchants, terrorists, incompetent, unwashed, carbuncular, tactless, deadly, filthy, poisonous, drug merchants, murderers, corrupt, ill-equipped, polluted, wired, kinky, perverse, disreputable, criminal, indecisive, slimy, sick, cracking up, diseased, insecure, intolerant, fattist, bad drivers, yobs, dopeheads, sex-crazed, cowards, loopy, suicidal and terminally silly.

We think you're going to love 'em.

November 1989

Supporters' Phrase-Book: German Edition

EUROPEAN SOCCER CHAMPIONSHIP '88

At the Stadium

Would you be so good as to direct me to a bunch of innocent bystanders? – *Würden Sie so gut sein, mir den Weg nach einer harmlosen Zuschauergruppe zu zeigen?*

Two tickets for the stand, please. – *Zwei Tribünenplätze, bitte, Sonnenschein.*

It's not a piece of bent pipe, it's a straw. – *Das ist kein Stück Krummrohr, das ist ein Trinkhalm.*

Because I'm thirsty, you winkle. – *Weil ich Durst habe, Windbeutel.*

Hello, officer. What a nice uniform. – *Guten Tag, Herr Wachtmeister. Welch eine prächtige Uniform!*

Bring me another knife (fork, spoon, piece of bent pipe). – *Bringen sie mir noch ein Messer (eine Gabel, einen Löffel, ein Stück Krummrohr).*

While I was dining someone has taken my piece of bent pipe. – *Als ich speiste hat jemand mein Stück Krummrohr gestohlen.*

What do you mean, the British Consulate has been struck by Legionnaires' Disease? – *Was soll das bedeuten, das englische Konsulat soll von Legionspneumonie geplagt worden?*

At the All-Night Chemist's

Can you give yourself something for constipation, you old bat? – *Können Sie sich etwas für Verstopfung geben, alte Schlampe?*

General Difficulties

Is this a twenty-hole golf course, or are those your nostrils? – *Ist das ein zwanzig Loch Golfplatz, oder sind die deine Nasenlöcher?*

He says I hit him with my safety triangle. – *Er behauptet, dass ich ihn mit meinem Warndreieck geschlagen habe.*

You have a blown cylinder gasket. – *Dein Vergaser ist kaputt.*

No, I mean you personally. – *Nein, ich meine Dich persönlich, Sonnenschein.*

The sheets in my bed are damp. – *Die Laken in Meinem Bett sind feucht.*

That is an insulting suggestion. – *Das ist eine beleidigende Anspielung.*

At the Police Station

I want to make a confession. – *Ich will ein Geständnis machen.*

Not *the* Jack the Ripper, *a* Jack the Ripper. – *Nicht* der *Jacktheripper*, ein *Jacktheripper.*

My documents were hoovered up in a pub. – *Meine Papiere sind in einer Kneipe mit dem Staubsauger abgesogen.*

Your foot made contact with my shin in contravention of the Treaty of Rome. – *Ihr Fuss hat mein Schienbein entgegen den Vorschriften des Vertrags von Rom gestossen.*

Bring me a copy of the Treaty of Rome. – *Bringen Sie mir ein Examplar des Vertrags von Rom.*

Honest, Sergeant, I have never hit anyone with the Treaty of Rome in my life. – *Auf mein Wort, Herr Oberst, niemals im Leben habe ich einen mit dem Vertrag von Rom geschlagen.*

Mavis is not drunk, she was hit by a rattle. – *Mavis ist nich betrunken, sie wurde von einer Klapper getroffen.*

Not a rattlesnake, you pillock, a football rattle. – *Nein, keine Klapperschlange, Wirrkopf, sondern eine Fussballklapper.*

Well, somebody must have one. – *Ne, einer gibt es doch, der eine Klapper hat.*

What's an anachronism? – *Was ist ein Anachronismus?*

Tarrah. – *Hau ab, englischer Scheisskerl.*

June 1988

'It's no good – I just can't seem to think of myself as a European *yob.'*

LUXEMBOURG R. G. WILLIS SCORING HIS FIFTH 999 NOT OUT IN THE TEST SERIES WHICH ENGLAND WON 5–0.

Mahood

WHAT'S IN IT FOR ME?

DENMARK THE TOURIST BOARD HAS RESPONDED TO BRITISH COMPLAINTS ABOUT THE COUNTRY NOT LIVING UP TO EXPECTATIONS.

FRANCE PRESIDENT MITTERRAND HAS CREATED A SKIERS' PARADISE ON THIS MOUNTAIN OF FROZEN BRITISH LAMB, THE FIRST OF A WHOLE NEW GENERATION OF PURPOSE-BUILT RESORTS FOR BRITISH FARMERS.

The Esperanto Song

YOUR HOLIDAY SONGSHEET

Ci tie ni funkcii giri!
Ci tie ni funkcii giri!
Ni volo nun kanti Esperanto.
Ci tie ni funkcii giri!
Ci tie ni funkcii giri!
Ni areo de magnifico Britisha Yobo!
Neniu de us iz de individuo.
Ni cio havi la cerbo de an oboro!
Ci tie ni funkcii giri!
Ci tie ni funkcii giri!
Ni areo hero de fankas de supra-loco!
De gobbo an pizzo el de hotelo fenestro!
Ni aero hero de scraubo, mangi an trinki nin idioto.
An moono fromo el pedalo an luado motorcyklo
An do fugaritos ela de restauranto
Ne de mentiono ponardo de odo Dago!
Ci tie ni funkcii giri!
Ci tie ni funkcii giri!
Ni iri eksterland de miskonduito –
Ni areo a bukedo de kamparano.
Ni navi ne intellectuo.
Ni areo de odori, malica bubego.
An ni pagi fora it cio mem nos senlaboreco Giro!
Ci tie ni funkcii giri!
Ci tie ni funkcii giri!
Ni penso gi iz vera malmolo
Teni homoj ver en nockto.
Pereigno de disco an baro
An kauzo an gusta genago
An uzi de abomina linguo
An generallo runiga ciu's fero.
Ne facto gi iz sub ciu niveto
Ne wondro ciu is goja iro heymo.
Ni areo moronico dickkapo.
Ci tie ni funkcii giri!
Ci tie ni funkcii giri!

(ENGLISH TRANSLATION)
Here we go!
Here we go!
We will now sing Esperanto.
Here we go!
Here we go!
We are the great British yob!
None of us is an individual.
We all have the brain of a lobster!
Here we go!
Here we go!
We are here to smash up the place!
To spit and urinate from our hotel window!
We are here to pork, eat and drink ourselves silly.
We do moonies from pedaloes and hired mopeds
And do runners from restaurants
Not to mention to stab the odd Spanish gentleman!
Here we go! Here we go!
We go abroad to misbehave –
We are a bunch of peasants.
We have no intelligence.
We are smelly, malicious louts.
And we pay for it all with our unemployment benefit!
Here we go!
Here we go!
We think it's really tough
To keep people awake at nights.
To wreck discos and bars
And cause a right nuisance of ourselves
And to use such foul language
And generally ruin everyone else's holiday.
In fact it's really quite pathetic
No wonder everyone's glad to see us go home.
We are moronic dickheads.
Here we go!
Here we go!

June 1988

David Thomas

PLANE SAILING

Something like 15,000 of the people who buy this particular issue of *Punch* will do so at a British airport. And for those 15,000 people I have one simple question . . . why?

Not, 'Why are you buying this magazine?' That's obvious; you're buying it because you are a person of rare taste and distinction, with a lively sense of humour and a much-better-than-average chance of belonging to social groups A or B. So why, then, is a nauseatingly successful and charming person such as yourself hanging around at airports?

It surely can't be because you actually want to go on holiday? Haven't you learned yet? Flying off to foreign parts in search of a little rest'n'recreation is just about the craziest possible way of spending your precious moments of freedom from wage slavery yet devised by man.

First you hang around in departure lounges for days on end waiting for a bunch of stroppy dago traffic controllers to end their siesta-to-rule. When you finally get on a plane you run an odds-on chance of having bits of wing, fuselage or engine drop off between here and Malaga. The hotel's foul, the pool's full of Germans who beat you to the chairs thanks to their souped-up Audi Quattros. If you get away from the Jerries it's only because all the rooms have been taken by drunken yobs from Chester-le-Street, all pissed out of their brains and out on the hunt for tarts whose knickers are as elastic as their morals. If you lie in the sun it gives you cancer. If you eat the food it gives you gyp. Jesus – it's bad enough we have to join their blasted Common Market. Do we have to visit them as well?

There has to be a less frenzied way of spending a vacation. And I think I may have found it.

The method in question comes courtesy of the 1989 summer tariff and catalogue sent to me by Halsey Marine, supplies of charter yachts to the moderately well-off.

It's all pretty familiar stuff to anyone who's seen a Bond movie. These are the kind of boats the baddies get to ride. You may remember Largo in *Never Say Never Again*; his little number had all the top mod cons, much the best of which was a gym with two-way mirrors through which one could view Kim Basinger working out. What more could a crook want?

This company can't provide young Kimmy, although they do have the sort of boats Pamella Bordes used to be flown out to in her previous incarnation as a human perk for businessmen. One of their yachts, for example, is *Katalina*, 'the ultimate in opulence afloat'. It has a crew of twenty, plus room for as many passengers.

Anyone who wants to keep in touch with the office will be pleased to hear that there are two direct-dial satellite communications systems on board, complete with fax and telex. For those in a more playful frame of mind, the boat has a gym, sauna, Jacuzzi, two power boats, three small sailing boats, four windsurfers, two canoes, two waterjets and a whole heap of diving equipment. And that's before you get onto the helicopter pad, the vast sundeck, the art masterpieces, the lavish drawing and dining rooms and bedrooms – cabin is far too meagre a word – that would do justice to the Savoy.

Now, *that* sounds better than a 6.00 a.m. flight from Luton and fourteen nights in the Hotel Miramar, doesn't it? And how much will it cost to you cost-conscious holidaymakers? Why, a trifle, a snip; to be precise $206,000 . . . per week. That doesn't include food (allow $20 per day per head of crew and $40 per day for passengers) or local taxes. But it is the top whack. If you don't mind sailing out of season they'll let you have *Katalina* at a giveaway $165K. And if you want to buy her outright, she's yours for a sum not unadjacent to $30 million.

Other highlights include *Lady Ghislaine*, which for a rate unspecified in the tariff provides a fascinating insight into the lifestyle of Robert Maxwell, who owns it. Run-of-the-mill plutocrats put their mirrored ceilings in the bedroom, but it tells you something about Big Bob that his is over the main dining table.

Dreary egalitarian cheapskates amongst you may even now be moaning about the disgusting élitism of the mega-yacht charter business, particularly when I tell you that Halsey Marine find they have no trouble getting takers for their gin-palaces. And I suppose I could try to appease some vestigial social consciences with the information that you can pick up a yacht – albeit a Turkish sailing job – for as little as $10,000 a week, which works out at $1,000 a head in real money. But, frankly, if you're going to play the boat game, then you might as well play it big.

That's what I was saying to Mrs Punch, anyway. But she wasn't having any of it. She didn't give a damn whether we could afford a yacht or a fleet of yachts. We had a duty, a mission to perform. We owed it to our heritage to pick up our big sticks and entertain the kiddies.

So this summer I'm dreaming of a cruise around the crystal waters of the Aegean. And I'm filling the magazine with satirical attacks on airports, planes and all who attempt to fly in them. But I'm spending my hols in just the same old way as usual – stuck inside a tent on the sands at bloody Margate.

June 1989

Lee Humphries

ONLY JOKING INNIT?

The Punch *Guide to who Jokes about Whom*

The Spanish make jokes about the English

The EC decides to investigate what would happen if a country's population was nearly wiped out by a nuclear attack. Three Germans, two men and one woman, are put on an isolated island. Similarly, three Spaniards and three Brits are put on another two islands.

Some years later, EC scientists visit all three islands to check progress.

On the Spanish island everyone is living together in a big house with lots of children. On the German island, the two men are living together and the woman has taken up knitting.

On the British island, they find a pair of identical semis. The woman, several children, and one of the men live in the right-hand house. The scientists ask them how they are getting on with the third man, the one living next door. 'The neighbour? We haven't been introduced.'

And the English make jokes about the French

Q: How do you tell if a Frenchman's been in your house?
A: The dustbin's empty and the dog's pregnant.

French tell (lousy) Belgian gags

A Frenchman goes to see a Belgian colleague in Brussels.

'Have you ever seen a donkey with a staple through its ear?' he asks the Belgian.
'No.'
'Then take a look at your passport photo.'
Next year the piqued Belgian pays a return visit to his French colleague in Paris. 'Have you ever seen a donkey with a staple through its ear?' he asks.
'No.'
'Then take a look at my passport photo.'

Swedes are remarkably gloom-free about Norwegians

It's the first Scandinavian space flight. The crew – two pigs and a Norwegian – are talking to ground control.
'Hello, this is Ground Control for Pig One. Pig One, are you reading me?'
'Hello, here is Pig One. Reading you loud and clear.'
'Pig One, how is everything?'
'Everything's fine, Ground Control.'
'OK, Pig One. Just to check: can you repeat your instructions?'
'Yes, Ground Control. When we come into orbit, press the square button, then the round one.'
'OK. That's right. Over and out.'
'Hello, this is Ground Control for Pig Two. Pig Two, are you reading me?'
'Hello, here is Pig Two for Ground Control. What can I do for you?'
'Pig Two, how is everything?'
'Everything is going smoothly, Ground Control. No problems.'
'Pig Two, can you also repeat your instructions please?'
'Yes, Ground Control. When landing, pull the red lever and push the blue one.'
'OK, Pig Two. That's right. Over and out.'
'Hello, this is Ground Control for Norwegian. Are you reading me?'
'Hello, here is Norwegian for Ground Control.'
'Norwegian, how is everything?'
'Everything is going fine, Ground Control. No problems.'
'Norwegian, please repeat instructions.'
'Yes, Ground Control. Feed the pigs twice a day and be bloody careful not to touch ANYTHING.'

Eastern Europeans tell jokes about the Secret Police (and now they can tell them in public)

Why do Secret Policemen have stripes round their elbows? So they know where to bend their arms.
Why do they go round in threes? So one can read, one can write and the other can keep an eye on the two intellectuals.
A policeman asks his colleague if the indicator on their car is working.
'Yes, it is,' says the colleague. 'No, it isn't. Yes, it is. No, it isn't.'
A Czech militiaman goes to the doctor with severe burns on both ears.
'How did it happen?' asks the doctor.
'Somebody phoned whilst I was ironing.'
'But how come both ears got burnt?'
'Well, after that I phoned the ambulance.'

Turks despise Lazes, their name for Black Sea Greeks

A Laz, finding his wife in bed with another man, seizes his gun and puts it to his own head. Amazed, the wife's lover bursts into laughter.
'Don't laugh, you bastard,' says the suicidal Laz. 'Your bullet's next.'

Greeks despise Pontios, their name for Black Sea Greeks

A Pontios and two Athenians go on an African safari. At the end of the first day, they sit round the camp fire discussing their bag.
Athenian 1: 'I got a couple of tigers and a gazelle.'
Athenian 1: 'I got an elephant.'
Pontios: 'I got two ant-eaters and seven nomisterakia.'

The Athenians aren't too sure what nomi-

sterakia are, but are too embarrassed to ask. For the next three days, whenever they discuss the day's bag, the Pontios always claims he has shot at least six nomisterakia. Finally, the Athenians cannot contain their curiosity any longer.
'Look, just what are these nomisterakia?'
'Dunno,' the Pontios replies. 'They're fairly small, black, and whenever I point my gun at them they keep shouting: "No, mister. No, mister."'

Yanks make jokes about Poles like Brits make jokes about Irish

A Polish couple, newly arrived in America, decide to try their hand at chicken farming. They buy two chickens and bury them head first in the ground.

Next day the chickens are dead and the Poles are puzzled. Undaunted, they try a different strategy. They buy two more chickens and bury them feet first in the ground. Again they die, only taking a little longer this time round.

In total despair they write to the Polish Consulate describing their problems and requesting advice. Within a week they receive a reply: 'Please send soil samples.'

But the Irish make jokes about Kerrymen

A Kerry hospital receives its first AIDS patient. A Dublin specialist phones to check on the patient.
Specialist: 'How's it going?'
Kerry doctor: 'Fine, fine. He's in isolation.'
Specialist: 'Good.'
Kerry doctor: 'And we've got him on a special diet.'
Specialist: 'Special diet – what special diet?'
Kerry doctor: 'After Eights and Cream Crackers – they're the only things we can get under the door.'

The poor old Kerrymen don't get to make jokes about anyone

The PUNCH Round-the-World Ethnic Gag Guide

JOKER	JOKEE
Scots	Aberdonians
Belgian	The Flemish
Dutch	Belgians (The Dutchies even have a special word for such jokes: *em Belgemoppen*)
Italians	Sardinia, Southern Italians, carabinieri
Sardinians	Lodè (a small town in the east of the island)
Danes	Århuisiens (inhabitants of Århus), Norwegians
Norwegians	Lapps
Finns	Karelians
Austrians	Carinthians
Poles	Russians
Eastern Europeans in general	Secret Policemen
Americans	Poles, Polacks, Mexicans
Russians	Poles
Brazilians	Portuguese
Mexicans	Spaniards
Australians	The English (Bruce vs Whingeing Poms)

September 1990

DAZED TRIPPERS

'Personally, I wouldn't recommend Spain.'

'Don't complain, I said . . . Leave it, I said. But oh no, not you . . .'

Julia Langdon

THE ERM TURNS

Our text for today, dear reader, is whether Britain's entry into the ERM or the EMS will affect the ECU and what it means for EMU. No, no, don't switch off, I implore you – this isn't serious. I mean, it is, of course – it's deadly serious – but this column is not about to be deadly serious about this really very serious matter. In fact it intends to be extremely frivolous about it. This column wants your sympathy.

Just pause for a while if you will and imagine what it is like being an ordinary, journeyperson journalist trying to explain to a largely uninterested public that the issue which is arousing most political concern is the EMS, the chances of EMU, the impact of the Chancellor's plan for a 'hard ECU' and whether our joining the ERM has changed the world. For the purposes of understanding this column it really doesn't matter in the slightest if you haven't the faintest idea what I'm on about. It doesn't matter if you do and I don't mind in the slightest either if you have no views at all about the relative wisdom of Delors Stages One, Two or Three. I don't care whether you want a single currency or a central bank, or if – like most human beings – you are not at all sure what either of them would imply.

I have to admit, however, that such is the folly of the furore created by the latest outbreak of Euritus that the other day I gaily jumped into the back of a taxi and actually told the driver – because it had only just happened and I thought he might not know – that we had just joined the ERM. And that was in Blackpool. 'The what?' he said.

So how does a poor journalist put all this into English for the readers? With great difficulty, dear reader, that's how. It beats me, though, why anyone ever bothered to invent Esperanto. If they had just hung around in Brussels for a couple of decades or so, they would have found it had just about all been done for them. Except the French put everything backwards, of course. Did you know that AIDS is SIDA in French?

There are some desirable aspects to Britain's membership of the EEC for politicians, anyway. It is a great relief to ministers of all countries when the presidency of the European Council (each of the 12 member states takes turns running things and hosting all the parties for six months) is held somewhere pleasant. At the moment it is Italy, which is very pleasant indeed.

Departmental ministers therefore have the far from arduous duty of visiting Italy at regular intervals in order to talk to each other. You can see, without my needing to explain this further, that, by and large, this is a better bet than, say, Luxembourg.

It is an even better bet if you happen to be the Arts Minister. Being Arts Ministers they always meet in very cultural surroundings – nice pictures, lovely furniture, that sort of thing – and have very civilised discussions. They even, apparently, have civilised disagreements.

Pity then, the lot of our man, poor David Mellor. He was attending an arts council of Ministers in Italy and when the business was done it had been arranged for them all to repair to Capri for lunch with Franco Zefferelli – well, he's arty, after all. Mr Mellor had to return to Nottingham for a date with Mr Arthur Scargill and others on *Any Questions*. Mr Mellor was a little sore about this.

November 1990

Oofy Prosser

MIXED DATES

What's the most boring number you can think of? Surely it has to be 1992? If ever there was a number to induce yawns the moment it is uttered, it is surely that one – conjuring up as it does scintillating visions of pan-European markets being opened up with boundless optimism, only to be strangled by pan-European bureaucracy.

As a businessman, I am supposed to be excited about all this. But the main benefit of 1992 to me is that the debate has solved that most difficult of social problems, how to get away from a dinner party that shows no sign of flagging. Simply start gassing about the Single Market and everyone will soon be saying, 'My, my, is that the time? Gosh we really must be going, whose turn is it to drive then, no, I did it last time, you must remember.'

The DTI (the people who managed to turn Enterprise into a dirty word) is trying to persuade us all that we don't know enough about the Single Market and that we are nowhere near as prepared for the great day as our Continental brethren. No doubt they will soon be running courses showing us just how to kiss Johnny Foreigner on the cheeks in advance of carving him up over some deal.

Yet there is one thing the DTI is keeping very quiet about, suspiciously so in my view: the real secret of 1992, the mysterious misconception under which almost everybody in this country labours, is not one the DTI is in a hurry to dispel.

Perhaps you are one of those people who consider themselves well up on Europe and all it entails. Perhaps you actually go so far as to read those interminable newspaper supplements about it, rather than using them to line the dog's basket like everybody else. But I'll bet that not more than one in ten of you can answer this simple question: just when exactly does 1992 happen?

Don't worry if you are humming and hahing about this. Most others simply get it wrong. Only the other night, some reporter on *The City Programme* said that there were now less than two years to go to the great day. Whoops. Wrong!!! There are now, in fact, almost three years to go to 1992.

Despite all the publicity about the bloody thing, the most important fact about 1992 – when it begins – is the DTI's best-guarded secret. 1992 does not, you may be surprised to learn, happen until midnight on 31 December 1992. Or at least that's the view of the bright chaps at the DTI. As far as the daft Continen-

'He's determined nobody's going to accuse him of not being ready come 1992.'

tals are concerned it starts on 1 January 1993 and so, with a peculiar logic, they all refer to the Single Market happening in 1993. We are, surprise surprise, the only nation in Europe that attaches a significance to 1992.

I can only assume that the DTI hopes that this subterfuge persuades the Brits to get ready a year earlier than everyone else. It is a strategy that could backfire terribly. Come 1 January 1992 (or as soon after the Bank Holiday as seasonal indulgences permit), every British businessman is going to be rubbing his hands together and raring to get down to it. When he finds out that he has got another year to wait, he may, as the DTI no doubt hopes, say oh goody goody, another 12 months to get ready.

It is far more likely, if you ask me, that he will say stuff this for a game of soldiers and order his secretary to put all the bumf sent out by the DTI through the shredder. It is a task that will take her well into 1993.

February 1990

Paul Jennings

TALK AND THE WORLD TALKS WITH YOU!

On het thirtieht anniversar of the funding of hte Unitted Slates of Europ, greelings to all our reabers! All-person yong and anctient can look mit prid satisfactioun on the extroardinar vapid developpment of Minglish into a mihgtig, flexile langage, easy beknowed to evrye constitung-poeple of Europp, wether it's matrix-tong was Italien, Franch, Duetsche or Anglish.

A vash, inopible tasking! A lingistic feet to mesh the braines of mastrephilologes! So mihgt spake such noncredent cyniqes of htirty annes agone. Und also treu migt be such prognostic if that operating, to froge a glossar-universel of universel of Evropean – putt in our head the versating Labor-dozen of Herkule! – was left to Academes! You may image it! Wat strifings, wat intermined commissions having discution, wat argusment, prehaps coming to blobs and strike!

We scrate in elder, dusted file-journales of France in such bypass daies, and find the scolar-puristic by everywere nevrose at such-called intrudels of *weekend*, *dancing*, *le steam-cracking*, *la manpowerisation* and many varigal ensemples of Franglaise. Hola, mann the barbicade and save-honor the pureness-clarety of smother-tong, crie scolardy Docteurs! And by this also, how shuold the German sprake wich have crafig declinings be mongled with the analytice, oddsome, unsynnetrcicale Englis word? Moreover pandits could bong their heads togather over like prodlematic, e.g. contrapunct of Englihs iambich-rythm and the musicale tenderose female-ending, all troochjee-meter, by Italiano. How by devils-name can any lerning enrond sich a pangloss?

Butt, neverstanding that Anglis-saxony posse a mundial spread, in USA nortamerican landes and Austral-antipods, also for commercials in Afrique trade, such a fearing it wuold impermate Enrope as jugglernaut, did swaftly proved a fools vaine, a chimeara of the intelligents.

For by all this so, its to ken by each person that our gloried Minglish universal-sprak is distinted quite OK from Enlgish-tong. Und why? To reponse is that in each terran, Spanien and Turc, Griesch too, outlands also in Commun-markt landes, were fecundating in each ressort, each panoram-delihgt, evry beauty-spo and thermale heath-plage or turist ruines of classics-tempel, grand daedal printers and auctors to guide boolets and turismo-informats. In such volcan-forg was the nice precis and lingafranc litter bonked, wich now bibble on the lip of childs from Bremen to

THE BRITISH CHARACTER.
SKILL AT FOREIGN LANGUAGES.

Naple, in total areage of our Continental.

So *Hopp!* it cried to professeur with bibliotek of lexicons and comparing interglossals to make from abstruct a Eorupemann's lingage. Be gone, mit all porings and schema from grammatiques wich run only in your heads! Here in pangraphic stile of brochure-leafs, and so of hotels-pubblicite, and noticaments to foreing-turistes in very nice vacacion sitts, here is new speaching-grund for conversating of all euRopeen gentrys.

No Englander, natal of such locale as Warington, Botle, Noneatun, Bis Hopstorfod or Londre himselve can say wit his poete Walther Scotch 'this is my owl, my dative tong'; as by seen anterior, Minglish is no Inglesh. Yet as thought by hug sobterranic forze, such a wording cognat to each turist from Amerik also and inteligent to all, bumped into existence fulsy maturn like Athena born. Miraculose of Europ psycheal! Grand fork of inspiration! Instant commune deal! As if by wading of magics wind, humbel and obscurse writers of spa-programs, menu traductions, public-affiches and museoguibes from Hellsinki to Sicel hat on the same herbal felicitie, the same convortion and distinged matter.

Yet truely, wen we make a stopp to bark this phenomenal, we arne't amuzed. Is it not by the communed tramping of grandiflored meals, by grande prospekt on sin-glozed beeches of Mediterran vacacion, by the ambiance-turist of her bushing citys and typical cathedrales that we have our hearting of Europa? Lingist is to yomp from experientrealitat; and fuller hoppiest realitey of manskind is not in the shouling clamant of the markt-place and diurne laboring. Never such! It is spirting in the foomy wavelets, it is sun-bashing in the tronquil baie, it is maiestic panoram from alpin-telepherique where his soul burst and wander.

And wider, a noval face of this self-forme uttering of Minglish litters is, you can uniquely deviate its orthograph to your voluntary. Which nobile complexity, to have such varies, to fit like fingers in your globe!

So is to reflexion the spewing aspects, like a million, of our continente; the grand porphyreal tumbs and billowed colonnades, the pintured gravity of the maestral renascimento of Italy! The somptuous edificacion and enlightened avenues of Paris, where you may see artist in his smack at work to strain the trembling coloures of the *ville lumière*! Or you could spun throuht its smiting paysage of fairies châteaux nodding their dreames by the Loire to the bostling chic of the Côte d'Azur, and busk in sinshine. Or you can cure athmsma and hyper-nevrose febrile at thermal balneic station, first class. Than you can gear to redonded curvature of Baroc-stil and onion-doms in a little valle of Bavaria. Hisht! You have nougt to hear but tinkel-bells of a cow mooching near. Now you see yong pople in a quant rustique dress jangle and lep in a folklor-typic dance from two hundred years. Now you blow your breath to inspice a grandly frawning vista from the mihgty Alpes.

All such divers, but yet its too a bee-hove commercial manufactory and negotiant communite. You can't expect it, how she pulsate, each time a change, so we could match Euorupes complice trails of strand with this pusty, varigous, fluvent now-sprech, the same wen you watch alwaies, yet never lagged by the binds of a wrotten orthographe-grammatical – our nobile, mobile tong of Minglish.

August 1970

George Mikes

WHO GAVE YOU GOULASH?

Britain, if the Prime Minister is unlucky enough to succeed, will join Europe; I represent, through my organisation, a country which has been more or less expelled from that Continent in spite of the fact that it lies in the middle of it.

Mr Wilson may indeed conclude successfully a decade of Tory-Socialist fight to become a member of the European Community. He will not be the first man to weather many a storm, master many a disaster and then be toppled by his greatest achievement and success. The British people find it hard to swallow the fact that instead of ruling an old Empire they have to become part of a new one; that instead of watching those curious aliens with wary eyes the whole nation, lock, stock and barrel, is to become a nation of bloody foreigners – because that is what joining Europe for millions of Britons means. Mr Wilson, as over-ingenious super-politicians are wont to do, is manoeuvring himself into a position in which he cannot win: if he succeeds in joining Europe, he may be judged to be a great man by history but a very small one by tomorrow's electorate; if he does not succeed – well, what do people think of a leader who has failed?

Hungary has suffered the reverse fate. When I was being brought up there, we believed we were part of Europe but we cared little about it. We acted as Europeans: we weighed potatoes by the kilogram and measured milk by the litre (except peasants who stuck to the pound and the pint, never even suspecting how terribly anglicised they were); we measured length by the metre (except carpenters who used the inch, the ell and the foot) and, most important of all, pushed decimal points to the right and left. Times of sweet and happy ignorance! Little did the Hungarians know that the great British nation regarded this shifting of decimal points as the most revolting manifestation of Continental trickery and cunning; and little did the British know that the decimal point was already looming over the lakes of Westmorland and the horizon of the weald of Kent.

Victorians and Edwardians used to say (in other words) that coloured gentlemen began at Calais. But the French were only tinted; real colour began on the Danube. The phrase 'Central European' always had a funny ring in Anglo-Saxon ears. A Central European was a man in a long coat, clicking his heels, drinking innumerable cups of poisonous black coffee and was ruled by the Habsburgs, the one dynasty the Hanoverians never intermarried with. Why, even Queen Victoria never had a grandson on the Austrian-Hungarian throne.

Then, after World War II, Central Europe suddenly disappeared; it was wiped off the map. Some gigantic super-Enoch did a thorough job: all the Czechs, Hungarians, etc. were expelled from Europe without even a repatriation grant. Today we have Western Europe and Eastern Europe, with no centre. Austria is West; Hungary, next door, has been relegated to Asia Minor.

That is why Hungarians were really *forced* to form the Hungarian Mafia. They dispatched a powerful Fifth Column to take over Europe, including Britain, as well as the United States and Australia. This was no crafty scheming but a pathetic attempt to keep a foothold in Europe. Look at the consequences in Britain alone. It is impossible, of course, to survey the whole field but a few examples will suffice. In literature and science we have Arthur Koestler to spread alarm and despondency and to undermine British morale. In music we have Solti and used to have Dorati (not speaking of countless performers) to lull Britain into a mellow mood;

'The Russians are years behind us in everything!'

others took over the Treasury and did their best to destroy the country's economy from within; but in case the economy survived, Prof. Dennis Gabor explained that even too much leisure will ruin Britain's future. And so on, indefinitely. If you cannot beat them, join them. Should peaceful means fail, Professor Teller in the States developed the hydrogen bomb.

At home, in Hungary, they made a different type of attempt in 1956 to return to Europe. And having failed in it, they still went on in the best European traditions and proceeded to transform their capital into a Western-type metropolis and today poor, deprived Russians and other Soviet peoples, about two hundred millions of round-eyed provincials, flock to Budapest as Hungarians would, if only they could, flock to Paris.

Both the Hungarian Mafia and the Hungarian Revolution, as well as Dubček's noble effort in Czechoslovakia, have failed and Central Europe is still out in the cold. These countries are very anxious to get back. Whether this effort is not altogether misguided, is quite another question. Our Europe, so great, so glorious, so supreme even in my youth, started shrinking, losing its power, its authority, its influence, its possessions a short while ago. Is it really wise for the countries concerned which seem to be lucky enough to find themselves in Asia, to make such great efforts to rejoin this shrinking Continent? Why not join Japan instead? Or Australia?

But we must get out of these objectionable, old habits. We must give people what they want for themselves and not what *we* think they should want. Central Europe wants to rejoin the Old Continent, so let them rejoin. I am authorised to speak only in the name of the Hungarian Mafia, so let me plead Hungary's cause.

First of all, Hungary claims to have defended Europe, quite successfully and at her own expense, against the Turks, for two centuries or so. That the Turks never reached Vienna is due mainly to the Hungarians. Magyar leaders of those times are recorded to have said: 'Let's defend European and Christian civilisation against the Turks and in a few hundred years, you will see, we shall be allowed to join the Common Market as our just reward.' But what is, in fact, really happening? The Turks themselves have been shifted up to the shores of the North Atlantic and accepted as a member of the North Atlantic Treaty Organisation while the Hungarians, right in the middle of the Continent, are being kept out of it.

Well, who gave goulash to the world? Goulash is one of the triumphs of the European genius, imitated, unsuccessfully, all over Europe. You go to Vienna, Germany, Scandinavia and many other places and you find that dish everywhere. But to call it *goulash* on the menus is nearly always an insult to the honour of the Magyar nation. They put tomatoes in goulash and change its nature, its profile, its vocation. I have to admit here, however, that the Turks have scored once again over us: shish-kebab is, for the time being, more popular than goulash.

The famous Tokay wine, for all I care, may be expelled to Asia Minor: it is almost as sweet as Turkish delight. (Oh, the Turks again.) Yet, Bull's Blood is practically the only drinkable red wine east of Burgundy. And the *csárdás*, Hungary's national dance, with its half-solo way of dancing, with its jerks, kicks in the air and individual embroideries, anticipated the modern way of dancing by about five hundred years. And when I walk along Carnaby Street I see nowadays blouses displayed, posing as the last words in subtlety: Hungarian peasant women have been wearing the same blouses for centuries.

Hungarian snobberies are also positively European. Hunting – for bear and wild boar – is the delight of West German businessmen and wild horses still roam the Great Plains.

And what about Hungarian women? They are too busy nowadays to spend unlimited time in front of their mirrors but they are still among the prettiest anywhere. You cannot expel them from Europe. They are ready to unite and fight. They have nothing to lose but their mini-skirts.

I appeal to the public: when redrawing the map of our Continent, remember the fringe-Europeans! After all, in this era of bureaucrats and Eurocrats, of jumbo-jets and of the decibel-explosion, of package tours and the rat-race, it is *goulash* and *scárdás*, the spice of paprika, the sound of gipsy music, the neighing of proud and free Magyar horses and the forms and curves of Hungarian girls, which could make this Europe of the Common Market a little less of a market and a great deal less common.

February 1970

Richard Mallett

THE TWO-WAY MIRROR

Now (as that weather-forecast man says to make it conversational), like all such inquiries, this one is bedevilled at the start by

the need for definitions. We – if you're still with me – are considering the influence on us of European films, and the influence of our films on Europeans; and this depends not only on what we mean by *European films*, but also, even more (I hesitate to mention this) on what we mean by *us*.

For argument's sake, take it that *us* means all of us, and that includes you. *European films* is not so easy. Do we include all films that are in fact literally European-made? That would mean, besides the Italian-Spanish-German imitation Westerns, practically everything in the way of foreign films except American, Japanese, Indian, Chinese, Australian . . . So for argument's sake (the same argument) take it that *European films* mean foreign-language films from any of those 3,800,000 square miles bounded on the South by the Mediterranean and the Caspian and on the East by whatever that place is. Perhaps on this occasion I ought to be limiting it to the Common Market countries, but an extra million or two square miles gives one room to turn round.

All the same – can you be sure of any way in which you've been influenced by European films? I very much doubt whether you or anyone else can judge whether what influenced you was European, or American, or Japanese (that *will* be the day – when we see someone influenced by Japanese films engaged in the violent and passionate undertaking of ordering a glass of milk, or asking the time), or on television, or behind a window.

If you *were* influenced – which (on previous form) you don't for a moment admit. Most people hate to acknowledge that they've altered their behaviour and habits as a result of anything, short of some celebrated character they want to bring into the conversation and boast about knowing. But even with subliminal influence there's the same basic difficulty: how to separate out the influence of European films from that of all the other moving pictures that diversify one's existence – let alone that of the real thing, whether seen on the spot or in Soho.

For in these over-communicative days,

anything influential is influential all over the world, almost at once. On the assumption that films were the only influence, you might suppose that the declamatory police-car took to using a nerve-shattering nasal *ee-aw* instead of a bell because the police authorities had seen a lot of French crime films; instead of which . . .

Instead of which . . . well, I don't know, and I'm not going to ring up their press officer and ask, because he might give me some simple fact cramping to the imagination. What I assume is that a delegation from Scotland Yard attending a conference in Paris found the *ee-aw* more impressive, audible at kilometres instead of thousands of yards and so still more useful when we go metric. If you happen to know, don't tell me. I'd rather think of those police delegates in Paris, in the Sherlock Holmes Suite at the Crillon or somewhere, having left their skeleton keys at the desk. A magnifying glass belonging to one of them, covered with historic bloodstains, is still – but I digress.

To be sure, there is fashion; but when was the last time dress was affected by a European film, and how do you know? The most notable recent example of fashion influence was *Dr Zhivago* (the dregs of whose inspiration, filtering down through the years, I blame for the maxi), which was three, not to say six, thousand miles from being a European film, even though it did have a British director.

Perhaps we could try an interview or two, in the Mass-Observation manner . . .

Woman, 38, housewife.
Oo, no, well I don't remember any European films even on the telly. A European film? What, you mean where they all talk different, and that? – and little bits of printing all along the bottom? Oo, I haven't the patience. Bad enough with the BBC when you have to watch all the time and don't get a rest in the commercials.
Man, 58, policeman's uncle.
I like them European films. What do you mean, how do I know? I can see when they're in Europe, can't I? All the cars driving on the right. Way they've influenced *me*, I'm not so rash. I wouldn't ask for trouble, I'd never drive on the right, if I had a car.

. . . Or perhaps not.

Where the influence is undeniable is not on our way of life but on our way of film-making. Think of the average British film something over thirty-five years ago – the *average* British film. No, I know you aren't old enough, but examples have been known to pop up on television. It was typically a drawing room (or bedroom – for what that was worth in those innocent days) comedy, a stage play photographed, lit like the corridors of a hotel, with a silvery gleam that intensified to a dazzling halo when the heroine was seen against the light.

She often wore a silver evening dress, so as to be a bit more luminous, and the uncovered bits of her might have been polished. Her lips, in that pre-Technicolor time, were like a large (or rather, small – they liked heroines with small refined-looking mouths) black leaf. Most of the men, too, except a few bits of comic relief who dropped their aitches and said 'Garn' or 'Cor', were to a considerable extent polished. Credit titles didn't go into as much detail as they do now, or they would have named the Director of Luminosity and the Sleekness Adviser.

As for the story, the action, the dialogue – these were the sort of thing characteristic of that sort of matinée-audience play; there was really very little difference. One even saw French windows and deep-focus pictures of baronial halls with butlers.

Now think of the average British film today, and you can't: there isn't one. Your favourite sarcastic summing-up with its references to the North, and ordinary people, and kitchen sinks, and back views of naked shoulders in bed (ah, bed!), applies to only a fraction of the sixty or seventy films made here annually. How do you fit in *Chitty Chitty Bang Bang*, or *Oliver!*, or *The Lion in Winter*, or *The Prime of Miss Jean Brodie*, or *Isadora*, or *Oh! What a Lovely War*, or *Room at the* – no, I mean *Saturday Night and S* – no, I mean *Otley*?

They're a miscellaneous lot, as they should

be, and certainly the influence of European (and for that matter, all other – but let's worry about one thing at a time) films has had much to do with the change; but in these over-communicative days, influence of that kind is mutual, what we have is a sort of two-way mirror. Though it's only quite recently, in the last thirty years or so – this is my week for talking like an archaeologist – that British films have shown qualities likely to have any influence, qualities worth imitating. Since, in fact, they've improved *partly as a result of* the influence of European films. Influence on something by which you've been influenced . . . The word 'incestuous' comes to mind, and the men in white coats are just round the corner.

I now realise I chose my title too hastily: it doesn't, after all, fit that mutual-influence situation. But I leave it there, because it's quite a good title (for *something*). And unlike the English title of many a European film, it wasn't deliberately contrived to mislead. If you read this because of it, let that be a lesson to you.

February 1970

Jeremy Kingston

ENTER STAGE LEFT: A SINISTER, MINCING, LECHEROUS, SCENTED, COMICAL FOREIGNER WITH A DAGGER

Luckily for us nations cannot sue each other for defamation of character. The English should be specially grateful because for centuries our playwrights have made their nastier villains foreigners whenever possible.

In Elizabethan days the traitorous beasts were usually Italians, with Frenchmen and Spaniards tying for second place. Other nationals came in for a slap from time to time, to show the audience their author knew his geography. Someone could be rotten in the state of Denmark; maids could be raped in Rhodes; Jews of Malta poisoned wells. But the Italians soared high above everyone else as the real nasties.

When a play's subject was English history some of the killers had perforce to be Englishmen. Even those who committed the worst of crimes, the killing of an English king, bore unmistakably English names like Tyrrel and Exton and Lightborn. The patriotic playwright had two answers to this awkward problem. He could make the killer suffer an instantaneous change of heart the moment the king expired, step back in horror, cry, 'Would the deed were undone!' and rush off the stage. This happens over and over again in plays of the period. On the other hand, if a killer's heart remained unchanged by his deed it is because, as Edward II's murderer explains, 'I learnt in Naples how to poison flowers, To strangle with a lawn thrust down the throat . . .' and numbers of other nasty arts besides. Arts learned abroad.

Italy was the root of all evil. Partly because Italy was where the popes lived and popes were dangerous things. Mainly because Italy was where Machiavelli had lived and Machiavelli was absolutely devilish. No Englishman would have thought of strangling with a lawn thrust down the throat but that was the sort of crime Machiavelli and the Borgias went out and did twice before breakfast just to keep their wrists in trim. Naturally it would be in some place like Parma that a brother would stride into a banquet hall with his incestuous sister's heart stuck upon his dagger. In Amalfi more brothers (and one a cardinal) would be content to occupy five acts tormenting a virtuous duchess. In Florence aunts are overcome by poisoned smoke while dispatching their nieces with poisoned showers of gold. And up and down Italy, in play after play, foolish husbands and fond wives die after kissing the poisoned lips of portraits of their false spouses.

How much audiences believed of what they saw on the stage is hard to say but the popularity of Italian settings for horror plays will have reinforced the preconceived idea (conceived, it must be said, with every justification) that south of the Alps princes were pitiless, prelates profligate and the whole area was to be avoided if possible. With comparably awful crimes going on in Amboise and Alicante the anti-European of the period had every reason to say that poisoners began at Calais.

A hundred years later all this had changed. The popes were too busy ordering baroque fountains to have time to threaten anyone except each other's offspring. So far as the English stage is concerned Italy had become a nation of opera-singers and music-masters.

The French presented a subtler problem. Invariably enemies on battlefields abroad, on fields nearer home, in Hyde Park, and the Mall, they ruled as the indisputable arbiter of taste. Captured French officers occasionally appear in Restoration plays crying 'Garzoon!' and kneeling at de feet of de English ladies. More often the French are a race to be lauded (by the fops) and mocked (by everyone else) for knowing little else than how to mount a pantaloon or fringe the latest glove.

As the plays of the period are almost always set in Hyde Park, the Mall and in drawing rooms thereabouts it is more common to find the French represented as valets mincing after their foppish masters than as important characters in their own right. The foreigners did their dirty work offstage, enticing Englishmen across the Channel and sending them back transmogrified into Foppingtons and Flutters, who sugared their chatter with French idioms, pranced about kissing men, but sneakily went for the ladies too. What began at Calais now was lack of moral fibre.

Not until the arrival of melodrama do Europeans people the English stage again in any quantity. The gothic novelists had set their lurid tales amid landscapes of spectacular menace, ruined castles beetling over mountain gorges, dark forests illuminated only by lightning. The hundreds of stage derivatives eagerly adopted these scenic effects and distressed heroines bemoaned their fate in front of a thousand bleak backcloths before running off pursued by baleful French counts, cowled monks intent on rape or fearsome bandits armed to the teeth. Corsica, Calabria, the Pyrenees, the Dolomites, all were places where the innocent were inevitably persecuted by somebody, tyrant or outlaw, or by *something*, because Germany at long last came into the act bringing vampires and monsters and all the heady excitements of *Sturm und Drang*.

All this and bad drinking water, too! Small wonder Britain took care to man her navy (if nautical melodramas are to be believed) with steadfast tars who kept one hand pressed to their hearts of British oak and the other ready with the cutlass to overpower smugglers, wreckers, pirates, corsairs and all other foreign wretches holding an Englishwoman, with or without her longlost babe, in durance vile.

As melodrama faded away foreigners were left stranded inside less violent stereotypes but their presence in a play continued – and continues – to signal danger more often than not. Modern playgoers will recognise the suave Frenchman, greying nobly at the temples, who agitates the becalmed waters of an English marriage by treating the wife 'as a woman'. And the commonest stereotype of all has become the glamorous, amorous au pair, short in skirt – sooner or later without any skirt at all – and especially attracted to married Englishmen twice her age.

And how, you may ask, have European audiences been led to see *us* all these years? The humiliating answer is that they have seen us scarcely at all. A tragedy by Schiller, adaptations of Scott, an occasional milord and the ludicrous family in Ionesco's first play who converse entirely in the simple sentences of an English language primer. That's all these foreign playwrights think of us, and what sort of an image is that to offer as an equal partner within a European community of amorous, long-legged, suave, suntanned, foppish, incestuous, pope-ridden poisoners?

February 1970

R. G. G. Price

TWO THOUSAND YEARS OF NEIGHBOURLINESS

One thing that will have to be changed if we enter Europe is our school history books. So *nobody* is offended.

Early Visitors

Many nations from overseas played a part in building the Britain that we know. The Romans were particularly helpful, showing all their Italian skill in building and engineering and covering their adopted country with walls, mosaics and hypocausts. Then came the Angles and Saxons from Germany and the Low Countries, with their love of music and poetry. The Jutes and Vikings came from the uncivilised north and contributed little to British Civilisation.

Our Norman Ancestors

Harold, the Anglo-Saxon king, who had the help of many skilful immigrants, was faced with a decision that would have taxed any man not of Teutonic stock. In the north there was a Norwegian army, which he easily put to flight; but things were more difficult in Sussex, where a French army had landed. (The Normans had originally come from Scandinavia but had long been settled in Normandy and were as *French as French.*) The Battle of Hastings was hard fought. Both sides were equal in bravery, equipment, tactical expertise and cunning; the result was a virtual draw. Unhappily, Harold was killed by a stray arrow, so William the Peacemaker took over his work of ruling the country and uniting English and French in friendship.

Joan of Arc

The Middle Ages were the time of Chivalry, when tournaments were held and English and French knights strove in rivalry in the field. During what was laughingly called 'The Hundred Years' War', captives were feasted and often lived with their captors as members of the family until a forfeit was paid.

Once a peasant girl told the Dauphin of France that the Voices of Saints had ordered her to make him King. Under the leadership of this brave girl, the French eased the English back across the Channel. Unfortunately, the Church convicted Joan of heresy, a mistake it later put right, rather splendidly, and handed her over to the rulers of the district for punishment. The local rulers happening to be English, they had to carry out the unpleasant duty; they were loyal Catholics and did not feel it was up to them to suggest that the Church might not be right on the point. However, perhaps if they had not martyred her, she might not have been canonised.

The Armada

Spain had been ruling the Benelux countries a bit harshly so naturally they looked to their English friends for help, which Elizabeth I was delighted to send them. In an attempt to get a footing on both sides of the Straits of Dover, Philip of Spain sent a great fleet to pick up an invasion army in Flanders and ship it to England. Fortunately, English guns, seamanship and sea dogs, with a helpful wind, put an end to the plan. This was not the first, or the last, time that we have played a leading part in saving the West from tyranny, a favour that, of course, the West has done more than return.

The Great Revolution of 1688

When James II tried to introduce undemocratic ideas into England, it was our good friends the Dutch who repaid our services over Spain by sending us their own beloved Stadtholder as King and providing troops to help him liberate us.

The Industrial Revolution

It is very difficult to find out who first made new discoveries in Science and Technology. The mechanisation of the textile industry, which we associate with Crompton's Mule and Arkwright's Spinning Jenny, may well have begun long before in remote areas of Western Germany, France, Italy, Holland, Belgium or Luxembourg. It is just that somehow we seem to have acquired the credit. The same thing applies to the steam-engine, railways, the ironclad steamship, chloroform, antiseptic surgery, penicillin and television. Who can be quite sure that we do not owe Gravity, Evolution, the Electron or the Genetic Code to the inhabitants of the Rhineland, the Loire valley, the Lombard Plain or the Ardennes? Do not forget that most electrical units are named after Common Market nationals.

Trade Follows the Flags

The overseas development of Europe has long moved on from conquering and ruling countries to trading with them. But, before opinions changed and Imperialism fell from favour, many of our neighbours joined with us in exploring and even exploiting other continents. Sometimes the first hardships of discovery were borne by one nation in Western

Europe, sometimes by another. For example, the French took the earlier burdens in Canada and India and Egypt, the Dutch at the Cape of Good Hope, the Germans in East Africa, the Italians in North Africa. Then Britain felt it was time to shoulder its share and replaced them, sometimes in due course relinquishing the work to the inhabitants. The bringing of European help to less advanced countries was a movement in which all our neighbours wished to play their part. There was, in fact, a good deal of healthy rivalry between us all.

Wolfe at Quebec

General Wolfe helped to win eventual self-government for the French Canadians by bravely capturing the fort of Quebec, which was held by supporters of the *Ancien Régime*, the cruel government which the French threw down in the revolution of 1789. Like the equally brave French general Montcalm, he did not survive to take part in the foundation of modern Canada. There is a story that, as he was rowed along the St Lawrence with muffled oars on the way to lead the assault, he recited from the works of Gray, La Fontaine, Walther von der Vogelweide (c.1170–c.1230), Dante, Hooft, Ruysbroek and an anonymous Luxemburger balladist.

Waterloo

This event can be taken as just one example of the way that people from various lands can sink their differences and work together. The French, whose will-to-win was weakened by worry over their Emperor's health, the British, who provided one of the day's best leaders and some of the steadiest men, the Germans – for we must not limit our gratitude for their all-important help just to the Prussians – and the Belgians, to whom the participants were indebted for the site of the meeting, all combined to make it a really memorable day in Europe's history.

Kings and Queens

Sometimes people think that history books should leave out Monarchs and concentrate more on the doings of ordinary folk; but our Sovereigns have always shown us the way forward to international co-operation. Henry

VIII took one wife in three from overseas. Charles II was half French. William III was Dutch. For the last two centuries or so our rulers and their consorts have often been German. On the other hand, this has not been merely a matter of Imports. We have supplied many thrones abroad with princesses, for example the mother of the well-remembered Kaiser.

Free Trade

In the nineteenth century, England decided to stop trying to keep out the products of other countries and led the way in convincing some of our neighbours that lowering barriers between nations would lead to more for everyone.

1914–18 and 1939–45

The astonishing feats of Germany in this century could have been performed only by a people who had brought organisation, discipline and military skill to the highest point. However, the dogged endurance and panache of the British, French, Italians, Belgians and Dutch managed to make things evenly matched. Foch, Hindenburg, Cadorna, Montgomery and their comrades are widely respected as Founding Fathers of what may one day become a true West European Army. Great advances in technology were made during these years, the Germans leading the way in ballistic missiles, the British in radar, the Italians in certain aspects of submarine work, the French with their famous field gun and the Dutch, Belgians and Luxemburgers with many improvements in the techniques of underground fighting. Good knocks were given and taken on all sides; some of the lands which took the worst are now the most prosperous.

President de Gaulle

During the latter period, when General de Gaulle was rallying the French, he lived in London and worked close to the British Government. Later he returned to France and never forgot all he had learned about us as a stranger in our midst. When he became President of France, he took a great interest in uniting all the countries of Western Europe. He was anxious that the Common Market should be a great success and insisted that it should not be started off at half-cock. He was determined to move slowly and, instead of including everyone in sight in the early days, preferred to leave it to our good sense to adjust our way of thinking to that of France. Soldier, statesman, writer, he is one of the noblest figures in recent history and one can hardly blame him for not further widening his vast range to include economics.

Other Friends

The United States, which has itself combined in a single country men of many different races, has on several occasions helped Europeans to help themselves. We may not need to call on their good offices so frequently in the future.

Some Famous Quotations

'This precious stone set in the silver sea,
Which serves it in the office of a bridge,
Or as a road conducive to a house,
Which links it firmly to more happier lands.'
Shakespeare

'Unroll the map of Europe.'
William Pitt the Younger

'In matters of commerce, the strength of the Dutch
Is asking too little and offering too much.'
Canning

'Here and here did Europe help me: how can I help Europe? – Say.'
Browning

'C'est magnifique, et c'est la guerre.'
French Commander on the Charge of the Light Brigade

'The lamps are being lit all over Europe; we shall not see them go out again in our lifetime.'
Sir Edward Grey

February 1970

Michael Parkinson

SOME CORNER OF A FOREIGN FIELD

Those lily-livered alarmists who believe that Britain will sell its body and soul to Europe have little reason to worry. There is one part of Britain that will remain ever so, one rampart of chauvinism that will not succumb, one group of people to whom a German will always be a Kraut, a French man a Froggy, an Italian an Eytie and anyone else a Wog. I refer to the sportsmen of Britain. These are the true Britons, the defenders of the faith, the disciples of nationalism. To these people other countries exist only to be trampled to death on the playing fields of Britain and as far as they are concerned that four bobs' worth of instant knowledge called All You Need To Know About Europe might have been written in invisible ink.

It is true, of course, that we already have strong sporting links with Europe. We play football against European teams and compete for trinkets like the European Cup. But it would be wrong to interpret this as a laudatory example of sport building bridges between different nations. The fact is we play soccer against European teams because there's money to be earned playing against eleven wogs. The average football fan who wouldn't turn out on a wet Saturday to see Sunderland play Crystal Palace is, however, lured from hearth and home by the promise of Sunderland giving a sound thrashing to The Sporting Club of Omsk. If the predictable happens and the Omsk goalkeeper goes home with a severe case of backache, then the average fan leaves the ground feeling good, his heart warmed by the knowledge that British is best. If by some mischance the foreigners dare to win, then the average fan is sure to blame the referee who in these games is always a bloody foreigner in any case.

The great Dixie Dean (and we must never tire of quoting the classics) once told a lovely story about playing in Europe which puts into true perspective the real attitude of British sportsmen toward foreigners. Dean was captaining a team playing in Germany at a time when the Continentals used a different size of ball to the British (typical of the awkward sods. Who invented the game in any case?).

Determined not to bow the knee to the foreign foe, Dean went to the kick-off carrying a football of British manufacture and size. Not surprisingly the Germans had a ball manufactured in the fatherland and a size smaller. 'Of course they can't speak English, the players or the referee,' says Dixie, shaking his head in disbelief. 'So a right old mince starts in the middle of the field. This German is holding out his ball and jabbering away and I'm holding our ball and telling him, "Save your breath, sunshine, because we're playing this game with Dixie's football." The ref doesn't know where he is so in the end we make signs and the like and it's obvious we're walking off to find the interpreter. So we go to the touchline and there's the interpreter and I'm telling him we're playing with our football and the German tells him we're playing with his and it solves nothing having the interpreter because we know what the row is about. Anyway I get a bit fed up with all the talk because it's getting us nowhere. So I says to the interpreter, pretending like to be interested: "Can I inspect the German football?" He gives the message to the German captain who is dead chuffed because he thinks I've given in and that I'm going to look at his ball and agree to play with it. So he hands it to me, dead pleased and I look at it for a moment. "Very nice," I say and then I kicked it straight over the bloody stand and out of the ground. "Goes a long way too," I said. We played with our ball.'

Dixie smiled at the remembered triumph of the moment. 'Tactics,' he said, tapping his forehead. 'British tactics.'

All that was a long time ago. Since, wars have altered the boundaries of Europe, visionaries have shown us the promised land where there are no Frogs, Krauts and Eyties, just Europeans. Politicians have pointed out the obvious advantages of Britons becoming wogs. Some sectors of our society have been persuaded by the argument, but not our sportsmen who still believe the gospel according to the great St Dixie.

What is curious is that although the average soccer fan would never admit that we had anything to learn from Europe, there are apparent signs that Continental influences have already affected our spectators and our players. Take, for example, the very un-British spectacle of husky athletes (male) embracing one another in midfield in front of sixty thousand people and wetting one another's whiskers with sloppy kisses. That is now common practice among our footballers and is to be seen any Saturday afternoon at any ground in the land. It was a filthy habit that we picked up from the foreigners who don't mind who they kiss or where. But how did it happen here? Then there's the business of British crowds adopting the dirty foreign habit of whistling to show displeasure. You don't need reminding that it was Britain that discovered the boo, that manly and entirely proper way of registering protest. Why do we need to whistle? And what about the shorts the players wear nowadays, those indecent armbands worn around the waist. A Continental fashion which caught on here. But why? What was wrong with those baggy pants our players used to wear which gave a proper covering to a man's mystique and an athlete's pride? After all it was we British who decided that sex and sport don't mix so why pamper to the poovy foreign trick of making our sportsmen dress like the girls in the Folies Bergère? Nonetheless, although the foregoing reads like a catalogue of concession, a sell-out to the foreigners, the fact remains that British soccer is really untouched by outside influences. The Continental gear merely alters John Bull's silhouette but not his heart and soul.

It is likely that in the future, when we are joined to Europe, British soccer, for all its fierce independence, will inevitably be painlessly absorbed into Eurosport. Soccer, whether we like it or not, is a common language nowadays and while the accent might be different the vocabulary is the same.

Our one real hope of keeping ourselves apart from the common herd lies in a game which we invented and which the Continentals have thus far not taken up: cricket. I have mixed feelings about the non-participation of other European countries in what I consider to be the greatest of games. I have always thought that the Germans might produce some of the best sloggers that the game has ever seen and that the Ruskies would certainly provide the most formidable team of women cricketers. Similarly it has always perplexed me that the French have never taken up a game which includes in its vocabulary such phrases as 'bowl a maiden over', 'fine leg', or that most delicious of sporting descriptions 'caught in the leg trap'. On the other hand I find gratification in the fact that cricket has defied the Continentals and is only played by chaps who speak English like a foreign native. It's not that the Froggies or the Krauts or the Eyties are more stupid than we are, it's simply that they are less British.

Any Eurosport who might think differently and who wants to indulge in a little missionary work must be made aware of the dangers. The fact is that we feel so deeply about this game that if the wogs got hold of it World War III would start over an LBW decision. Best to leave things as they are. Join Europe by all means but leave Lord's out of it. *Vive la différence*, as they say in Pudsey.

February 1970

'No mixing, Damen and Herren, no mess, no bother – just spray it on your haggis!'

Donegan

ICI ON MANGE ANGLAIS

'That's the kind of ruthless marketing we're up against, Crosby.'

Humphrey Lyttelton

EAT AND THE WORLD EATS WITH YOU!

Call it the quest for truth, a social survey, masochism or just plain curiosity, but the other day I got this study group together to undertake one of your searching probes into British food. The brief, in a nutshell, was to find out why, in the London section of the Good Food Guide, one has to wade through an Agra de Luxe, an Ah, Bistro!, three Alpinos, an Alvaro, an Amalfi, an Angelo, an Andrea's, an Antoine's and a Portuguese Arabelle before reaching one modest little outpost serving British fare. (On Horseback Through Tagliatelle, Taramasalata and Tandoori to Steak and Kidney Pie! I mean to say, is it our country or isn't it? Steady, men, let's keep it scientific.)

My research team consisted of three young Europeans living and working in London – Martine from France, Mario from Italy and José from Portugal. We met for lunch at the Baron of Beef in the City, where the idea was that they should be subjected to typical British fare and should then speak their minds on London food in general. In the taxi, I asked if any of them had been to an English restaurant before. I was prepared to hear that, in their respective countries, there are no restaurants specialising in English food, though I have myself visited a Scotch Tea Hoose in Nice as late as 1948. But it shook me to hear that they did not know that English restaurants existed in *England* outside of the unmentionable sausage-egg-and-chips belt. I began to feel like a tourist guide taking a party to see 'ze folklore'.

My team's first impressions of the beefy,

'All right – find me some British salamander tails and I'll buy 'em.'

super-pub atmosphere of the Baron of Beef were quite gratifying. Both Mario and José were surprised by the sight of a roomful of Englishmen all bellowing at the top of their voices and revealing uncharacteristically pliant upper lips in the noisy consumption of food. Martine seemed at first rather taken aback to find that men outnumbered women by about fifty to one. I was in the middle of explaining that the City is a predominantly working area and that most of the men would be discussing business when a waiter bustled up and, with a flourish, presented her with a nosegay of snowdrops on a velvet cushion.

It was at this point that I began to suspect that my well-laid plans might go astray. If my research team's deliberations were going to be subverted by these un-British gestures, we should get nowhere. The menu tended to confirm my fears. While I was persuading Mario to try cock-a-leekie (which I had never eaten in my life), Martine sidestepped neatly on to the neutral territory of an Avocado pear. Clearly, the meeting had to be called to order, so when the waiter took orders for the main course, I said, 'Roast beef, everyone?' in an empire-building sort of voice. Cabbage and sprouts were resolutely avoided. I pointed out to Mario that the sundry Spaghetti Houses in London are practically built on sprouts, but he cried, 'Never have I seen a sprout in Italy!' with such passion that I dropped the subject. So it was Yorkshire pudding, roast potatoes and spinach all round. With a politeness which one would expect from our oldest ally, José cleared his plate. But both Martine and Mario, while applauding the beef, firmly piloted their potatoes and Yorkshire pudding to the side of the plate. Lest you should think me pusillanimous in the face of criticism, I do recall some animated exchanges on the lines of 'I'll swap your rotten old polenta for Yorkshire pudding any day!' But I must confess that neither spuds nor Yorkshire pud were like Mum does them.

And this episode raises two interesting points. Martine alleged that in France roast potatoes are cooked in the home, never eaten in a restaurant where pre-cooking has to be done. I added that the same goes for Yorkshire pudding, which tends to turn into suede if kept hanging about. But if we relegate these specialities to the confines of home-cooking, what are typical British restaurants going to serve? I can't see a chain of Steak and Kidney Pudding Houses catching on, and if you start mucking about with courgettes and ratatouille, there's your trad image gone for a Burton. The second point is more far-reaching, and can best be posed in the form of a question. What do the British do when confronted with something which is, to them, uneatable? They eat it. Whether through politeness, a horror of 'scenes', immolation of the flesh or sheer absence of mind, they shovel it all in regardless. This led us to a general discussion from which we concluded that the British regard food as fuel rather than as something to be enjoyed, lingered over and paid for. They all agreed that in their respective countries, no one would expect to eat out for under £1 a head, nor would they regard a lunch-*hour* as adequate. The kind of cheap and nasty caffs which will feed Mum, Dad, Ron, Ivy, Granny and Auntie Flo in twenty minutes flat for thirty-five bob exist here and nowhere else because the British will eat muck if it's cheap enough.

By this time I was feeling rather depressed. The time had obviously come to counter-attack with a barrage of delicious apple pie, a volley of splendid British cheeses. But while I was studying the menu for these reassuring delights, a squad of waiters swooped on the table with baskets of exotic fruits. 'Here is something I would never have in Italy!' cried Mario in ecstasy. I feel a twinge of renascent patriotism until I looked across and saw that the fellow was eating mangoes! Really, it was too bad. Here was I in the heart of traditional London making a serious social experiment, vital you might say if we are soon to join the Common Market, and my guinea-pigs were escaping all over the shop. I hurriedly summoned the coffee and set about reaching something in the way of findings.

It appears, then, that Europeans in London avoid eating bad English food – and bad American, come to that – and have little interest in looking round for good English food. I put it to Martine and José that French food is expensive and Portuguese food relatively rare in London. They agreed, and said that for a reliable cheap meal, they would go to an Italian restaurant. If we add that sophisticated Britons do exactly the same in their own country, it's not hard to see why, in the food guides, foreign restaurants outnumber the native establishments by three to one. I got little joy on the subject of English beer. They all confined their beer-drinking to lager, and mention of a pint of bitter drew universal expressions of disgust. I thought I might be on safer ground with cheese, but apart from José, who named Danish Blue as his favourite English cheese and then hurriedly corrected himself, they had nothing to say other than that they believed that English cheese is very strong. As Chairman of the meeting, my recommendation is that a study group be set up to determine first of all what British food is, and that strenuous efforts should then be made to sell it to the British. And I hereby append a minority report to the effect that German beer tastes like zeppelin fuel, that when you've tasted a hundred yards of spaghetti you've tasted it all, that Britain never, never shall be slaves and that, by Gad, they can say what they like about our Yorkshire pudding but we do know how to serve a mango!

February 1970

Pierre Daninos (creator of 'Major Thompson')

HAS ENGLAND CHANGED? OUI . . . ET NON

It is possible to get rid of a mosquito, a battleship, even a woman. It takes a second, hours, half a lifetime. The one thing ineradicable, the thing that a man's lifetime is not sufficient to eliminate, is a preconceived idea.

When one grew up, as I did, in a domain of geographical clichés, where in the same fashion as in botanical gardens on scrolls, labels remind you that Germans are quarrelsome and obsequious, Americans big children (except for cooking where they are savages), Poles drunkards, Russians unfathomable, Italians versatile, Chinese indecipherable, Argentinians gay goers, Spaniards proud (always-noble-even-their-beggars), Arabs lazy, Swiss slow (but-always-clean), Dutch heavy, Jews Jewish, English hypocrites, tenacious, phlegmatic and, that, in the centre of this hostile and venomous world stands France, eternal hexagonal France, chivalrous, gallant, the dove France, gentle prey exposed to the rapacity of Americans, when she is not done for by Lloyd George and perfidious Albion – something remains, even fifty years later.

Particularly when History finds on her way a providential General who knows how to revive the most worn-out clichés, making England appear as a ship temporarily anchored across from Calais, ready to sail for her usual destination: westward.

This is how an important diplomatic officer just spoke to me about the English on the subject of the Common Market: 'But, mon cher, you know better than anybody: they are like no one else, they will never be like anyone else, they are a different sort . . .'

Perfidious Albion still alive.

I am forced, and regret it, to observe, that in a recent poll organised by *Le Figaro*, Great Britain comes after the United States and Germany among the countries considered friendlier by the French. After Germany . . . One must be dreaming . . . A bad dream . . . It is so, it is not easy to give up the part of *l'ennemi héréditaire* – presently vacant – that one held for centuries. The Hundred Years War continues on sports fields, whether at Wembley or Colombes. Should our XV win? It is Rocroy. Should it lose? Waterloo. Besides, it could only lose because of a bad fate or a neutral referee – English, Welsh or Irish – which inflicted an unjustified penalty. Thus French papers explain it the next day:

Incredible bad luck
and a strange arbitrage
by the English M. Lamb
YES, L'EQUIPE DE FRANCE
DESERVES ONLY
CONGRATULATIONS

England does not change: their indifference is a stone of touch. The first reaction of a Parisian having his hat blown off, is not to look for the hat that a taxi just missed, it is to find out if anyone has witnessed his mishap. I often wondered, looking at a man training for a foot race, in shorts, in Bayswater Road, around 5 p.m., in the midst of heavy traffic, nobody paying any particular attention in the buses or on the sidewalks, what would happen to a Frenchman arriving Place de l'Opéra, in casual wear, at small canter, around 6 p.m. . . . He would not only be circled by passers-by but probably arrested by policemen.

On the dancing floor of a San Remo Palace, some weeks ago, I saw an old lord in evening attire planted with a red carnation, sweep off his septuagenarian half, rustling in *baby-blue* taffetas adorned with cherries from head to breast, in a delicious waltz. Little were they concerned to be the object of interest of the assembly. They were dancing for their own delight, not for that of others.

England does not change. When in London, in 1936, 1949 or 1970, the newspaper I read seems the same. I know *The Times* (still venerable in our vocabulary) did not hesitate after a hundred-and-eighty-two years of meditation to take off his shirt of personal columns publicly, to display to the general view the womb of his informations. Otherwise, the ingredients composing *The Times*, the *Daily Mail* or the *Mirror* seem to me the same: north-east of Aden the situation is serious (north-east of Eden or south-west of Khartoum it will always be so, never comical). The Queen will spend the holiday with her family at Balmoral. Princess Margaret inaugurated a school for nurses in Sheffield. A sadist killed a fourteen-year-old schoolgirl after raping her. Another pulled out the claws of his cat. In the personal ads, a repentant driver offers publicly his apologies to the owner of the Bentley LXO 85 with whom he had a word a little too brisk on Piccadilly. Another citizen celebrates in three *in memoriam* lines Valhalla, bull terrier of noble character, his best friend for fourteen years. Underneath, another *in memoriam* dedicated to Caesar (Caius Julius), madly assassinated in the Senate in Rome, 64 AD. In spite of the love for animals, a lady traveller complained to British Railways because she travelled in the corridor of the train from London to Edinburgh while dogs were seated in the compartments. The British Railways answered awfully sorry, but the dogs had booked.

England has changed. Barely ten years ago when an Englishman, full of evil, went to one of the dirty libraries of Charing Cross Road, packed with *French books* exclusively *made in England*, he would pay and furtively slip the *Kama Sutra* inside the pocket of his MacFarlane. Today he may hesitate, choose, look through the *Epitome on Whipping among Victorian disciples of Sacher-Masoch* or *Sexual Behaviour of the English Female* at leisure, on the sidewalk racks of these shops: nobody

1970

2000

UNITED STATES OF EUROPE?
(as seen in 1970)

cares. He could even hold with one hand a *Lexicon of Exotic Potions* and in the other one of your miniskirted little red riding-hoods, willing to be devoured by the big bad wolf, nobody is shocked.

England does not change. On that same visit to London, my publisher invited me to his club, the Garrick: we had lunch in the *Coffee Room* and had coffee, early in the afternoon, in the *Morning Room*. Previously I had been at Dunhill, Duke Street. How could I call clerk, the elegant fiftyish gentleman who greeted me in the Cigar Room? Measured in his motion, chastised in his language, it was I who felt like a pedlar, a lost, poor fellow asking for 'havanas' when there were Larranaga, Bolivar, Hoyo de Monterrey, Ramon Allones . . . He spread ten sorts in front of me. 'Those,' I hastily said, like a child eager to get his cake. The *cigar*-master curbed the unruly pupil: 'I am afraid, Sir . . . I could not possibly. Not quite ripe.'

Had I been properly trained, I would have known that cigars from *Seleccion Suprema for Connoisseurs* cannot, under any circumstances, be sold before having followed their twelve months' classes in the *Maturing Room*. What a Boeotian! I held out my lighter – a flat, golden treasure – asking for a flint to be fitted. The man did not want to touch it. 'My hands, Sir, must remain virgin for the cigars. I shall take you to the *Pipe Room* where this little thing can be fixed.'

England has changed. We built barricades without a revolution. You had a revolution without barricades. A revolution which should deserve an eight-column title: *England has changed Sovereigns*. For although there is still a queen in Buckingham Palace, her power is inferior to that of the mighty unions; without their agreement nothing is possible. Not even in an hotel, to have the valet change an electric bulb. Politely, the valet told me that he could not touch that sort of thing without being in trouble with the electricians' union, itself divided in six or seven underunions, according to the voltage, or the specialty involved. I had to wait for the presence of the unionist. That is only a trifle. I know of a car manufacturer who started a strike in his factory by reducing the team of specialists, highly qualified, in charge of distributing the tea to the chain workers, from twelve to eight.

After the publication, in the *Sunday Telegraph*, of two anecdotes about belching in public places in England, a reader wrote me: 'I enjoyed your article very much and would like to explain that your belcher of a soldier and your other two young belchers probably belong to the new enchinesed castes (half Chinese). I take the liberty to remind you:

1. It is polite to belch in China.
2. Great Britain has become an Afro-Asiatic dependance.'

I do not say that. I cannot be too worried about the question of how you will behave when you will be given your European identity pass. I am convinced that you will be as cunning and dishonest as the others (except for France, naturally: France is the only nation in the world which never does anything out of selfish interest, but in the interest of the whole universe).

The day of the accession of Great Britain to the only club, at the door of which it was kept stamping, will be a glorious day for the whole world and for yourselves. For me it would be a sombre day if it should modify your demeanour. My diplomat friend was not altogether wrong . . . In this world shrinking a little more every day, where one goes to Tahiti as one used to go to Naples, there is not one other nation susceptible to remove one from his usual habits, more than any of the Tuamotous, an ultra-civilised nation, whose customs remain more bizarre than that of the natives of Sunda Islands – yours, unique State in the world which allows one to feel out of the planet without leaving it.

Stay that, stay what you are, and what you are not.

February 1970

John Wells

BREAKAWAY BRITAIN

Brussels, Thursday – Federal Leader General Charles de Gaulle today dismissed as 'mischievous rebel propaganda' allegations that millions were still starving inside the former British enclave after last week's successful final push by the German Fourth and Fifth Panzer Divisions of the European Federal Army. Commenting on a report by the New Zealand Red Cross which criticised the Federal Government for not allowing relief flights to use the former rebel airstrips at Heathrow-London, Birmingham and Glasgow, situated as they were at the centre of the worst-affected areas, and for insisting on what aid it accepted being channelled through Brussels and then taken in by sea, road and rail, the General emphasised once again that this was now a European problem, and advised foreign 'nosey-parkers' that such outbursts could endanger their trading position in a re-unified and prosperous European Federation.

Meanwhile there was still no news here of the whereabouts of former rebel leader James Harold Wilson, who was reliably reported by the Federal Government's Press Office last Friday to have fled the country in a two-seater Meteor jet, taking with him two white Rolls-Royces, four tons of gold bullion, and over three hundred aides, hacks, whores and dependents, including his chief adviser Colonel A. Douglashome, himself a prominent member of the rebel governing clique. Portugal, South Africa and Bolivia have all been suggested as possible destinations, and an unofficial report from Jordan suggests that he may be offered temporary asylum in Amman. In Brussels, General de Gaulle has lost no time in condemning Wilson as being solely responsible for the three-year war in which it is estimated over two million have died in the former 'British Isles', blaming it on the secessionist leader's 'insensate greed, ambition and lust for power'.

It is now over three and a half years since the events took place which the rebel public relations firm, the so-called 'Foreign and Commonwealth Press Office', have repeatedly exploited and exaggerated to justify the illegal act of secession from the Federation. In an atmosphere of growing crisis throughout the newly unified States of the European Union, a handful of English businessmen – the number was certainly not more than a few hundred – were murdered in several major cities from Hamburg to Marseilles. Complaints about English 'cockiness' and cheek were familiar, and the incident did not attract much attention at the time; but when a perfectly justified threat of legal secession by the former Western German State necessitated a sudden increase of Teuton representation at the European Parliament and a more realistic approach to the role of private finance in politics, the English reaction and that of the Scottish and Welsh minority tribes was hysterical. Reckless allegations were made. The innocent wife of a Teuton politician was accused of having spent funds raised for charity on a solid gold bed, intended, according to the London propaganda sheet, *Daily Telegraph*, 'to form the centrepiece in a private brothel'. Decent citizens of Paris were described as 'corrupt'. London's share of the Federal cake was said to be minimal. Suddenly, without warning, a bloody coup established the Englishman Heath as President of the Federation. The ugly face of Anglo-Saxon ambition was unmasked. Revenge was not long in coming. In one swift and clinical operation Heath and several of his Ministers were shot, and shortly afterwards a larger number of English and Celtic Minorities businessmen – twenty thousand at most – were massacred throughout Europe in a spontaneous eruption of popular resentment. Again the reaction from the rebellious offshore islands was prickly and brooding. As General de Gaulle was recalled from retirement to preside over the vigorous young Federation, self-styled Prime Minister Wilson returned from the political wilderness to grab power for himself and his rebel gang in London, officially as Governor of the Western Maritime State (later 'Britain'), in fact in preparation for the criminal act of secession. Outrageous demands were made in his name, including an offensively worded request for a Federal Inquiry into the so-called massacres. Resolving to slap down the 'uppity' Anglo-Saxons once and for all, General de Gaulle responded by creating a new and more compact Western Maritime State, giving the old 'Home Counties' to Paris, and the coal and natural gas rich East Coast to Bonn.

Wilson needed no better excuse. By an act of insane folly and maniacal arrogance, he officially declared the Independent State of Britain, coolly announcing that he intended to take the islands' valuable coal, natural gas, and heavy industry with him. From that moment the podgy white Hitler was doomed. With the armouries of the former Colonial Power thrown open for their use by the Pentagon in Washington, the European Federal Army flung a stranglehold of death round the beleaguered islands, imposing a total blockade of rebel ports and cutting off altogether all food, ammunition, arms and medical supplies coming from abroad. Anxious to preserve her influence in Europe, the USSR provided her latest bombers to strafe and pound the foolhardy secessionists into submission. At the same time both Russia and the United States made the strongest representations to the Red Cross and the Church Aid Organisations, pointing out that the clandestine supply of food to the besieged rebels could only prolong their agony. In the event only a trickle of contraband food and blackmarket weapons was flown into 'Britain' by evil mercenary nurses and arms dealers, and the majority of right-thinking charitable organisations threw their weight behind the policy of a 'Quick Kill'.

Despite this, the self-styled 'British', drugged with their own propaganda, held out for almost three years in a crazed, masochistic ritual of racial suicide. Invited to Peace Talks again and again to proffer their unconditional surrender, coaxed into a more reasonable attitude by bombing raids, rocket attacks, and the ever-tightening ring of small-arms fire and artillery barrage that drove the civilian population before it into the English heartland of Yorkshire and Lancashire, the stubborn, intransigent islanders fought back with the vilest tactics known to man. Disgusting photographs of starving children, bombed hospitals, and dead civilians were circulated by their Public Relations Office in Whitehall, ludicrous claims of genocide were made to neutral governments, and it was only thanks to the American Foreign Secretary's impassioned oratory on the dangers of balkanisation that no interventionist spanner was thrown into the Federal fighting machine. Four military observers visited the battle zone, and were able to set at rest absolutely the conscience of the world on every score.

Now, as the massive aid operation begins to gather momentum, the shattered ruins of Wilson's dream 'United Kingdom' bear silent witness to the fate that waits for those who having once set their hand to the European plough dare to look back.

February 1970

'Mark my words, there'll be all those foreign influences creeping in . . .'

'I don't see why it shouldn't work . . . I've always got on awfully well with my au pair girls.'

Graham

INTO EUROPE

'You know what I'll miss? – Bringing back all that duty-free booze.'

'This summer Giles intends to make what he thinks may well be a last gesture.'

EUROPEAN TIMES

Incorporating Le Monde, The Times, Die Welt, Corriere Della Sera, etc.

EUROPEAN ECONOMY: PRESIDENT WARNS

Ermano Izquierda, compromise Andorran President of the coalition European government, yesterday issued a reminder that our balance of payments was still open to overland competition. Speaking to Sicilian Young Conservatives, he recalled that it was not very many years ago that Europe was known as the sick man of the Old World.

"We must not let ourselves be fooled by last month's figures. They are good, but only because of the Mediterranean dock strike, which has held up imports, and because of the sale of Finland to Russia. The basic situation is not altogether healthy even if it is not exactly whatever the Sicilian for unhealthy is."

Our Bonn correspondent writes: It seems fairly clear the President Izquierda was referring obliquely to the present industrial unrest in England where the car industry, now entering its third week of strikes, is in a desperate position.

Owing to a printer's dispute, the first editions of the European Times failed to appear yesterday. We apologise to those readers in Scotland, Gibraltar, Heligoland, Greece, the Alps and Brittany who did not receive copies.

Our London correspondent comments: There will of course be attempts to link the President's speech with the English motor strike, but as our motor industry now only employs five hundred men, chiefly to supply spares to the Italian tractor trade, this is hardly relevant. What must have been uppermost in his mind is the continued inability of the French to stem the outward flow of capital.

Our Financial Editor adds: Mostly to Africa.

Our Paris correspondent writes: Yes, this was a speech to make one think. As we stand on the threshold of a new century, perhaps a century of glory, perhaps a century of gloom and despair, we find ourselves faced with questions so momentous that even a philosopher, even a French philosopher, would find it difficult...

Our Brussels, Oslo, Madrid and Vienna correspondents write: A timely warning.

Horror Killings in Naples, Godalming & Hamburg

Police began investigations yesterday in Germany, Italy and England into the deaths of Siegfried Gottburg, Luigi Cattalchi and James Farley, who were found murdered in their boarding house beside the autostrada and in the back yard of a pub. Police suspect foul play, brutal murder and funny goings-on.

Luigi Cattalchi was last seen by his friend Elsa Moravo at three o'clock in the afternoon walking down the street. "He waved and smiled and seemed quite alive at the time. Siegfried Gottburg? No, that doesn't ring a bell."

Whereas Cattalchi was stabbed to death, Gottburg appears to have been struck with a blunt instrument and the death scene was described as

Continued column 1, page 2

PLANNING DECISION:

New Protests

The British plans to demolish Belgrave Square in order to make way for the Piccadilly Underpass By-pass have met with hot opposition from the Club de Preservationistes de Town-planning de Clermont-Ferrand and the Stadtgebieterhaltungsverein of Kassel. Both associations are keen to preserve outstanding examples of early nineteenth century speculative building and are shocked by the English decision.

"Zis is an outrage," said a spokesman in Clermont-Ferrand last night. "We shall fight tooth and nail, and leg and claw to make sure that Belgrave Square survives. In the whole of France we have nothing like this."

"Nor have we in Germany," said a spokesman in Kassel last night. "Have you taken leave and said good-bye, senses? Next thing, you will be knocking over St. John's Wood. This is a sad day for lovers of diplomats everywhere."

The Historic Building Preservation Society declined to comment last night, being currently totally engaged in trying to save the remains of the Eiffel Tower.

continued from column 3, page 1
the worst they had ever seen by eye witnesses, none of whom had been to Godalming. But it is the motive that puzzles the police most. Was this an inter-state plot aimed at liquidating barbers, student and building workers? Was it simply a case of mistaken identity (all three victims were, strikingly, men)? Or was there, bafflingly, absolutely no connection between the three crimes, despite the incredible organisation this would have involved?

One small clue comes from Gottburg's landlady, who describes hearing loud noises in his room "like a team of sportsmen kicking a ball around." Gottburg had no interest in sport, but Farley was a rugger club member and had in fact been drinking with them when the accident occurred. Is it possible that Farley was killed in Hamburg, Gottburg in Germany, and that the bodies were then exchanged? And if so, who was Cattalchi exchanged with? Or was his a quite private murder?

It was announced late last night that a man is helping the police with their inquiries in Hamburg, Naples and Godalming.

EUROPEAN RECIPES

No. 31: *German style cod pilaff a l'ecossaise with gnocchi.*

4 cod fillets	salt & pepper
1 lb rice	gnocchi
8 knödel	optional national
I cup oats	flourishes

Cook, cool, flake, fry, mash, rip, toss, add, simmer and stand well clear. Then serve piping hot, or spaghetti bolognese would do very well instead.

COMMENT

We have reported elsewhere President Izquierda's comments on the state of the European economy. The problems for ourselves are obvious; what needs discussing is its effect on our overseas policy.

For the last twenty years Europe has been efficient and prosperous, and the effort of underpinning the American economy has been bearable. But with a recession on its way, is it not time that we considered again our commitment across the Atlantic? Everyone knows how much we owe to America, which during the middle years of the century just past was the mistress and peacekeeper of the world. Those days are now past and America has become an empire without a role to play, a vast sprawling exhausted nation. So far we have protected her with loans, defended her with our soldiers, and invested in her industry.

But now we have troubles of our own. Our war in Vietnam drags on from year to year, the gap between generations increases, the erstwhile spirit of the U.S.E. has slumped to near gloom. Might it not be time that we expected America to look after herself? What does she give us beside pornography, cheap holidays and the heritage of our history? The United States of Europe are still young, while America is old and tired. It would surely be fairer to her to give her another chance to revive, to find her own resurgence.

Europeans, it is now widely recognised, are not popular abroad. We are resented as upstart, nouveau riche tourists. Well, let us at least take advantage of this image and begin now to reserve our largesse for ourselves.

SPORT

West Germany 2: Italy 1

(from Alan Craven)

It was a great shame that anyone had to win, but there it is—in the closing minutes Scholl slipped, fell and knocked the ball by accident into the Italian goal and all his apologies could not alter the score-line. Germany desperately tried to give away an equalising goal in the dying seconds but the effort was too much.

As for the performance of the Dutch referee and the Scottish and Spanish linesmen, no words of praise are too high; their flag control and whistling was of the highest order from beginning to end. Nor let us forget the Tyrolean ballboy squad or the Alsatian dog which ran on in the second half—all combined to make this a memorable evening. I typed till the tears ran down my face.

Letters

Sir,

It is not quite true to say, as some of your correspondents have suggested, that there was no opposition to Neville Chamberlain in 1938 and 1939. One of the doctors who attended the English leader in those days told my uncle many years ago that in fact a loyal group of civil servants had planned his assassination down to the last detail. A bomb was planted in his umbrella several days before Munich, designed to explode when it fell to the ground. Unfortunately the damp in the umbrella affected the mechanism in the bomb and when Chamberlain next opened the umbrella he suffered nothing worse than a badly bruised big toe.

I am &c,

Charles Seagrave, SW3

Sir,

I have just seen the first swallow of winter.

Yours faithfully,

Manuel Garcia, Barcelona.

Alan Coren

THE WOMEN OF EUROPE

The Frenchwoman

The Frenchwoman proper, if that's the word, began in 1914, when she took to bathing in mill streams behind the lines, and leaping up and down in the water, waving at Lew Ayres and Slim Somerville, and mouthing, through bee-sting lips, such eternal verities as 'Wot 'ave you done wiz my cloze, you naughty Tommee?'.

When the war was ended, the Frenchwoman got out of the water, lashed herself into her waspie, and went back to sitting behind an estaminet till, from which fortification (she kept the keys between her breasts, an indulgence she allowed to nothing else) she ruled the family with an iron rod, called the franc. Her daughters remained chaste until 1925, when the first wave of young American novelists struck the country, whose need for first-hand material was such that by 1929, there were fewer than ten virgins in the entire country.

They held out until 1931.

During the latter thirties, so deftly chronicled by Renoir and Gabin, Frenchwomanhood was rigidly trifurcated: they were either (1) dressed in berets and fishnet stockings and thrown through the windows of the darker nightclubs, still smoking, or (2) married to Adolphe Menjou whose own impeccably clad assignations (he is rumoured to have worn tails in bed) forced them into one passionate affair with a frail bronchitic pianist that ended in the rain, or (3) living in such grey conurbations as Metz or Valenciennes where they became pregnant at the hands (and so forth) of Parisian travelling men with pencil moustaches who had a habit of shooting their cuffs and leaving their playmates to die in childbirth.

None of these women, i.e. all Frenchwomen, ever enjoyed sex at all. It was mainly a source of grief, frustration, and disillusionment. All it had was a thin edge over drinking alone.

The World War II years were somewhat better for the Frenchwoman, since she would either collaborate, in which case sex, however miserable, meant stockings, chocolate, sable, and riding around in a Mercedes; or she could work for the Maquis, which meant a lot of fresh air and cycling, and Doing It In A Good Cause, i.e. sleeping with RAF rear-gunners awaiting repatriation.

After 1945, Frenchwomanhood underwent (choosing one's words carefully) a sexual revolution, in that enjoyment crept into bed. In the Bardot years, busts got bigger, clothes came off (pre-war, much of the sex-life of the Frenchwoman took place in evening gowns, well-cut of course, but complex and noisy), and men started looking like Belmondo and Delon, instead of like brick outhouses in blue vests. Coyness disappeared (the French, contrary to their winking, louche image, have always had more sexual hang-ups than any race on earth, with the possible exception of the Urak islanders, who will only make love in shallow water, at night), and a jolly good time was had by all.

All this came to an end with the *nouvelle vague*, a period, starting in 1957, when Frenchwomen grew pitifully confused, unable to distinguish between husbands and lovers, lovers and lovers, and husbands and husbands. Most of the time they wandered about on the terraces of the more decrepit castles, trying to sort things out.

Of late, as you will have seen in the newspapers, poisonings appear to have begun again, a bad sign. However, another war might clear the air a bit. Frenchwomen seem to thrive on wars.

The Luxembourgoise

There are nine women in Luxembourg, and they are kept pretty busy making stamps (see pages 13–14). They all look rather alike, except for Tante Marie, who has a wall-eye, the inaccuracy of which restricts her activities to gumming.

Sexually, their lives are somewhat limited, there being only six men in the Grand Duchy, and not too many places to hide; in fact, there is only one eligible bachelor, Armand Arfamault, and one copse, so that he is kept pretty busy. He is also attacked by incensed husbands with pitiable regularity, and being too tired ever to defend himself, is growing less and less eligible with each passing night.

Given these extreme spatial limitations, the Luxembourgoise is sadly cut off from many of the thrills which her European sisters enjoy: not for her the dirty weekends (anyone attempting to pass themselves off as M. et Mme. Smeeth is unlikely to fool the other thirteen inhabitants), not for her the regular hot afternoon trysts (Armand Arfamault being available, at best, one afternoon in nine, and then only when his work as an album-binder is over for the day), not for them the billets-doux slipped to milkmen in the empty bottle (the entire population lives in one small block of flats, and shares the step), not for them the heady escape to mountain retreat or country cottage (there is only one mountain in Luxembourg; it is some eight feet higher than the rest of the country, bare as an egg, and commands an uninterrupted view of the only cottage, some six yards away).

It is hardly surprising, then, that the romantic life of the Luxembourgoise is spasmodic, fraught, and unfulfilled. She is, in consequence a dour and unrewarding mistress.

The Fräu(lein)

It was Bismarck who welded the German woman into a fighting unit. Until the 1870s, she was a disparate collection of conflicting characteristics: buxom, flaxen peasant wench; brooding saga-heroine given to liaisons with owls and dragons and headless horsemen; fierce earth-mother waggoning her children from dukedom to dukedom, dirndled and parthenogenetic; randy noblewoman in the habit of savaging booted lieutenants on the sideboard; melancholy riparian songstress; and single-breasted artiste of the sabre.

It is not to be wondered at, therefore, that the German woman emerges in the early twentieth century as a figure in a top hat, black tights and a baritone voice, with a penchant for lashing out with a stockwhip and seeing, at the same time, that the boys in the backroom want for nothing. She is currently seen at her best upon the Reeperbahn (pronounced, for reasons which became obvious at Number 122b, second floor, Raperbahn), where, for a small consideration, she will wrestle in mud, spit rivets through sheet ply, and perform a number of interesting tricks with ordinary household objects, like men. Beyond the Reeperbahn, German womanhood has undergone the well-known *Fräuleinswunder*, indistinguishable in essence from the equally famous *Wirtschaftswunder*, in that it merely means that they are bigger and stronger than you are. Provided you stay away from mud, however, this need not be to your disadvantage, but take a friend along. They are also the most sexually liberated women in Europe, which is fine, since it keeps them from marching on the Sudetenland; what happens to the New German Woman when society channels her vigour into alternative areas may be seen from a glance at her East German *Schwester*, whose energy manifests itself in terrifying ways; unless you happen to like hanging around girls who can chuck a hammer into the next county, that is.

Connoisseurs of such things say that the German woman reached her apogee (often several times a week) in the last days of Weimar, when the decadence was so thick you could slice it like knackwurst, and everything went, including, unfortunately, the mark, with all that that entailed. It is worth remembering, therefore, for anyone with residual doubts about the economic stability of the EEC, that there is always a bright side to German inflation.

The Dutchwoman

Dutchwomen fall into two quite distinct physical types: the small, corpulent, red-faced Edams, and the thinner, paler, larger Goudas. Having evolved underwater, the Dutchwoman is, perhaps, a trifle less hot-blooded than other European ladies, but this is more than made up for by her expertise on the bicycle, an invaluable instrument for getting away quietly at night.

Which cannot be said for the clog.

There are one or two drawbacks to more serious and longer liaisons with Dutchwomen, prime among which is the fact that Queen Juliana is the richest woman in the world and her less elevated countrywomen have not been slow to see the advantages of the folding stuff. Couple this to a healthy appetite (for food) and a blasé attitude towards flowers (sick of tulips and their ilk, the Dutchwoman will rarely be satisfied with anything less than orchids or long-stemmed roses out of season), and you will observe that anyone with an overdraft should step warily upon disembarking at the Hook.

'You the owner of the car number OYW 872R?'

La Belge

Everything that the Belgian woman is has come about as a direct result of Belgium's being the most densely populated country in Europe. A woman for whom her native agronomists developed the sprout, this being the largest cabbage a busy housewife could possibly manoeuvre through the packed Brussels streets, will accept almost anything. It is those same teeming roads, crammed buses and trams, and general nose-to-ear social conditions that have made her so sexually sophisticated; since a lifetime of being wedged up against men on public transport has left her with few naiveties.

The obverse of this otherwise encouraging coin is that it is practically impossible to get her alone. With nary a spare millimetre of soil between Ostend and Liège, the chance of achieving a rendezvous is extremely remote: arrive thirty seconds late at the appointed spot, and you will find that your date has been shuffled on by the crowd, to be lost for ever (they tend to fetch up eventually at the German border, weeping; which makes Aachen the lugubrious place it is, except for the week in the year when they throw their *Witzfest*, and God knows they need it).

The Italian Woman

Ninety-eight per cent of Italian women go around in black bombazine; it is the two per cent who go around without it with whom we should concern ourselves here.

Little was known about Italian women until 1951, when the first of them was spotted, standing in a rice field with a wisp of hair blowing into her incredible velvet eyes, and her dress tucked into her knickers. Since then, we have never looked back; except, of course, when driving too fast past rice fields. Sadly, the ubiquitous pasta has seen to it that rice remains a minor crop; despite the general feeling that if the entire country were put onto a rice economy, it would be no bad thing. The other villainy wrought by pasta is entirely dietetic: the beautiful, lissome, delectable Signorina of nineteen can, in the space of a few short years (or, to put it another way, thirty-eight tons of fettucine) become an unbeautiful, unlissome, undelectable Signora beneath whom many a gondola has sunk like a brick, raising the water level to disastrous heights and threatening, very soon, to turn Venice into nothing more than a campanile or two poking above the surrounding silt.

The grafting of the Lollobrigidas, Lorens, Cardinales and so forth onto the cultural tapestry of the most sin-conscious country in Europe has done nothing for domestic calm, and foreign visitors should tread with care: visiting women may be turned, in an hour or so, into a mass of bluish-black bumps by frustrated local fingers, while visiting men, surrounded by the busty untouchables with which the landscape is dotted, may, in the same period, end up as hollow-eyed, dry-mouthed wrecks. The introduction of divorce a year or so ago should not be taken as an encouraging sign, since the traditional customs prevail: international brotherhood is one thing, but international Brotherhood is something very different, and one of the things known to mar a night of unbridled passion in Italy is a knock on the door in the small hours heralding the arrival of a brace of Cosa Nostra members. Cosa Nostra means 'our thing', and good luck to it; but when they do their thing to you, and it becomes your thing, and medical science shakes its head and walks away, you may well find yourself asking whether Italy shouldn't ban the production of rice altogether.

Scandinavia

At the time of going to press, the women of Scandinavia were uncertain about entry. They fall, therefore, outside the scope of this survey, if they fall anywhere.

October 1972

'If we'd stood firm over their French Golden Delicious, they might have thought twice about their Exocets.'

'Oh God! Not another sand dancer!'

'Don't get excited – it usually turns out that all but two of them are dead.'

'Gentlemen, the fort will have to be evacuated – it's just been bought as a holiday home by a couple from Altrincham!'

Hector Breeze

DESERT FROGS

'And now Captain Le Marchand will demonstrate how military strategy can be fun.'

2

THE CHANNEL TUNNEL

Miles Kington
CHANNEL TUNNEL
Progress Report

1802. A scheme for building a tunnel under the Channel is submitted to Napoleon. Nothing happens.
1830s. French engineers make exploratory surveys. Nothing is done.
1880. The construction and final completion of the Channel Tunnel Company. Nothing happens immediately.
1881. Work begins at both ends!
1883. Work stops at both ends after protests from House of Commons and the Army.
1914–18, 1939–45. Channel Tunnel Company shares relatively inactive.
1968. New preparations are halted on account of political unrest in France.
1970. Under the leadership of Leo d'Erlanger, grandson of the original founder, the Channel Tunnel Company celebrates another year of existence with another annual general meeting. D'Erlanger prophesies that a tunnel will unquestionably be built by the end of the 1970s. To mark their ninetieth anniversary they hold the time-honoured ceremony of announcing no dividend – shares change hands at 23*s*. each, but dealings are quiet rather than frenzied.
1972. A Government Commission is set up to consider the possibility of a road tunnel link with France. In evidence, Leo d'Erlanger testifies that it is getting less possible all the time because of rising costs, but that if they act immediately it may not be too late. Channel Tunnel Company shares rise to 25*s*.
1975. The Commission receives a sarcastic birthday card from Leo d'Erlanger.
1976. The Channel Tunnel Commission goes public; shares start modestly at 10*s*. and slip unselfishly to 1*s*. 9*d*.
1977. A rumour goes round the Stock Exchange that the Commission is about to produce a report and many people dine out on this hilarious story. Many dinners are ruined by the news that the Commission has indeed produced a report. It weighs 4½ lbs, cost 3 gns, and, if the pages were laid end to end, would stretch from Calais to Dover, drift on to Hastings beach in a sodden mess and involve the Government in a new pollution scandal.

The report recommends that a tunnel

should be built under the Channel as soon as possible by a joint effort of the British and French governments, and any others who care to join in. Commission shares shoot up to 2*s.* 4*d.*, the Company's shares rocket to 27*s.*, d'Erlanger forecasts a tunnel by 1985 and all national dailies print the same photograph of a hole in the ground near Folkestone.

1979. The British and French governments announce a joint plan to build the Tunnel de Manche and start work from each end on a six-lane highway. Every national daily simultaneously coins the term six-lane lowway, except the *Guardian* which, worried by the two adjacent w's, christens it a six-lane deepway.

Undeterred, the British Prime Minister drives a ceremonial two miles under the sea and back again, a feat only rivalled by that of the French President who has done the same a few months earlier slightly to the south.

1980. Centenary year of the Channel Tunnel Company, or would have been if it was not nationalised in 1978. Leo d'Erlanger forecasts that they would have paid a dividend in 1987.

1981. A world-wide recession halts work indefinitely on the Tunnel. To make use of the section built already, the British end is converted into a combined submarine research/seismology unit.

1982. The French end is converted into a rival submarine/seismology establishment. The British Government starts negotiations with the French to co-ordinate the research work of the two stations, but no agreement is reached.

1983. An improving world situation allows work to restart on the Channel Tunnel, despite organised protests from seismologists and marine researchers the world under, and a further three miles are completed in both directions before an unusually heavy spring wage claim stops progress. Both termination points become customs-free areas and the five-mile drive under the sea becomes a common weekend expedition for both nations. Though the main object of reaching France has not yet been attained, the Tunnel is now beginning to earn a little money.

1984. Five more miles are dug, making the Tunnel unquestionably the longest underwater tunnel in the world, or rather the two longest underwater tunnels in the world.

Costs by now have risen to £5,000,000,000 more than the original estimate and a *Times* leader seriously questions the wisdom of going on. Encouraged by this sign, the Government goes on.

1986. On 4 April the two sections of the Tunnel finally meet, causing great draughts in

Folkestone and celebrations elsewhere.

On 17 April the Prime Minister of Britain and the President of France set out from opposite sides of the Channel and meet in the middle to shake hands.

On 19 April the new Tunnel is opened to public traffic for the first time, it having been agreed that vehicles will drive on the right, as they have been doing in Britain since 1981.

On 20 April the Tunnel is closed for structural modifications. There are no fundamental changes to be made, but it is found that the engineers had not made allowance for several inconveniences:-

(i) the tendency of a large pool of oil and water to gather at the lowest point.
(ii) the accumulation of almost unbearable motor noise.
(iii) a smell of garlic in Kent with a southerly wind.
(iv) the mass hysteria among fish in the Channel caused by vibration.

1987. The Tunnel reopens to take ordinary traffic.

1989. As twenty-mile traffic jams and customs area congestion become more frequent, it becomes apparent that the original Tunnel was not large enough for the volume of traffic using it. A commission is set up to determine whether it would be wiser to widen the Tunnel or build a new one alongside.

1990. At Easter weekend, the Tunnel is entirely blocked for forty-eight hours and all cars abandoned. The national daily insists that this must never happen again.

1991. In its report the Commission describes the cost of increasing the Tunnel in any way as prohibitive. It recommends consideration of a new plan to build a hoverbridge to France. A commission is set up to consider a new hoverbridge to France.

1993. The Commission reports in favour of a new hoverbridge to France and the Channel Hoverbridge Company is nationalised.

1999. The new twelve-lane hoverbridge to France is ceremonially opened and the old Channel Tunnel ceremonially blocked at both ends.

2045. The Elizabethan Preservation Society agitates for the reopening of the Channel Tunnel as a national monument to twentieth-century engineering. The Government argues that the cost would be astronomical and that all available finance is needed for the airborne twenty-four-lane skyway being rebuilt to replace the old Hoverbridge.

2056. An enthusiastic businessman, Mr Joshua Betjeman, puts up the money to drain the Tunnel, restore it to its former condition and preserve it as a national institution of some kind.

2070. Currently, the Commission to decide the eventual function of the old Tunnel, the negotiations with the French over the financial load-sharing, and the inquiry to determine how to replace the old inadequate twenty-four-lane skyway, are all still in session and there is no immediate prospect of a decision from any of them. We will inform readers as soon as there is.

July 1970

Sean Macaulay

SO WHY *IS* THE CHANNEL TUNNEL SO EXPENSIVE?

Machinery

Really big digger-trucks, like the Tonka ones you used to get for Christmas only loads better. £40,000 each from your local Scammel dealer

Radio signal booster for use underground to pick up Radio 1. £1,000 upwards

Huge, specially designed wooden horse for

'I must warn you – that estimate was drawn up by someone at Eurotunnel.'

workers to jump over while tunnel is being dug. £9,000 from Colditz Crafts Ltd

Anglo-French Pneumatic Donkey Jacket Delouser. £150 from top branches of Millets

Safety Equipment

De-luxe water-wings in case there's a bad leak halfway. £4.95 each from all leading department stores

Scuba equipment in case that leak gets any worse. From £250, extra with built-in Walkman

Luminescent hard hats. Available in a variety of colours and all with 'Acid Tunnel' smiles on front. £39.95 from Camden Market

Canary in cage for any ageing, nostalgic miners among the workforce. £50 from your local pet shop

Staff extras

Three Yorkie bars per worker daily. 22p each

Acne cream to counteract all that chocolate. £1.50 from all leading chemists

Daily copies of the *Sun*, pre-folded for easy back-pocket insertion. 22p each

All rights in the disaster movie *Tunnel '89* currently being made by Dino Di Laurentiis. $2m

Sundries

Berlitz French phrase book for those other tricky encounters halfway. £3.95 each

Large girlie calendars from local road haulage firm. Free, but you have to take advertising

Models hired to walk up and down tunnel and be whistled at. £200 per hour

Berets and stripy Breton T-shirts. £19.95 by post, coupon in back of the *Observer Magazine*

October 1989

Jonathan Sale

MISSING LINK

At least the rails are the same distance apart. The entire land surface of South-East England may have to be removed to make way for the Chunnel, but there is one thing in its favour. Two if you count both rails.

The gauge is the same for BR and the Société Nationale de Chemins de fer Français. This has not mattered much since the days of the Golden Arrow, when the entire train was driven over the edge of the docks, onto the ferry and off at the other side of the Channel, without the bone-idle passengers having to leave their sleeping-compartments. (Incidentally, do not be fooled by the Orient Express, the rolling-stock of which screeches to a halt at the coast, approaching no nearer to the Orient than East Sussex and leaving the passengers to amble around on the ferry like all the proles.)

But it matters now. British trains will be able to start their dive in what was, in pre-Chunnel days, scenic English countryside with hardly a touch of concrete, and emerge in the middle of France. Unfortunately the

space provided in our existing tunnels is not enough for the overgrown French *wagons* with their larger dimensions which would have the corners knocked off before they had penetrated far into Kent, leaving the shocked visitors crouching on a large skateboard. The plan is for new, customised trains to be knocked up in time. These are early days yet.

The other area where there are a few details 'still to be ironed out', in the words of the Department of Transport, is that of the by-laws relating to, say, the war wounded who have their seats specially reserved on the Continent but not here. When the train has completed half its submarine run in the direction of England, what happens to *les mutilés de guerre*, not to mention blind folk who have been nowhere near any fighting, the victims of industrial injury, pregnant women and others whom the chivalrous French have insisted must be allowed to take the weight off their feet? Will they be booted out at the halfway mark by men whose injuries owe nothing to armed warfare or by women who have been on the Pill for years? This would certainly provide a taste of life in the Thatcherite Britain that they are about to experience.

The taste of gastronomic riches is a service promised by the SNCF *Première* class: 'A prodigy of culinary virtuosity' – I translate, though not very well – 'made real by Joël ROBUCHON, the best craftsman of France and a cook blessed by the critics.' And the bar is no BR-style place where thirsty folk bump against each other while being told, 'Sorry sir, we've closed.' It is 'a harbour of relaxation where it does well to find oneself'. As you would expect, the first-class area is 'designed by François CATROUX, inter-

nationally renowned decorator, where a cosseted atmosphere makes the voyage an exceptional moment'.

We shall have to wait and see what happens to M. ROBUCHON's *Etuvée de Langoustines en Civet* when the White Cliffs of Dover loom over the horizon. Hurled out, probably, to avoid showing up the work of the British culinary prodigies that are internationally accursed by the critics. Likewise the designer seats of renowned M. CATROUX. Dumped in the guard's van until the return trip, *mon vieux*.

Take the case of the typical Frenchman on a bicycle with a string of onions round his neck. In the Brave New World of sub-Channel travel, where does he stand (apart from in the corridor)? I'm not sure about that bike, *monsieur*. My local cycling pressure group is asking the Dept of Transport about the chances of bicycles being allowed to make the trip, but in general BR's international prodigies of design forget to leave room in the van. SNCF offers a Train 'n' Pedal service that hires out *vélos* to tourists; the nearest mainline station to this office refuses even to accept my machine in the Left Luggage.

In rail travel, you gets what you pays for, and SNCF told me that its customers pay two-thirds of the fares of their British counterparts. Agreed, the subsidy is twice as big but so is the country.

Working out who pays what is hard enough, given our system of Awayday PersilCards for Senior Citizens visiting grandchildren of student age on Rogation Tuesdays. It is no easier with the French system of railcards, which enable passengers to save francs francs francs for young people, for families, for those making a round trip of at

'There's a red light at the end of the tunnel!'

least 1,000 kilometres, for salaried citizens on their annual holiday.

There are reductions for 'Numerous Families'; France is a Catholic country. There is money off for couples who are not legally coupled but who present *un certificat de concubinage*, which is what it sounds like; France is a romantic country. There are cards which, among other benefits, bring reduced entrance fees to the National Railway Museum at Mulhouse. On the debit side of the ledger, there are supplements bumping up the fares of some trains – but, astonishingly as the news strikes Britannic ears, these are reimbursed for arrival times of over an hour late (half an hour in the case of the crack TGV service).

It is more complicated than that, though. Like Picasso, French rail travel has its Blue Period. Unlike him, it also has its White Period and, unfortunately, its Red Period too.

The French railways colour-co-ordinate their timetables. Most trains speed away in a time-band painted a fetching shade of blue, i.e. off-peak, which attracts the lowest fare. That section designated as white signifies rush-hours such as Monday mornings, for which the price is higher; and national holidays, when it is fighting-room only in the corridors, are livid red, like the bank balances of anyone making a habit of these dates.

Today, *mercredi*, is a bargain basement blue throughout, as is tomorrow. Journeys postponed until the afternoon of *vendredi*, however, run up against the less economical white. And those delayed until 3 p.m. this time next week are slap into one of those truly red-letter days. The Numerous Family and Concubine Cards slot into the colour system in a way that can be explained, given that you have on your hands the sort of time needed for a round trip of not less than 1,000 km, with or without designer cooking.

BR's arrangement of Cheap Day Returns on Routes With (a) Busy Peak Period and (b) No Busy Peak Period, is probably just as complex but not as colourful. It is anyone's guess exactly how the two systems will be plugged into each other. It may be rather more difficult than making sure that the tunnelling machines from both coasts manage to meet in the middle of the Channel.

The SNCF brochures which I asked for arrived by the next post. The BR leaflets took a week; 'We're getting there,' said the envelope. Eventually. As their French colleagues could have said but didn't, 'Nous sommes déjà arrivés.'

April 1986

Tim Heald; illustrations by Paul Cox

WHO SAYS THE FRENCH ARE BORING?

It was *un de ces jours*. M. Vidal sat slumped at his desk having a telephone conversation with Colonel someone from the Elysée. The conversation was very one-sided. Occasionally he would grunt and raise his eyes to the ceiling as he sank deeper into his chair.

The problem was the President's boots. M. Mitterrand was arriving in two days' time and he would need boots for keeping the mud out. Forty-three boots. Or was it 43 pairs? My French wasn't up to asking if there was a one-legged person on the presidential staff.

Monsieur Vidal is the site director on the French end of the Channel Tunnel, a harassed figure with just a touch of Tati. Not only was the President coming – with the minimum of notice – but the first of his crucial TBMs had just arrived from Oregon. A TBM is a 'Tunnel Boring Machine' and it weighs 380 tons. The Calais Harbour Master had just rung to say that it would be docking at ten. A convoy of low-loaders would have to bring it to the access shaft in the middle of the night. Then they'd either have to get it into place before the President arrived or leave it at the top. Maybe the President would want to bless it. He'd been keen to take holy orders early in life. M. Vidal shook his head. 'What I like to do,' he said, 'is to play eighteen holes of golf in the morning, then drink a lot of wine and beer and then play another eighteen holes in the afternoon.'

Since work began on the Channel Tunnel, Gérard Vidal's golf has suffered badly.

The French and the English have been talking tunnels since 1802. The 1802 project was actually a Napoleonic invasion scheme but the 1882 and the 1974 schemes were born out of *entente* and foundered on the traditional Froggye-Rosbif mutual suspicion. At M. Vidal's headquarters, a newish villa in the rather forbidding, high-roofed style of the Pas de Calais, he and his number two, Bill Coleman, produced an old *Punch* cartoon of 1882 which shows hordes of heavily armed Frogs emerging from under the white cliffs of Dover with the obvious intention of running amok through England. M. Vidal thinks something of the same attitude persists today with the interesting difference that English xenophobes assume that the invading Frogs will all be carrying Aids.

Nevertheless the newest tunnel really is showing signs of getting built. M. Vidal's

HQ, recently purchased from its builder, a M. Pau, is the most modern item on the French site, which in a few months has grown into a veritable moon city on the foothills behind the bleak seaside village of Sangatte.

After our frantic briefing from the preoccupied M. Vidal, Bill took us up to the *puits*, which in this instance is French for 'hole in the ground'. An efficient security check to get us through the *Accès Interdit* signs and then up to the visitors' dressing-room to put on hard hats and the boots which had been so exercising the colonel from the Elysée. '*Avez-vous lavé vos bottes?*' asked the notice. 'Put on your wellingtons or napoleons,' said Bill, who is a story in himself. His English father was an engineer on the cross-Channel ferries, his mother was French; he did national service with the RAF, transferred from Canberras to Aer Lingus, where he flew transatlantic 707s, before retiring to run a not very successful family business in Boulogne. He has an Irish wife and a son who is a French cavalry officer. He sticks up for the French in England, the English in France and the Irish everywhere.

I think he's my first European. When the tunnel's finished there'll be more of him.

'Quite an impressive hole,' he said, employing some English understatement as we reached the edge and peered in. It was one of those occasions when the statistics, if not damned lies, are quite simply meaningless. Overhead ran a vast metal support which, in tests, had carried a thousand tons. You can't visualise a thousand tons – all I can say is that it exuded strength like no man-made structure I'd seen. Other cranes lowered girders, planks, cement-mixers and sundry apparatus into the depths. Men scrambled in the safety netting, went up and down in the cage opposite, welded and fitted, carried and surveyed, in an unending multi-tiered frenzy. It was like an animated Bosch without tears. Bill said it reminded him of his boyhood Meccano set.

After the illustrator had done his illustrating we had a quick look at the remains of the 1882 shaft nearby – clearly only meant to service the Victorian equivalent of an underwater Pennine Way – and took a quick shufti through the village of Coquelles where the terminal will be built. The French answer to Ashford. A windmill, a farm selling *endives*, cemetery with ruined church tower, the remains of German runways used in the Battle of Britain, *Café d'Agriculture*, *Café de la Marie*, *Hôtel-Gril*. Then on to Calais harbour to see the TBM arrive. No such luck. An assembly of low-loaders from Dessinier Zucconi squatted by the quayside, behind a sign saying *Convoi Exceptionnel*, while two pterodactyl cranes scooped buckets of sand aboard a beaten-up boat called the *Chris of Napoli*. The TBM was standing off out at sea, waiting for the *Chris* to leave. Would it get there before M. le Président and the 43 boots? Tension was mounting.

We lunched in the canteen. *Quel canteen! Quel charcuterie! Quel rosbif!* The wine, perfectly palatable, came from a tap and most people poured a two-glass carafe. The atmosphere was convivial but businesslike. If the tunnel facilitates an invasion of French works canteens, then *tant mieux*! The one question

on every lip was, 'When is the TBM arriving?' 'Just like a baby,' said Bill, 'everyone has to know when is it coming, when is it coming!'

Before going down the *puits* ourselves we went up to the *belvedere* on the approach to the hills. This is where the 'spoil' from the excavations will be deposited. Three German blockhouses, the remains of the Battery Lindeelmann, will be submerged under the salty waste. The entire hillside will be reshaped and then sown with grass. Perfect for a new golf course dedicated to M. Vidal.

And then down in the cage to the bottom of the *puits*. It was quite eerie looking up at the descending hardware swaying on its chains, seeing the statue of St Barbara (patron of miners and artillerymen) guarding the tunnel entrance, standing under the sign saying *Douvres 38 km*. Suddenly, in that ordered subterranean chaos of hard-hat Frogs, one began to think that, yes, actually, it's going to work this time.

And whatever one feels about the romance of the sea, isn't it time it did? We sailed back on the *St Christopher*, past the marooned TBM, feeling as if we were on a slow theme pub to Dover. Once there, it was bus to terminal, serried ranks of Customs and Excise, bus to the Western Docks and a 'fast' train to Victoria. On the platform a resplendent buffet attendant swaggered. No buffet car, but a well-armed trolley, he promised. Five minutes out he appeared clanking down the aisles. We both bought drinks. Five minutes later he reappeared and asked if we gentlemen would be requiring anything else. 'Not just yet,' we said. 'Maybe next time.'

'There won't be a next time,' he leered, 'that's why I'm asking. I have to cash up.'

Oh, roll on Froggies, roll on tunnel. *Allez la France*. And I do hope they found 43 gumboots for Mitterrand and his entourage.

February 1988

Bargepole

BETWEEN THE TUNNEL AND THE DEEP BLUE SEA

Full fathom five thy Father lies and so do the politicians and greedy buggers whose baby this ridiculous Channel Tunnel is. To that, I have no objection: if they want to creep about like worms 'neath the nether surface of the vasty deeps, constrained within their dark and dripping tube, then I will do absolutely nothing at all to stop them and indeed will help them get down there and stay down there.

But the excuses, as always, are pathetic. The promotion of free trade. Integrating ourselves into a United Europe. Acknowledging that this is the twentieth century and no man is an island.

Hopes and Fears, or,
a Dream of the Channel Tunnel
(1882)

Butcher. 'HAS YOUR HUSBAND GOT ANY WORK, MRS GREEN?'
Customer. 'NO, 'E AIN'T DOIN' NOTHIN'. YER SEE, 'E'S BIN WAITIN' FOR YEARS EXPECTING TO START ON THE CHANNEL TUNNEL.'

Tommyrot.

We have spent hundreds of years fighting the French, and why? Because we do not like them. And don't talk to me about the last war. They were lucky. We would have attacked them had the Germans not got there first, and when did you hear *anyone* express disapproval of the German invasion? Not at all.

France is there to be invaded and we might have been slightly jealous of Germany having a crack at our private preserve but certainly there was no sense that they were doing something they shouldn't have.

I am afraid that the Channel Tunnel is a wrong-headed idea in every way. Currently it is awfully romantic to take a girl to Paris for the weekend. You fly there and it's exotic or you appear in a trenchcoat and wide-brimmed hat on the platform and she arrives at dusk:

'If the scheme is turned down, mind if I take the model home for my lad for Christmas?'

a glimpse of albino mink through the crowds, hand brushing on the suitcase-handle, a long dinner involving heavy-lidded eyes, lascivious flirtation, Beychevelle '66 and buttered asparagus, and the tantalising question: *will she or won't she?*

Well, of *course* she bloody will, as you know and I know, and the neighbours will be hammering on the walls by 2.00 a.m., but that's not the point; the point is, how do you achieve any romantic effect at all if it's preceded by a raucous, honking, hypertensive shuffle through South London in the bloody car, followed by an encounter with the slack-jawed malevolent subhumans of BritRail and then the carnage and anxiety of the French roads, reeking of blood and hot, torn metal?

You don't. The truth is that the Channel Tunnel is a late efflorescence of Victorian technology; appropriate for our present ailment of metaphorical metonymy: the substitution of the symbol for the thing symbolised. Victorian tunnels symbolised their world: not only the great substratum of proles toiling away in as nasty and dirty circumstances as possible so that the rest of us could have fun, but also the sense of subterranean mysteries measurable by man, of great gleaming tunnels and mysterious transportation systems sliding smokily therein, or drawn by great greased leather washers through a vacuum. They would have built the Underground under ground even if there had been ample room on top.

We ought to wait for the new technologies. Teleportation, for example; that would be fun.

I teleported home one night
With Ron and Sid and Meg.
Ron stole Meggie's heart away
And I got Sidney's leg.

Perfectly possible, too; there are two ways in which it might work. One way would be to use wormholes in space, where you just go down one of them and pop up at your destination without having traversed the intervening distances, which is a bit dull and offers little chance to buy duty-frees. Or you could disassemble the *information* contained in a human being and reconstitute it at the other end from new materials. Which would be the real person? I don't know; you would erase the original before building the copy, otherwise you literally wouldn't know whether you were coming or going. You might think that any form of transport which required the nuking of a perfectly good human being in order to preserve equilibrium was a touch brutal, but perhaps you haven't flown the Atlantic in tourist class recently or you'd know what *real* brutality was.

Real *brutalism* on the other hand is the Channel Tunnel. A bridge would at least be *elegant* and how do you instil elegance into a long pipe full of trains and leaking seawater? You can't, and I suppose that's one of the attractions for this Government of pushy beasts and their constipated, straining hangers-on. Thatcher's People are no doubt in for a fascinating experience in the psychologically-rich environment of the Tunnel, with its overtones of birth and death, but how do they think they will go down in France?

Despite all the blather about New Internationalism, we have never been more insular. God made us an island because He thought it was a good thing to do, and will not be mocked. The more we venture abroad, the more we stick out, with our inability to hustle, our strange table-manners, our high whining voices and pasty skins, reddened at the neck by contact with our cheap clothes; pottering helplessly in our plastic shoes, waggling our little collapsible umbrellas in impotent fear and incomprehension, unable to obtain our usual 'food' and dazzled by the unaccustomed sunlight, we lurch and twitter from crisis to crisis, despised, traduced, exploited and sodded-about by all. The meanest salesman on his little jaunt to Poitiers or Karlsruhe anticipates some sad or passionate romantic *excursus* but what foreign woman will look at an Englishman unless he pays? Thatcher's People may buy Charvet shirts but they retain Marks and Spencer minds and that's that.

And why France, of all places? It's close, true, right next door, you could almost reach out and touch it, on a good day you can see it on the horizon, but the same could be said of bankruptcy or death and we do not deliberately cultivate those. The French are noisy, rude, and smell of garlic and caporal tobacco; their police are offensive, their men lazy, vain and full of honey and also allegedly the worst lovers in the world, and their women are dirty and promiscuous, nor do they shave their armpits. Their teeth are all rotted from constant drinking and they lie abed in the daytime, shutters closed, on huge lumpy mattresses stuffed with undeclared income. They run the worst airport in the entire world, ignoble, shabby and misbegotten Charles de Gaulle, and there is no reason to think that they will be any better at running a Tunnel.

If we *must* have a damned Tunnel (and I do not see why; if the silly boys want to dig, let them do it on the beach) why do we not dig one to Australia? It would be huge and bottomless, with lots of room for everyone one would like to put down a hole, all the politicians and bureaucrats, contractors, permanent secretaries, traffic wardens, market researchers, chief executives, directors of tourism, travel agents, Esperanto-speakers, Eurobond-brokers, 2CV drivers flaunting *Atomkraft? Nein Danke!* stickers, and anyone else you want to stuff in an oubliette and shut the lid upon.

Enough of all this awful Euro-ism. Back to Battleship Britain, beleaguered and alone. Who wants to see the light at the end of the Tunnel? I don't even want to see the Tunnel.

August 1987

Libby Purves

STILL WATERS

The English Channel, 51°04′N, 1°16′E, 0330 hrs

Somewhere down there, they are tunnelling. Men in donkey-jackets and *bleu de travail* are boring their way towards one another, hoping to meet in the middle. Fat chance, I should say, knowing the Anglo-French capacity for mutual misunderstanding; we shall more likely end up with two parallel tunnels. But dig on, old moles, and if you notice the ceiling start to drip, or find barnacles scraping at your hat, point the machine down a bit. Up here, we need all the water we can hang on to. Tunnelman, spare that sea.

You may like to know that it is raining up here. Big, fat, splashing drops that make pockmarks in the waves, gather in wobbling rivers on the lower rim of my spectacles, and nip behind my ears when I look up at the streaming sails. It is also rough. God knows why it should be, when there hasn't been much wind for hours: perhaps the Channel itself feels heaving unease at being, literally, undermined. It throws the boat fretfully from side to side as we creep forward at about three miles an hour, corkscrewing along against a tide that runs at two. It does not take a microchip to work out that during the two hours of my cold night watch, we have travelled a mere two miles over the actual sea-bed. Still, only another sixty-three to Harwich. Super.

The tide will, of course, change in our favour. Probably just when we have to stop dead and jill about in circles for half-an-hour outside Dover harbour, watching a procession of fat, complacent ferryboats thundering in and out, and being carved up by the Folkestone Pilot boat on its way to welcome in a bulk-carrier of cat-litter from Bilbao. Then we shall sneak across the harbour entrance, enjoying a brief frisson of terror as the first hovercraft of dawn roars up from behind to brush us with its giant rubber skirt; and at last be flushed remorselessly into the Thames Estuary, where all the sandbanks are so amusingly named after wrecks.

Still, I don't care. I shall be off watch by then: I will have joyfully thrown a boot down the companionway to rout my soulmate from his dry sleeping-bag, and gone dripping and shivering into my own Terylene pit. I may spend a brief moment looking at the soggy copy of *Options* I bought on the train down to Brighton marina; earlier on, when I was wondering why I kept on coming to sea, I opened it at a most heartening article about acquiring a Good Self-Image. It quoted, admiringly, a career woman called Claudia who has 'a small, neat message taped inside her Filofax. It says "Warm, loving woman".' This, the writer explains, is to help Claudia remember that under the Power Suit she is a warm, loving woman. I read this and fell asleep quite content with my lot, realising that it is better to sleep in damp clothes and be sick in a bucket than to become so mad that you have to tape notes into a leather binder to remind yourself you are human.

Anyway, I shall think fondly of Claudia and drop into a creaking, fitful half-sleep for a few hours while Himself has the fun of getting through the sandbanks, making manly decisions about whether to 'nip through inside the Fisherman's Gutway' or 'risk it over the good old Swin'. He will probably be a bit grumpy on first discovering that I have eaten the last Penguin biscuit, but I shall sternly remind him that we are, after all, British. What are upper lips for? Tape it in your Filofax, man.

There is an hour to go, yet. Well, fifty-nine minutes. Sing a snatch of a Channel shanty to cheer myself up:

We sail-ed past Beachy, past Fairlight and Dungeness
Until we brought to by the South Foreland light.

Fifty-eight minutes. I'm not bored. I can

A PLEDGED M.P. (1869)
MP's BRIDE. 'OH! WILLIAM, DEAR – IF YOU ARE – A LIBERAL – DO BRING IN A BILL – NEXT SESSION – FOR THAT UNDERGROUND TUNNEL!!'

watch the baffling lights of the cat-litter ship, now gyrating threateningly, and stare with wary mistrust at something else whose lights indicate either I AM PAIR TRAWLING or SORRY, I HAVE FORGOTTEN TO SWITCH OFF MY PAIR TRAWLING LIGHTS. And I can brood on signs and portents and changing times as the little ship lumbers faithfully along beneath me.

Nor am I alone. Up and down the uneasy Channel on this night, countless other amateur sailors must be brooding, too, as the headland lighthouses blink fitfully and the sails rattle in the wind like sad ghosts. Each of us is an island of frowsty solitude in the night; some huddled over a Pot Noodle off Portland Bill, some staring disbelievingly at the Eddystone light (where can the Isle of Wight have got to?) and a few fossicking grimly through a lockerful of spilt coffee and mouldering cucumbers to find a match by whose light to re-connect their battery leads. Only our unquiet thoughts escape, and mingle, over the waters.

For even apart from the dark tunnellers below, funny things are happening. Unsettling things. The other day, a two-and-a-half-thousand-foot waterspout appeared off the Isle of Wight. The papers reported it in that tone of tolerant amusement reserved for singing dogs: after all, a grey funnel of cloud that descends to earth and sucks up the sea and, ho-ho, rains fish, is classic August stuff. To agnostic modern wallies, anyway. It takes a superstitious sailor's mind, unshackled by weariness and flashing lights and looming 8,000-ton ships, overdosed on Cup-a-Soup and seasick-pills, rightly to appreciate a Portent these days.

There was one yacht actually knocked over by it, according to witnesses, but the skipper 'made it back to harbour and went on his way

STRAIGHT THROUGH FROM LONDON TO PARIS. –A SUGGESTION TO MR. JOHN FOWLER. (1870)

WHY SHOULD NOT A TRAIN BE MADE TO RUN SO FAST THAT BY MERE VIRTUE OF ITS ACQUIRED IMPETUS ACTING ON THE SQUARES OF THE DISTANCE, MULTIPLIED BY THE HYPOTHENUSE OF THE INCLINED PLANE &C., &C., &C.? (WE DON'T PROFESS TO BE PRACTICAL ENGINEERS, BUT HAVE NO DOUBT THAT A GLANCE AT THESE DESIGNS WILL SUGGEST VALUABLE NOTIONS TO THOSE WHO ARE NOW DEALING WITH THE VERY DIFFICULT QUESTION OF THE PASSAGE ACROSS THE CHANNEL.)

Mr Dibbles (at Balham). 'AH, THE OLD CHANNEL TUNNEL SCHEME KNOCKED ON THE HEAD AT LAST! GOOD JOB TOO! MAD-HEADED PROJECT – BEASTLY UNPATRIOTIC TOO!'

Mr Dibbles (en route for Paris. Sea choppy). 'CHANNEL TUNNEL NOT A BAD IDEA. ENTIRE JOURNEY TO PARIS BY TRAIN. GRAND SCHEME! ENGLISH PEOPLE BACKWARD IN THESE KIND OF THINGS. STEWARD!'
Goes below.

without leaving his name'. Perhaps his name was Jonah: probably he thought the whole thing was his fault: yachtsmen are like that. They read endless reproving articles about the duties of seamanship and the heinousness of not mousing your anchor-shackles correctly; they agonise and apologise about their TBT antifouling. They are not like the cheery merchant fleet, doors askew and oil a-dripping, who bang into one another regularly in radar-assisted collisions and hurl the blame round courtrooms like confetti: yachtsmen are natural penitents. Poor old Jonah probably thought he caused the waterspout himself, by missing one night of his Meteorology evening classes.

Sorry. A long, moonless, sleepless, dripping night watch in the Channel leads the mind down all manner of dark alleys. Usually there is nobody to listen, so it doesn't matter. But if the waterspout was indeed a portent, I doubt whether it was aimed at poor Jonah. More likely it was a momentary flicker of divine irritation at the increasing division of twentieth-century man: a few of us scrabbling around confronting the elements in unreasonably primitive conditions on top, sailing or abseiling or growing organic leeks; and a huge technologically arrogant establishment down below, thinking it clever to tunnel beneath wild grey waves, to concrete over green grass, and fatuously to build nuclear power stations as monuments to the theory that Sod's Law has been permanently suspended by the microchip.

Probably the waterspout had just heard

about the new plan to switch out lighthouses in order to save money. Merchant ships, says a report by a chap called Strange (as well he might be), now navigate in a far 'safer and more reliable' manner by using electronic systems like Decca and Racal. Therefore there is no call for them ever to look out of the window. Therefore, money could be saved by switching off lighthouses and buoys. Pleasure craft pay no light dues, so it is none of their business, says the report. (It is not that yachts have refused to pay dues: it would simply be 'impractical' to tax them – this from the good people who brought you VAT.)

Yachtsmen should shut up, implies the report, and grope around Beachy Head and Dungeness as best they may. (They can, of course, buy Decca Navigator boxes themselves. These work fine. Well, they do until your brother-in-law goes for a wee over the stern and steps on the plug, thus causing an agonised bleeping below and the rather insulting flashing legend, ANTENNA FAIL.)

Anyway, big ships don't need lights any more. Any more than big-time, experienced, professional ferry operators needed alarms on their bow doors. In the darkness, the sea rising, I wearily tack the boat round to avoid a looming Sealink, and sing a sad catch from the old school hymnal:

Brightly beams our Father's mercy
From His lighthouse evermore,
But He leaves within our keeping
All the lights along the shore . . .

More fool Him.

Sorry. Tired, dark, blasphemous, confused. Of course the tunnellers and the PWR builders and the lighthouse accountants must be right. There are so many of them, and they have briefcases. There is no room for the opinions of 'pleasure-boat' owners, people who splash around in uneconomical little wedges with outmoded sails, rolling on the dark waters of the Channel merely because they like stars and dawn landfalls and winning small battles with bits of wind. Perhaps in the end they will leave us altogether alone with our Channel: as the remaining freight of tourists and fluffy dice and surplus grain takes to a system of submarine tunnels, and the last lights go out along the shore, the old waterway will be ours alone: darker, more dangerous, back five hundred years. Perhaps monks will once again set up wood-fired light towers on the headlands to save small ships from ruin. Perhaps the talking briefcases (each bearing its neat taped slip saying, WARM HUMAN PERSON) will all slide under us, on robot trains, and leave us up here to take our final leave of twentieth-century reality under the wise old Channel stars.

In a way, I hope so.

August 1987

F. F. Gillespie

CHUNNEL VISION

Breaking the Euro links

I had hoped to spend a quiet weekend visiting my lads Horace (16) and Hamish (15) at my former and their present place of education, the remote and intensely disciplinarian School of Hard Knocks. However, my longed-for Highland retreat was disrupted by two most alarming items of news in the local paper, the *Kyle of Minogh Free Press*:

Ron 'No' to Super League

Western Alliance Albion FC manager Ron Thatcher yesterday delivered a firm rebuff to plans unveiled this weekend for a new, one-nation European 'Super League'. In a calculated snub to his Continental rivals, he described the plan as 'preposterous' and 'quite clearly the idea of someone other than myself'.

The plan, which envisages all the leading European nations merging to form a single League, is the work of two of Europe's leading clubs, the

OUR NATURAL ADVANTAGES.
M. le Comte (who has come to London for the Season of 1888). 'AH BAH! YOU ARE AFRAID OF THE CHANNEL TUNNEL! *Quelle bêtise!* VY, IT IS NOT YOUR "SILVARE STREAK" ZAT PROTECT YOU FROM ZE INVASION, *mes amis!* IT IS YOUR SACRED DOG OF A CLIMATE!'

Berlin-based Hohen Zollern SV, and the Vienna team Anschluss Dynamo. Burly Hohen Zollern manager Helmut Kohl yesterday told reporters: 'What we have in mind is a League embracing all the big European teams. For example, our team might play in Prague one weekend, then in Warsaw the next, then in Paris, and so on for a thousand years or so. It would be a little like the last World War . . . I mean Cup.'

Herr Kohl said he hoped to be able to persuade English teams to compete in the League. 'For 76 years we have been looking for an away victory against Albion,' he commented. 'Still, "third reich . . . er, time lucky" as you British say.' Whether his hope will be fulfilled remains unclear however. Following the appalling hooliganism of Albion supporters at Bruges last year – when French fans were bombarded by handbags and other projectiles – all English clubs were banned indefinitely from European competitions.

Meanwhile a large question mark hangs over Ron Thatcher's future following revelations that he and other Albion directors have been betting on their team to lose *the 1992 Cup Final. The Albion manager refused to comment on the allegations, but goalkeeper Ken Baker admitted: 'With an own-goal record like ours, you'd be a fool not to have a flutter. Even I've been playing Spot the Balls-Up every weekend since the season began.'*

This story was enough to make me choke on my porridge. But imagine my anguish when I turned to the Business Section, only to see this horror:

Investors Switch to Eurowall

Shares in the troubled Channel Tunnel firm Eurotunnel last night plummeted yet further following news that two rival cross-Channel ventures are to be launched. The first, Eurowall, is known to have the personal backing of Prime Minister Margaret Thatcher, whose scepticism about the Anglo-French Chunnel has been evident for some months.

Whereas Eurotunnel envisages linking the English and French coasts by an undersea tunnel, Eurowall proposes, according to a spokesman, 'to cut the Continent off from the British mainland by constructing a 15-foot-high concrete wall around the European coast from the Baltic to the Black Sea'.

Mrs Thatcher yesterday warmly endorsed the project, calling it 'essential in the interests of our national security'. Speaking at a meeting of the Little England Ostrich Fanciers' Club, she declared: 'We cannot sit idly by while the French attempt to poison us with their Perrier. It is time to pen the Continentals in before we are swamped by their noxious beverages.'

However, Eurowall was not the only new Channel-oriented company to be launched yesterday. Shortly before the close of trading, the German company AWP (Aufwiedersehen Pest) announced that it was ready to invest DM20bn in a mysterious new company calling itself Anglowall AG. City analysts last night confirmed that Anglowall's plan is to construct a 15-foot-high concrete wall around the English coast. A spokesman for the company commented: 'It is not so much splendid isolation we have in mind for Frau Thatcher as ignominious quarantine.'

What, I muttered to myself, are we denizens of the North to make of all this? And, quite suddenly, it dawned on me. Seizing my serviette, I began scribbling the following *Address to the People of Scotland* (henceforth *Schottland*):

'My fellow countrymen. It would have been nice to have celebrated the tricentenary of the Act of Union; but the time has come to file for divorce. Association with England has ceased to bring us the benefits we expected from it: indeed, it has now become a source of nothing but embarrassment.

'I come to you not as a romantic nationalist, but as a realist. Look at it this way. The West German Government is in an expansive mood. Dr Kohl seems ready to exchange good Deutschmarks for bad East German monopoly marks. Is he going to turn up his nose at our nice, green Scottish pound notes? And can anyone think of a better solution to the German Question than an Act of Union with us tolerant Scots?'

Further details of my proposed scheme for German-Scottish unification next week. In the meantime, practise singing: '*O Blume von Schottland/Wann werden wir deines Gleichen noch einmal sehen . . . ?*'

'Are you sure you haven't broken through?'

3

LE MARCHÉ COMMUN

'Personally, I'm dead against a single European currency.'

BRITAIN

IS SO FILTHY

Peter Barnard

NEITHER NOWT NOR SUMMIT

I was sitting beside a sherpa at 29,000 feet: did that make me Sir Edmund Hillary? Alas and dammit, no. This sherpa would not be caught dead on snow that wasn't within easy reach of a condominium in Aspen, Colorado and she (oh, yes) probably regarded Nepal as being terminally deficient in the gross national product department.

Sherpas, in the jargon of modern diplomacy, are the summit meeting dogsbodies, the small-print shufflers and comma shifters who toil through the night and rush from room to room in hotels like London groupies on *Band Aid* night.

I met one, an American, in the window seat on a flight to Williamsburg, Virginia, back in the heady days of Reagan-Thatcher hand-holding. But she was too busy to talk to the likes of me. She was up against a deadline – two days to go until the G7 summit and the final communiqué not even half finished. As she thrashed away at a lap-top word processor, I saw through a wandering left eye that much use was being made of a key on the far right of the second row of the keyboard, home to the normally relaxed square bracket symbol. This confirmed the lady as a communiqué draftee, for should you find a succession of summit communiqués leaking all over your lap (and boy, do they leak) by their square brackets shall ye know them. These are the vital brackets which delineate passages in the communiqué that have yet to be agreed.

Already the flood of square brackets is pouring out of the Maastricht sherpas, so much so you would think the Euro-summit being held in the small Dutch town on 7–8 December had already finished. On the evidence presently available, there will be an opening square bracket just below the date and closing one just above the signatures.

Fear not, however. All summits agree something, whether they be Group of Seven (Western industrialised nations), EC or super-power. The G7 is a cakewalk by comparison with Euro-summits. For one thing, G7 is run by America. If the Americans want a square bracket removed, they'll let you know, OK? Some years ago, G7 got in a terrible tizzy over some arcane nonsense about central banks intervening to stabilise currencies. Washington wanted none of this but the cowering Euro-wimps with their silly little currencies persuaded the Americans to make a harmless concession, so the final communiqué talked about a commitment to 'intervene in a disorderly market'. The then US treasury secretary, Donald Regan, whose manner is to diplomacy what loan sharking is to assisting the disadvantaged, was asked to define this phrase. 'A disorderly market,' he rasped, 'is a disorderly market. Next question.' Sure was nice to have that cleared up.

And so to Maastricht. The Dutch, who only own the place, seem to say 'Ma-strish', whereas the nicest of the Mister Men, Mr Major, appears to think he is in for some corrective discipline in downtown Amsterdam. Ma Strict? Certainly Major could find himself more flagellated than flagellating.

Maastricht is a border town, which makes it an ideal place for an EC summit: every other person there speaks a different language. One man's federal is another man's inviolate national sovereignty. The trouble with the name is that it sounds awfully German. This concern, however, is merely cosmetic: the outcome of an EC summit held in Wootton-under-Edge would sound awfully German. The Germans are to EC summits what the Americans are to G7 ones: dominating, a word which appears in *Ridley's Thesaurus* against such synonyms as 'bullying', 'expansionist', 'wild' and 'domineering'.

The real measures of Maastricht success

'We've been waiting to see how the EEC Summits go before we decide.'

and failure will have nothing to do with whether we shall soon be paying for English muffins in lire or whether the Queen will be obliged to move to Berlin (thus saving her family a lot of travelling at Christmas). No, only two things really matter: can the sherpas get the square brackets down to single figures and will the Dutch hosts avoid The Great Polyester Tie Calamity?

The square brackets, at least the English ones, are in the hands of an acronym: UKREP. Any non-British Brussels diplomatic wife who is told her husband is just nipping out to see UKREP knows she will next see him a lot later wearing a frown and bearing yet another set of drafts. Sir John Kerr, UK Representative in Brussels, has been this way before, and before and before. Sir John is adept at producing what diplomats choose to call 'a suitable form of words'. Gobbledegook? I wouldn't say that, not least because it might catch on and become the Euro-currency. Quite how many gobbledegooks you would have to fork out for a polyester tie is difficult to say with the markets so disorderly but what the host country contrives as its commemorative summit gift (not least to the media, but also to the summiteers) could decide whether Maastricht gets its name on a treaty or returns to being just another Dutch town where sitting below the salt requires the ability to swim.

In the Thatcher era, EC summit 'home matches' gave the British capital the sobriquet Polyester City. Grossly unfair, but there you are: put a polyester tie in the know-your-summit kit and that is all the gratitude you get. As one Foreign Office wallah put it: 'One felt there were times when efforts to reflect Margaret's attitude to both the press and the EC were perhaps a little over-zealous.'

Oh, surely not. But this helps to explain why from the fringe participants' standpoint the perfect summit is impossible, for it requires joint hosts: the Italians and the Irish. Neither of these were top of the tree with Thatcher, given the Italian propensity for sandbagging her at the final plenary session and the Irish habit of producing off-the-wall schemes out of nowhere just to check that everyone was awake.

But to hell with politics: the Italians always take over a Venetial lagoon for the summit and the last time the Irish hosted one they gave each of the participants and their 200 best friends a bottle of Jamesons and a side of smoked salmon.

All Maastricht needs is the Italian location policy, the Irish gifts policy and that wonderful Brussels invention called stopping the clock, whereby the 12 pledge themselves to do a deal by midnight and then stop the clock at 11.55 p.m. until the deal is actually done. With those ingredients, the summiteers could stay in Maastricht for ever while we get on with living. Who says pan-Europeanism can't work?

November 1991

Keith Waterhouse

LIKE TO BE AN MP IN THE EUROPEAN PARLIAMENT?

1. This directive is intended for the guidance of candidates desirous of contesting the direct elections to Europe, by whatever electoral method.

2. This directive is not intended as campaign literature. Campaign literature, printed in five languages, may be obtained from the Manifesto Secretariat in Brussels. When applying for campaign literature (application forms may be obtained from the Application Secretariat in Luxembourg) please state which grade of manifesto you require. Four grades are available as follows:

(a) TOWARDS A BETTER EUROPE (You are totally in favour of the EEC but think the Common Agricultural Policy could be slightly improved.)

(b) OUR FUTURE IN EUROPE (You are totally in favour of the EEC but cannot be doing with the butter mountain.)

(c) EUROPE FOR THE PEOPLE (You are totally in favour of the EEC but believe it may be getting a shade too bureaucratic.)

(d) EUROPE – VISION FOR TOMORROW (You are totally in favour of the EEC but think that Scotland should have parity with Denmark in the European Parliament.)

3. Rosettes are available from the Rosette Secretariat in Strasbourg. Please state colour preference.

4. Door-knocking. Under the provisions

'And now, double or nothing. For £1,000, who is your Euro MP?'

of EEC Directive 048/67893012/B, door-knockers in the European Community will be phased out by 1979, when the standardised bell-push will be common to all households. Door-knocking will then be known as bell-pushing. (Research shows that householders answer a ring at the bell by up to 0.46 quicker on the Offenbach Time Measurement Scale than they answer a knock on the door, thus enabling a candidate to canvass 32 more prospective voters per hour.) In the case of the forthcoming election, however, many old-fashioned, anomalous, time-wasting stupid door-knockers will still be in use.

The procedure is as follows. Grasp the knocker firmly with the right hand, and knock loudly enough to produce a reading of 3^H on a Baumann Noise Measurement meter. Wait until an old lady answers the door.

The candidate should identify himself to the old lady – in other words, announce that his name is Smith (or Corcoran, or MacFarland) and inform her that he is her candidate for the European Parliament.

The old lady will then say: 'But we had a Mr Jones (or Thoroughgood, or O'Riley) round not ten minutes ago, and he said *he* was my candidate for the European Parliament.'

The candidate should reply: 'Yes, madam, there are four of us fighting this particular seat, if you wish to include the Liberal and the loony representing the Freedom Through Bicycling Party.'

The old lady will say: 'But if you all support the Common Market, there's no difference between you.'

The candidate should riposte: 'Oh, but there is, madam. For one thing, I have a moustache. For another, where one of my opponents makes snide jokes about Roy Jenkins's salary, I never make snide jokes about Roy Jenkins's salary.'

The candidate should then give the lady a copy of the appropriate manifesto, and proceed (at a run, if the *Panorama* team are recording his progress) to the next house.

WARNING: Do not get involved in doorstep arguments about the Green Pound. It wastes valuable time, and anyway the old lady doesn't know what she's talking about.

5. Slogans. These are available by the tonne from the Slogans Commissariat. They are mostly on the lines of 'Smith (or Donaldson, or Llewellyn) believes that proposals tabled by the Agricultural Commission would diminish our fishing rights off the north-west and south coasts of Ireland. Do YOU?' There is also one about dairy-fat content in cream crackers.

6. Mass meetings. These should be held in very small halls. A quorum, as defined by the Quorum Commission, shall consist of the candidate, the candidate's agent, the candidate's wife, the caretaker, and an old lady who believes she is attending an amateur production of *Ruddigore*. This may very well prove to be the same old lady who was so tiresome in the doorstep interview in paragraph 4. Rule her out of order before she starts making noises about this here metrication.

7. Hecklers, other than the old lady. It is no longer permissible for hecklers to throw fruit grown outside the EEC countries, except

'Take him. He has a pad in the Dordogne, another in Tuscany and he's anti-EEC.'

where such fruit is not indigenous to the EEC countries. e.g., tomatoes grown in the Canary Islands, or from plants imported from the Canary Islands, may not be thrown. But pomegranates, whatever their point of origin, are for the present allowed. This should be pointed out to hecklers before they commence asking how much you will be getting paid tax-free for sitting on your backside in Strasbourg with a bit of plastic flex stuck in your ear-hole.

8. Baby-kissing. The EEC has not, so far as it knows, any official policy on this question. Contrary to public belief, candidates of individual member-countries may kiss babies or not according to national custom, always provided that the Common Health Regulations are not infringed.

9. Apathy. The interim report of the Common Apathy Commission has not yet been completed – in fact it has not even been started. However, it is anticipated that an ignorant minority of voters might not comprehend the over-riding importance of the direct election, so remedial steps must be taken to jockey them up a bit. The Remedial Steps Secretariat have suggested the following:

(a) Make grossly offensive insinuations about why your opponents are desirous of dipping their snouts in the European trough. If libel writs are issued, so much the better.
(b) Promise that you will screw social and regional funds out of the Community for the exclusive use of your constituency.
(c) Discover that your most dangerous rival failed an 'O' level in geography. Suggest that he thinks Strasbourg is in Austria.
(d) Accuse any or all of your opponents of supporting French proposals to put garlic in the drinking water.
(e) Suggest that the old lady who featured in paragraphs 4 and 6 is being intimidated by the other candidates.

10. Election broadcasts. These, in the interests of democracy, should last about an hour each, so you will have ample time to put your message across. It would be useful to the European Commission if you could chuck in the point that it is impossible to turn back the clock. Try to be homely. Avoid facts and

'That's at least one useful function of an MEP – reducing the level of the wine lake.'

figures, which are only confusing to the viewers. Show them a picture of a cow.

11. Committee rooms. Minimum standards are laid down for the size and quality of European Parliamentary candidates' committee rooms, and they are a far cry from the back-street hovels from which conventional elections are fought. A complete floor of your local Hilton or Holiday Inn is what you should aim at. Specifications may be obtained from the Prerequisites Secretariat.

12. That butter mountain. There is only one answer to this. 'It is to eliminate follies of that kind, friend, that I wish to represent you in Europe.' Boom boom.

April 1977

Peter Tinniswood

AND THE LIVING IS EC

It was a day of cold-nosed snow and weasel-toothed, needling draughts. At every street corner the wind pounced at the scruff of your neck and took savage nips at your Europrivates. Indoors, I found myself walking down a long, hot, soft-carpeted corridor with many closed doors. I was looking for Great Britain.

No sign of it. Not a whisper.

There were dollops of Luxembourg and a few helpings of France. I was lost. Totally.

In desperation I pushed open a door and grunted myself inside. A young lady, dark-haired and plump-cheeked, was sitting behind her desk filing her nails (not necessarily in alphabetical order) and eating a chocolate cake the size of a loofah.

'Sorry to bother you,' I said. 'But I'm looking for Great Britain.' 'I'm not Great Britain,' she snapped. 'I'm Turkey.'

Then of an instant she softened. And so did her cake. She took me gently by the arm to the door and said: 'I'll show you the way. Walk to the end, turn left and you'll find Great Britain next to the ladies' toilets.'

It was. I think the gents was next to Liechtenstein.

I was, of course, in search of the press office in the European Parliament in Strasbourg, that great natural abattoir for the gently browsing Eurobrain, that giant food processor that pounds and pulverises the intellect and the imagination and spews them out in a vapid, tepid pea green soup.

In that vast building, like city-weary dray horses let loose into plump summer pastures, the MEPs frisked and gambolled, the lobbyists munched through their juicy, beguiling goodies and the pressmen wallowed in the fat of their hand-outs.

Time to take stock.

The day previously I'd woken up in the early hours to hear some sanctimonious twerp wafting incense and glucose through the inside of my wireless as he droned on about the Gulf War.

'Lord, communicate with us, we pray. Show us the way and guide us. Oh Lord, we beseech Thee, communicate with us.'

Later on in the plane to Strasbourg I reflected smart-arsedly that if the air traffic controllers were as competent as God in the communications business we'd soon find ourselves charred debris in a mangled metallic cat's cradle on some mist-shrouded knoll in the heart of the Vosges.

No such doubts seemed to bother my companions. They were the army of British Euro MEPs on their way to their monthly coven with their Eurochums in that lovely, beguiling gracious city of soaring spires and cackling, sated geese.

They were all communicating like billyo. Good old jolly Ian Paisley, dear old rumpled John Hume, avuncular Henry Plumb – oh my gosh and oh my golly, how they communicated. Jabber, jabber, jabber. It was like being on a bowls club charabanc outing to More-

'Between you and me, the Common Market subsidies are getting to be a bit of an embarrassment.'

cambe. And I was lucky to be on the leading coach with the committee members, and we'd got all the beer crates stacked in the back and we'd have first use of the toilets when we stopped off for a swift pint and meat pie.

Their eyes glinted, their cheeks twitched and their lips glistened with the excitement of men bound for a week's earnest discussion of fishing agreements with Senegal, brucellosis and enzootic bovine leukosis and the definitive Commission statement on wave energy.

And, of course, when they got to Strasbourg and had to find a common policy on the ghastly, needless catastrophe of the Gulf War, all the poor boobies could come up with was a statement as potent as a damp, hamster-chewed, india rubber.

But we must not be too harsh. We have no right to expect anything more from a convention of street-corner Wavy Line grocers whose imaginations stretch no further than a battered supermarket trolley stacked with the transfrontier movement of hazardous wastes and final proposals for the exact length, consistency and colour of the new Eurosnot.

Some nights later sanity was restored in Schiltigheim, a brown-and-white timbered village a couple of miles outside town.

I found myself in an inn surrounded by the superb, slithering, lilting, soft accents of Alsace, stroking the ears of an enormous curly-black dog that looked for all the world like a hand-knitted coal scuttle.

'Was für ein Hund ist das?' I asked its owner.

'Prima Vermischung, mein Freund,' said the man proudly, 'Prima Vermischung.'

First-class mongrel – and that is precisely the nature of Europe. But try telling that to the MEPs in their great circular throbbing boil of a chamber as they try to turn the romping, bounding, comical, infuriating, lovable mongrel into a Cruft's Champion as bland and as characterless as a water polo player's kneecap.

That chamber! A handful of delegates who all looked like Alf Roberts, the *Coronation Street* grocer, yawning and scratching. The footmen in their frock coats strutting solemnly like the chorus in an Ivor Novello operetta.

And those simultaneous translators. All women and sounding just like Louise Botting on *The Money Programme*, so fluent, so confident, so precise.

How on earth did they do it, I pondered as I slumbered, twitched and jerked through at least three decades of a German stuttering and blundering through a discourse on, if a shell-shocked memory serves me correct, luncheon vouchers and temperance crèche facilities for traffic wardens guaranteed free from salmonella and terminal radish thrip.

And then it came to me in a flash – it was the translators who wrote the speeches. That's why they were so brilliant. The MEPs simply turned up to perform them like an itinerant band of grumpy, rumple-chinned, redundant mummers.

Actually the linguistics cause very few problems. You simply consult the linguistic colour code, which I think took the delegates 17 years to formulate.

Each language has its own colour. Britain's is mauve.

Mauve! After the heroics, the hardships, the sacrifices, the miseries and agonies of Blenheim, Trafalgar, the Somme and Dunkirk we've ended up with mauve.

What kind of patriotic fervour can that possibly create? Can you imagine a group of port-sodden, Blimp-necked Brits high up in the visitors' gallery of the chamber rising to their feet and chanting: 'Come on, you mauves. Come on, you mauves.'

In the lavatories on the second floor there was a complete absence of mauve toilet paper. I apologise profusely to Greece and the last soggy remnant of Belgium.

In the Parliament buildings everyone is so kind. Everyone is so desperately anxious to please. You know instantly that, if you were absolutely at the end of your tether, all you had to do was go to the Commissariat and say: 'I'm homeless and destitute. Please, please, can you help?'

And some kindly, homely lady smelling of Lancashire hotpot would sit you down gently in a self-righting, inflatable armchair and say: 'Never mind, dear. Not to worry. We've got something right up your street on the top floor. What would you like – a two-bedroomed apartment with somewhere to air your singlets or a three-bedroomed maisonette with gold bath taps and an en suite butler who looks just like dear old Stinker Murdoch?'

Leave the building and step outside into

'Six months?! – But I've a business appointment this afternoon!'

Strasbourg. Look. Listen. This is the real Europe.

An elderly lady, elegant and dignified in a plush brasserie just off the Place Kléber takes out from her handbag a sandwich wrapped in tinfoil, eats it fastidiously and then with infinite grace raises the right cheek of her bottom and breaks wind as sweetly as a nightingale.

In a droguerie I ask diffidently for a bottle of hair shampoo. The young girl smiles at me sweetly and says in impeccable English: 'Certainly, monsieur. And how often do you want to wash your horses?'

The sign outside the station which, with my perfect French I translate, reads: 'It is strictly forbidden for two ancient roués to pose outside the taxi rank.'

Well, if you're a truly integrated European you can afford to crack pathetic little jokes like that – particularly if they're written in mauve.

February 1991

Simon Fanshawe

PRAISE DELORS!

According to the *Sun*, 80 per cent of British people think that the ecu is a bird. This is not true. The emu is a bird. Ask Michael Parkinson. But what may be confusing people is that the ecu is part of EMU and if you're Norman Tebbit your big fear in life is that Helmut Kohl is about to do to us what Rod Hull once did to Parky.

Ever able to adapt his style to his audience, the Chingford Challenger began an article on the subject of Europe in the *Guardian* the other day by comparing the Treaty of Rome to the Booker Prize. However, this attempt to appeal to the liberal values of the *Grauniad*'s pâté-loving, futon-sleeping, Beaujolais-slurping *nouveau riche* deserted him just a paragraph or two later. The mask of tolerance slipped away and a few hundred words into the piece, we were back in the old territory of the so-called Euro-sceptic, the defence of '. . . rights which have been ours for centuries . . .'

What the Battling Bootboy thinks we need is the stout defence of all that is Great and British. Down with quiche, salami and workers' protection! Up with woad, badger baiting and the House of Lords. I ask you.

However articulately and politely Essex Man tries to put it – and one should never make the mistake of thinking that he can't put it very politely and articulately – he is nothing more than an unreconstructed Protestant xenophobe. Down with the Kraut and the Frog. Suffer to be British. That's what won two world wars. Be proud, says he, to live in a country with almost permanent unemployment and drizzle, because that's what sovereignty is all about. Beware the Foreigner with his modern ways, his Social

Charter and his Single Market. We are British and if we stand our ground the rest of Europe will have to let us alone. Just sit in the corner of the nursery and hold our breath until we die. Then Jacques Delors will be sorry.

All this would be thoroughly admirable if we were staving off a Viking invasion, fighting the Armada or trying to get a decent cup of tea in Spain. But we're not. According to a recent poll, only one per cent of people think that we will suffer any loss of national identity by 'going into Europe' further. Admittedly that includes the people who think the ecu is a bird, but it also includes people who get take-away pizzas in Bolton, order garlic bread and drive Volkswagens.

In truth, things have changed. No one I know is prepared to go out of their back door, let alone to the ballot box, to defend the retention of the pound coin or the fiver just because they are British. Perhaps if this government had made it possible for more people not just to see but to hold on to more of them, we might be slightly excited. But we aren't. It's only because you can fold a tenner and make the Queen's neck look like her bum that gives it any value at all. And I have no doubt that if we ever have an ecu note to fold up, someone will find a way of making Oliver Reed's penis out of the Eiffel Tower. Or Brigitte Bardot out of the Alps.

'I think you're mean putting Tony and Giuseppe on cider apples.'

We all feel European. If Norman Tebbit had wanted to stop the rot he should have cancelled the ferry that brought all those other Normans to Hastings. Or he could have shot Freddie Laker in the early seventies. Now, too many people have flown Laker Air on a Thomson tour and peeled in Majorca, frozen in Gstaad or put weight on in Rome for us not to belong to Europe.

To most people the single European currency is not an invasion of sovereignty. It is a blessed relief. It means that every holiday will no longer begin and end in unintelligible conversation at the bureau de change/cambio/wechsel on the railway station. It means that the raffia donkey will be priced in a currency average travellers understand and there won't be large groups of Englishmen outside the AC Milan ground complaining that, in lire, a can of coke and some chewing gum cost over a thousand of the things.

What Norman should also have done is to stop that nice Mr and Mrs Major from going to Spain for their hols. Our PM is nothing if not pedestrian in his thinking and I'm sure the chance to escape the particularly inclement weather here and the fuss with all those fiddly little coins influenced his attitude to the Maastricht summit and convinced our John and Norma that Europe and the single currency was a jolly good thing.

Incidentally (and not a lot of people know this), when Guy Fawkes set off to blow up the Houses of Parliament, he sailed from Maastricht. That may be an ugly rumour circulated by Mr Tebbit to prop up his old-fashioned views about parliamentary sovereignty. But you have to remember two things about Guy Fawkes. One is that every year the British celebrate his attempt on the House of Commons (so much for our love of Parliament). And the other thing is that he didn't succeed. And neither will Jacques Delors.

November 1991

BLANDANAVIA
North Sea
HERE BE IRISHMEN (God help us...)
Dominic 'Bloody' Lawson
HERE BE PETER LILLEY (Not Me)
Here be Unelected Reject Politicians
Brussels
HERE BE DRAGONS (Aggressive, Bullying Egotistical etc...)
HERE BE POODLES (Fawning, Obedient etc...)
HERE BE ITALIANS (Cowardly, Unreliable..)
HERE BE SPANIARDS (Nearly as Bad as Poodles)
Mediterranean Sea (Stinking, Filthy Cess Pool...)
INK
Rothmans
20

Thelwell

EURO-FARMERS

'I notice you're always off to block the roads at Nice or Cannes or San Remo.'

'Disastrous floods in Westphalia, pitiless drought in Calabria – it's ruination.'

'Heads, I spray Longmeadow. Tails, you go shopping in Ostend.'

Julia Langdon

CONTINENTAL RIFT

A journalistic colleague who used to cover the European Parliament in Strasbourg once had an outline plot for a thriller based there. The first chapter saw the murder of a British Member of the Parliament, found dead in one of the interpreters' booths. The headphones had been left on, mysteriously turned to Danish. Interplod was sent for and arrived post-haste from London. He examined the scene of the crime and then turned to his assistant. 'The real puzzle is,' he said, 'why on earth should anybody bother?'

That was the end of the first chapter, but alas the book was never written. We laughed about it a lot, but didn't take it any further. That was the point, really: there just wasn't any more to say. He had already encapsulated the irrelevance of the Parliament and its Members, at least as far as the British press viewed it.

This was in the early days, soon after the first round of direct elections to Europe ten years ago. At the time most British newspapers and broadcasting organisations made a determined attempt to cover the Parliament with the seriousness that its Members demanded. We all trooped out to Strasbourg every month to report on their week-long sessions and very pleasant it was too.

You may have heard, perhaps, that there are a great many fine restaurants in the city. There are also excellent ordinary restaurants on most street corners. There is very pretty countryside all around, dotted with picturesque *auberges* where the food is equally wonderful in the snows of winter or served outside beside a quiet river in summer. The local Riesling is served in chubby, brown jugs and is set on the table with the crusty bread as you sit down to eat. Strasbourg is also a

'You qualify for the silver bells and cockle shells subsidy, but I'm afraid you're on your own with the pretty maids all in a row.'

very beautiful city, boasting some fine architecture and a magnificent cathedral. There is, in short, lots to do and see – but generally this did not include much politics.

Mind you, the politicians themselves all take it very seriously indeed. If you have ever run into a Euro-fanatic you will know what I mean. If you have not so far done so, I advise you to proceed with caution next time you meet someone who might qualify for such a description. It is a bit like some obscure religion: if you are not yourself of the faith, it all seems very mysterious. They speak a language of their own – almost completely incomprehensible to the layman. They frequently have that mad light of the fanatic in their eyes. It is a very alarming condition and it can affect people who may appear to be otherwise completely normal, and who may be perfectly charming company as long as they are discussing something else. I even have friends who suffer from it and I have thus studied its extraordinary impact at close hand. Nevertheless, I still do not understand what possesses them to become so *serious*.

One particular couple, with whom I have twice taken holidays, are notable case studies. Most of the time they seem to be quite sane and talk about the kind of trivialities that occupy most people: What shall we have for supper? Is there any retsina left? Is that a cloud over there? What about another swim before lunch? Then they disappear for a long period and everyone tactfully assumes that they are making the most of their holiday. But no! On the contrary, hours later they will be discovered down at the bottom of the olive grove, deep in an intense discussion on the need for an intervention agreement on the grape seed oil controversy.

It gets them, of course, as soon as they get there. Even the most ardent former anti-Marketeers are soon turned. Barbara Castle was one example. She left the House of Commons, was elected to Strasbourg and marched into Europe proudly waving the banner of her beliefs. Once there, she quite understandably devoted her considerable energies to making the EEC work better for Britain. She was doing her job, but in doing it (even if it was unwitting) she invested the Parliament with a credibility that she had never previously accepted. I remember bumping into her in the Ladies at a Labour conference shortly after she had gone to Europe. The party, as usual, was in the throes of crisis and normally one would have expected Barbara to pass a remark about whether the Boilermakers or Sewage Workers were going to support the composite, or some such. To my amazement, she told me instead what the Competition Commissioner in Brussels had said about the future of the budget.

The Europeans among you will be deeply annoyed by all this. But the fact remains that the European Parliament is still little more than a talking shop with the political legitimacy of a bratwurst. That may change in 1992. That is what the British Government is bothered about and why the Conservative Party in Britain succeeded in mismanaging their campaign for this year's elections as badly as they did. It was all very unfortunate for them, but it was no one's fault except Mrs Thatcher's. It was she who articulated her anxieties about the encroaching powers of the EEC, the threat to British sovereignty and, especially, the danger for her personally contained in the sizeable socialist majority within the European Parliament – not to mention all those dreadful left-wing governments all over the Continent.

The wonderful irony of it all was that the Tory Party was meant to be the true European party. Its instincts 'communautaire', it took us into the EEC in the first place and signed the Single European Act in the second. And yet in this latest election Labour was able to portray itself as the party that was – relatively – united on the issue and which had a positive policy on the future of Europe. Even so, none of this mattered much to the Great British electorate. In the words of our unwritten novel: 'Why on earth should anybody bother?'

June 1989

David Thomas

DECEIVING YOU LOUD AND CLEAR

The fact that one has been defeated in conventional warfare does not necessarily mean that all is finally lost. A guerrilla campaign may still pay dividends.

This, at any rate, is the direction in which my thinking on Europe – sorry, but it won't take long, I promise – is rapidly moving. The train, boat or cross-Channel ferry of federal union has set off on its lunatic journey and, no matter what happens at Maastricht, there's not a lot we can do to stop it leaving with Britain on board. However, there's a very great deal we can do to ensure that the journey ends up at a destination of our choosing.

The crucial point is that we have to learn to cheat. I have long been convinced that one of the reasons that the EC so consistently acts against Britain's best interests is that we assume that they do things like us. We naively persist in the notion, for example, that appointments within the Community bureaucracy are made on the same basis that they are in our cricket-playing Civil Service: that is to say, on the basis of seniority, performance and a suitable Oxbridge degree.

This is a dangerous misapprehension. In actual fact, the boys and girls at Berlaymont make their way into the perk-laden, holiday-rich upper reaches of the commission using the sophisticated, nay, Machiavellian methods evolved in Europe over many centuries, to wit: corruption, nepotism and political patronage. The mandarins of Whitehall would do well to stop playing with quite such a straight bat and start chucking in the odd googly. (They could also try using many more incomprehensible cricket metaphors when conversing with our 'partners' – that should show 'em.)

Once we've set the first few bureaucratic booby-traps, we should find that the EC becomes altogether more agreeable. But, on the off-chance that the odd, disagreeable directive sneaks by undetected, there is a simple fallback position that the Government should immediately adopt: ignore the damn thing.

This, I feel, is where our membership has really come unstuck. Most members of the EC will happily talk all day about the ideals and destiny of our glorious federal future. That's because, underneath all the rococo rhetoric, they are sensible, realistic people who have no intention of doing anything that doesn't suit them. We, however, take the view that laws should be obeyed by everyone except for the chairmen of major supermarket chains. So when a new measure gets passed that bans Curly-Wurly chocolate bars, or threatens the Englishman's freeborn right to stuff his face with hedgehog-flavoured pork scratchings, we get terribly upset. The Government then sighs deeply, shrugs its shoulders and appoints a team of inspectors to ensure that all 55 million of us toe the line pork scratchingwise.

As if this was not bad enough, Britain is full of people who believe that they live in a democracy. What is quite clear from the slightest perusal of writings by European journalists is that they labour under no such delusion. They know that their parliaments are meaningless talking-shops (the French, for example, rarely debate anything to do with Europe on the grounds that it constitutes foreign policy and is therefore under the direct control of the President), running countries that are mostly the inventions of nineteenth-century politicians, without any real identity beyond their airline and their football team.

Over here, however, we have MPs who continually refer to their constituents' wishes when debating in the Commons. And we have

'It'd be nice if the Soviets could join. I rather fancy the idea of a caviar mountain.'

constituents who feel that their wishes are of primary importance, no matter how international the issue.

The consequences of this can be seen in the endless reprimands given to Britain on account of its environmental policy. Signor Ripa de Menea can only make pompous pronouncements about the ecological effects of our new roads or railways because British campaigners have alerted him to Government action and the Government has taken their protests seriously. No French administration would ever pay a moment's attention to the sort of Barbour-clad bourgeois types who try to protect our environment. If the Prez has decided he wants a motorway round Paris or a railway line to the coast, he just goes ahead and builds it willy-nilly. Does he get reported to the EC? *Mais, non!* Would he give a monkey's if he was? *Non, non, non!*

So, here's a tip for Major's men: ignore everyone – community bureaucrats, voters, you name it – and just do whatever the hell you feel like until someone comes along and kicks you out of office. Of course, it isn't very democratic, it threatens the very fabric of our nation and it makes people embittered, angry and profoundly disillusioned with the political system – just like they are in France, *bien sûr* – but what the heck? It worked for Mrs Thatcher, didn't it?

Well, okay, it didn't. But let's not be picky.

PS. I promise, really and truly I do, that this has been absolutely the last, final and ultimate word that this column will have to say on the subject of the European Community for a very considerably long time indeed, oh yes.

Well, quite a long time.

Probably.

December 1991

4

THE *ENTENTE CORDIALE*

'The other English couple want to know if you'd like the menu translated by their little boy.'

Alan Brien

PARDON MY FRENCH

The Fall of France . . . In May 1940, the phrase kept bowling round inside my head, setting echoes flying along the empty, labyrinthine corridors. All my friends in the Upper Fifth agreed there was no other country whose over-painting on the map of Europe could cause us such pain. *Ze Furl urv Fraunce*, we intoned to each other, simultaneously shrugging, winking, gargling, staring right out of frame, hand cupped on left breast, hamming it up a bit but also genuinely moved.

The possible invasion and subjugation of Britain seemed much less cataclysmic – after all, it would (*surely?*) also entail the cancellation of the School Certificate exams. We were very pragmatic and unsentimental about our own country, a bloody awful place, anyway as seen from the forsaken promontory of Wearside and Sunderland Bede Collegiate Boys' Grammar School. A decade-long slump was tapering off. But it had taken a war to give work to many fathers and uncles for the first time in ten years. As for us, we had hived off to the safety of the Yorkshire moors, where anyone under the age of 18 was an invisible supernumerary, like blacks below the old Mason-Dixon line or women in the East.

There was not even a name for us. The word 'teenager' did not exist because the concept did not exist. We were either in the oratorical, inspirational singular, 'Youth', a good thing invoked by politicians and clergymen, or 'Youths', in the pejorative, admonitory plural, who were spoiling everything for everybody else simply by gathering anywhere in our twos and threes, as identified by police constables in court or editorialisers in leader columns. The rumour that 'Youths' had been seen massing on the outskirts, or moving across the landscape, had much the same effect on the burghers as sightings of wolves near Siberian hamlets.

But the Fall of France. As soon as I heard about it on the wireless, I founded the French Club. The first few members were the stickiest to enrol. Like all English persons who have spent five years, four or five hours a week, learning French, none of us could speak more than a couple of sentences extempore. I had to swear that candidates would not have to stand up and hum eccentric vowels through their nose while the rest of us sniggered.

This was a French Club in England and English would be the language of our meetings. The qualification was simply to answer '*oui*' or '*non*' to a series of propositions. Eighty per cent in favour and you were in. Each prospective member was asked to show a preference above all other possible competitors for: French knickers, French kissing, French dressing, French leave, French letters, French windows, French bread, French horn, French cricket, French toast, French mustard, French chalk, French beans, French doors. Everybody passed, even though many of us were not exactly sure what each item signified.

For example, French windows turned out to be, confusingly, the same as French doors, that is, pairs of head-high, fully-glazed frames opening on to balcony or garden. Raised in a climate where everyone who could afford it muffled both doors and windows with heavy veloured and bobbled drapes against the winds from the bone-numbing, snot-green North Sea, these did not seem very practical conveniences. If Captain Oates had been unwise enough to exit through French windows/doors around us, except in the shallow depth of summer, he would soon have been shattering his icicled mitts within minutes against the panes, begging to be readmitted. Still, the very improbability of the suggestion evoked a tropic Gaul where the interior was not inevitably chillier than the exterior, all the year round.

Foods of any kind hardly needed the French prefix to interest growing boys, even if many of us were being better fed in the first year of Forties rationing than in the last year of Thirties depression. Still, I had to search far for any homes familiar with more than one of our list – French bread, dressing, toast, mustard or beans. But then who had ever enjoyed a desirable eatable, come to think of it any desirable possession, which was dubbed British or English?

French bread we had at least seen at the pictures. Usually it was being carried home, protruding from a leatherette shopping-bag, by a black-garbed, bespectacled gorgon, her loaf to the Anglo-Saxon eye more like a large dog-biscuit in the shape of a human thigh-bone. So far was it from our own mahogany brick, that there were even some among us who pretended to believe that they were really dildoes. (This was a wild flight of imagination inspired by a boy who had been brought up in Turkey and claimed once to have overheard his father vainly trying to explain to his mother why bananas, unless sliced, had been forbidden entry to the old Sultan's harem.)

French dressing aroused little interest. I wish I had a silver sixpence for every boy who asked – don't you mean French un-dressing? Even when I found the recipe in *Chambers Encyclopaedia*, there was no way of trying it out. All British adult males rejected salads as 'rabbit bait' so none of us dared lose caste by eating it. The women and girls preferred their lettuce and half-tomato naked or with a dab of long-hoarded Heinz salad cream. When I mixed some and handed out spoons-full, it was the oil not the vinegar that made the tasters shudder. French mustard was allowed to be superior on the sweet palate of youth because milder than the harsh, eye-watering, nappy-yellow stuff slabbed by our elders on everything. Beans? Well, the only beans that attracted boys came from a tin. Otherwise, it was just another inedible, good-for-you green to be concealed under itself at the side of your plate.

French toast (thanks to *Chambers*) was a great success. Gorgeously messy to make, it quickly consumed a whole lot of scarce ingredients your hated hosts had put aside for treats of their own, behind your back.

Do the French, I wonder, realise how deeply embedded in the Anglo-Saxon psyche is the conviction that 'French' means erotic means dirty means gorgeous means suitable only for abroad? By the time we had got through the neutral entries on the list, such as French leave, French chalk, French horn (some disappointment here), both the vetting committee and the proposed entrant were in such a lather of innuendo it was difficult to deny that French polishing was a massage by naked can-can dancers in a bath of perfume and champagne.

Our admiration for French as the language of love was heightened by an anarchic teacher, just off to join the forces, who taught us the invaluable lesson for all translators – the more two words in different languages look the same, the less likely they are to mean the same. He explained that your French waiter never asks a female diner if she has '*fini*' but only if she has '*terminé*' because otherwise he would be asking her if she had completed her orgasm. Even in France, it seemed to us, there was hardly likely to be much confusion between the two enquiries. But oh! to imagine a race which considered such niceties in its official grammar, that deployed such *délicatesse* in its public vocabulary.

We went on to luxuriate over French knickers. So far as we could observe, no manufacturer in Britain had ever thought of producing garments to arouse, and facilitate, sexual pleasure. From all we ever saw on catalogues and in advertisements, British underwear was more like something Boadicea wore over her armour. As for French kissing, the words were scarcely printable in English. The actuality, practised on a pair of bribed local girls, exceeded all our expectations.

'My God, Fiona, I think you've rescued the French franc single-handed!'

There were even a couple of Club members who forswore any further, future sexual delights beyond French kissing on the grounds that their nervous systems would not stand the sensual shock.

It seemed appallingly unjust that a people who clearly exceeded all other nations in its appetite for physical pleasure should be so deprived by the Hun. We hoped that this magic country, which appeared to be able to supply within its own borders every agreeable climate, scenery, wine and food, would find a way to evade Nazi restrictions. After all, and this was then perhaps the most popular item on our list – they were the people who made the French Revolution. At the time, I was afraid even the French could not help having their bright dazzle scratched and clouded by Hitler. Now, I am not so sure.

According to the *Hachette Guide to France 1985* entry on Paris,

> During the German occupation (June 1940–August 1944) a time of strict rationing, fear and Gestapo raids was offset by glittering and provocative night-life and real artistic and intellectual creativity.

Reading that, I must admit my Francophilia buckled for a moment. Isn't there something a bit suspect about a capital city that can make such a boast *in* such *extremis*? London was hardly noted for what is usually called nightlife, or for much artistic creativity during those war years. And then, I thought, neither was it in the years before or since. Good luck to them.

Forty-five years later, my eye is always caught, my attention is instantly lured, by and large my anticipations fulfilled, when I follow the word 'French'. Even in English.

April 1986

Libby Purves

ENFANCE TERRIBLE

I was ten years old when I first realised that it was going to take more than a tunnel to join us to France. I lived there, then; I was a Foreign Office child, a diplo-brat, and had not yet reached the age where they send you to boarding-school on the Boat Train; so I was enrolled in a convent school at No. 66 rue Royale, not a croissant's throw from the Consulate. The language had been no sort of barrier; a nine-year-old can learn a foreign tongue in three months flat, well enough to manage *la Géographie* and exchange whispered insults in Chapel, anyway. The divisions between me and my classmates were less tangible, more fraught: a matter of atmosphere and expectation and unspoken, iron-hard conventions.

Anyway, I can remember the moment when I first understood the breadth of the divide between us. It was when a formal embossed invitation-card came from my friend Véronique, to attend her lofty town-house *'pour le goûter et pour disséquer un ver'*. To Tea, that is, and To Dissect An Earthworm. Véronique, you see, had a scalpel of her own, and our biology class was just tackling invertebrates. In immaculate parental script at the bottom of the letter, it said, *'Prière d'apporter votre microscope.'*

Young as I was in the ways of the world, I dimly saw that this invitation, so formal, so improving, so punctilious in delineating the nature of the proffered entertainment, was something not quite English. On visits home we had met English schoolchildren, and knew

'Stop complaining about the smell – people will think you're English.'

something of their ways. We observed that after school they drifted round to one another's houses, fought, lounged, reluctantly completed homework, and drifted home again. Véronique and I, however, were clearly in for a session of informed worm-dissection, book in hand; followed by a chic tea, laid on a white cloth, including creamed mushroom sandwiches and paper-thin sponge cake washed down with Grenadine. I cannot even remember whether we were yet on terms to call one another *tu* rather than *vous*, probably not, since I had only been at the school a year. The time of my expected departure was firmly included on the embossed card, and woe betide any poor Daddy held up at the office and failing to remove me on the dot of *cinq heures*. I knew the rules, by then, as well as I knew the pluperfect of *avoir*.

And because I lived by these rules for three years, I have always considered that I know more about the French than any pâté-guzzling, Renault-owning Hampstead poseur with a time-shared gîte in the Dordogne and a few misty-eyed memories of school trips to Paris. In national childhood you find the unchangeable foundations of national character; and I had a fair slice of French bourgeois childhood. I was an *écolière*, I wore a pale blue overall and belonged to the order of St Aloysius; I learned one whole *Fable de la Fontaine* and ten Departments of France every night, venerated the Congo Martyrs, and did eurhythmics in a flounced white tunic. I dipped chunks of buttered bread into my morning bowl of coffee after early Mass, and drank my share of the beer routinely provided at school dinner (one litre between a table of eight). And on Thursday afternoons (*le jeudi*, no afternoon school on Thursdays, show me your vinous gîte-dweller who knows that) I went to the parties.

Véronique's little gathering was entirely informal, of course. I seem to remember that in honour of the earthworm, we actually wore commonplace school skirts and clean overalls. Had it been a birthday party, we would have been done up in party frocks and long white socks (short white socks, of course, being merely for school) and would have brought along an overall for sandpit wear. Had it been Sunday lunch in the country with a family of private bankers, things might have been relaxed to the point of, say, coloured socks; but still the convention and the *placement* (all worked out round *la Grand-mère*, who owned most of the shares) would be rigid; and children would sit, swinging aching legs, through all the endless courses. At school we still read the Comtesse de Ségur's *Les Malheurs de Sophie* with no sense of satire or of its values being dated; the whippings and lockings-in-cupboards meted out to Sophie might have declined, but the prevailing pressure upon little girls to be *correctes et gentilles* was identical. It is as if English parents were to point admiringly to the virtues of Little Lord Fauntleroy.

Formal events marked the passage of childhood. I was confirmed in a froth of white net, by the Bishop in the Cathedral, as was perfectly normal for a Catholic child; a cake was iced and neighbours sent me sugared almonds in boxes with curly string. Had I stayed another six months I would have been plunged into the vastly greater (and entirely French) ceremony of the *Communion Solennelle*, which in terms of dress, veil, church etiquette and general hysteria is nothing less than a full dress-rehearsal for a girl's wedding, only without the encumbrance of a bridegroom. On school prize days we walked across glittering parquet in our white gloves, and curtseyed like débutantes of the 1920s; parents watched critically from the sidelines, weighing up our Correctness. Only a Republic born of violent revolution could possibly mind so much about being Correct. It has driven me into a life of hideous incorrectness and odd socks, ever since.

But do not think the French are cissies. French children are brought up to be tough. While we went on holiday with our parents, and tried a bit of everything rather badly, our schoolmates spent the long summer *vacances* specialising. Off they went to the *École de*

Voile or the *Cours de Ski* by the sea or in the mountains; if they later rejoined their parents at a seaside resort, they would be enrolled immediately in the Club Mickey, and spend the day behind a wire fence making brilliant sand models and doing physical jerks, while we pottered freely around making inefficient dams and reading comics. On the other hand, when we were tucked in bed full of bread-and-butter, they were draped in napkins in the hotel dining-room, eating *quenelles de brochet* and telling their parents about their latest ski grade or judo belt.

After three and a half years, we moved on. The shallow layer of French childhood was covered by other influences; I grew less tough, probably; certainly less correct; far less industrious once the memory of two hours' homework a night wore off. But it takes only a glimpse of a *Pschitt!* poster, a sniff of the Calais drains, or the sound of a high fluent complaining French voice in a shop, to whip me back; I have walked all night round Paris in a happy daze, buying *gaufres*, I have lain eight months pregnant in a lonely hotel in Brittany with nothing to read but *Les Malheurs de* bloody *Sophie*, so nervously transported that I forgot what story my employers had sent me there to cover in the first place. I love France desperately; but am always glad, after a while, to put twenty miles of clean, rushing salt water between me and any risk of Révérende Mère or Véronique's Grandmother noticing that my socks are not correct.

'Do you walk on other people's food in England?'

I can barely face the idea of looking down into a concrete hole in the safe, familiar Kentish hills, and knowing that They are just at the other end. I am not at all sure that, this time, Mrs Thatcher knows what she has bitten off.

April 1986

Michael Bywater

SUR LE PONG

Evil Frogs in old novels of suspense always smelt. Stank, actually, as Johnson would have pointed out, and as indeed he did, of rank sweat, rutting fox and trouser, I imagine. Somehow that is all right. Jasmine isn't, nor various exudates like whale sick and stuff from rat's bottoms.

I am not sure about rats. It could be deer. Or ox. Is there a musk ox? If so, that could be it. All I can remember, off the top of my head, is that the odour which persuades is derived from the bottom of something called the Musk Something. Nobody ever says how the Musk Something feels about it all. We had a dog once called Fred. Gosh phew what an ozzard pong. Maybe he was a Musk Dachshund and we were sitting on a nasty little gold-mine, but we never investigated. One wouldn't.

Nevertheless it seemed to work. Any dachshund which can dislocate a hip by falling off a wall upon which it was standing to boff an Alsatian obviously has something up its sleeve. I may have restricted my adolescence by cowardice. A quick rub of the blighter's hindquarters behind the ear each morning and it could all have been a different story.

As it was I was a singularly – some might say overpoweringly – sweet-smelling youth. This was due to reading (a) old novels where wicked Frogs stank of scent, and (b) Frog novels where (oddly enough) scent was never mentioned, but an awful lot of time was spent being French.

This seemed to me better than being English, where it rained and the chances of a romantic entanglement were minimal. We didn't have an *heure bleue*. We didn't even have that many Alsatians, in those days.

Snappy sort of chap I was, with the intellect. Combined Bad novels and Frog novels, put two and two together, got three. Others fell under the spell of Kafka and shuffled bleakly about in long raincoats, coughing. I, on the other hand, acquired a *fin-de-siècle* scent spray, Frogs for the use of, and used it. Liberally.

The Da did not approve, not at all. 'Filthy foreign muck,' he would snarl. 'Pooh.'

The Da was, of course, a White Man. I, on the other hand (also on the nape of the neck, the face and all those other heart-warming pulse-points), was an exotic little poof who had long ago fallen under the influence of *The Hairless Mexican* who was not only Hairless but also Fragrant, but I suppose if W. S. Maugham had written *The Fragrant Mexican* it would have let the cat out of the bag, what with the Villa Mauresque and all those nice young men.

Wagner, too. Used to sit around on a velvet *chaise longue* sniffing Otto. Of rose, that is. That was all right but he also had a scrubby little beard, one of those perverts' ones that goes around the chin like a sort of residue. Presumably this showed that even though he sniffed scent he was no Frog.

Nevertheless, he did very well, did Wagner, with the girlies. I don't know how he fitted it all in. As it were. If it came to the crunch, I would have let the music slip, myself. You can't do everything at once.

Queer, though, him not being a Frog. The Frogs are supposed to do awfully well while the Germans sit around being fat and stolid and having 21 children, like Bach, who never wore a drop of the soft stuff in his life, though Gott knows what he got up to in the organ-loft. He may have been up there absolutely *redolent* for all we know, Old Wig with a *Wurst Hund* stuck behind each ear, exuding.

I suppose one was, um, multi-cultural. As a youth. German music, Latin pornography, Turkish tobacco and French knickers comprised the sensual panoply which I hungered to don. Unfortunately, the exigencies of adolescence being what they are, the French side of things really never got a look-in. The nearest I got to delicately-scented peach-bloom skin, or indeed d-s.p.-b. underwear, in the early years, was intermittent and hateful sightings of Holloway's jockstrap, which was possessed of the mysterious power of ubiquity, turning up in all sorts of unexpected places, as a kind of counterbalance to its owner, who was not to be found anywhere, most of the time.

A Brut man, Holloway, as I recall. You may remember Brut. It was considered pretty exotic when it first came out, before 'Enery got in on the act, thus confirming the Jockstrap Connection which had already been clearly formed in my mind.

Images of shifty Frogs in immaculate waisted hopsack shimmered in my tormented brain, oval Turkish fag held poised in a beautifully manicured hand as they snorkelled at a *café-cognac* and lavished languishing Gallic glances on elegant bints whose *haute couture* concealed a veritable Niagara of intimate garments. (The fact that the prevailing impression would have been one of Boyards and bogs, I conveniently suppressed, due to what psychiatrists have now identified as 'ignorance'). Who, I wondered, could set himself up in such a *milieu* reeking of Brut?

Holloway, evidently.

I, on the other hand, bided my time, waited

for the market to mature and in due course became a Nine Flags man.

Nine Flags, for the olfactorily disadvantaged among you, was a range of Nine shaving colognes (they were actually just colognes, but they stuck the word 'shaving' in for marketing reasons) representing the Flags of various nations. Ireland was there, oddly enough, not being a country you would naturally associate with good grooming, represented by Green Moss. I tried it first, along with a touch of brogue, until the inamorata of the day (a svelte, grey-eyed honey manufactured out of velvet, liquorice and titanium) said: 'Is there something wrong with your throat? Only you smell of linctus and you're talking so strangely.'

Sweden came next. Wild Spruce, as I recall, a colourless preparation smelling strongly of gin, which was immediately stolen by The Da on the grounds that he liked the smell and that if people said, 'By God, old man, you are wearing scent, you evil Frog!' he could say, 'No, I am not, I have just been drinking.'

I worked my way through the lot until I ended up with France, which was the colour of old burgundy and offered an exotic, sweet scent like a mixture of amber, patchouli and ylang-ylang. This yielded the best results. 'I am so glad,' said the object of my affections (a lithe coupée of a girl, built of silk, cinnamon and whipcord) 'that you do not wear after-shaving lotion. My stepfather does, and he is such a repulsive old roué, just like a wicked Frog in a book.'

My ardour undaunted, I continued my researches. Fetishism, I suppose you would call it, though strangely distorted: instead of her shoes or something, I became fascinated by the accessories of her pursuit, i.e., going out at strange hours smelling differently all the way down, Patou on the mug, Guerlain at neck-level, Rochas slapped on the burgeoning paunch, and so on right down to This Little Piggy Went Wee Wee Wee (Houbigant from choice).

The *chien saucisson* never stood a chance.

Thus it was galling to discover that the evil Frogs never wore the stuff at all. My wife told me this. 'Oh no. They don't need it. They have charm. They gaze into your eyes. *You* never gaze into my eyes. And anyway scent is not erotic. It covers up the natural pheromones.'

Natural pheromones, eh? I wonder where you can get those. And how much?

April 1986

'Pleading insanity got me nowhere.' (1985)

Caroline Ross

THE DUCHESS ON THE ILE SAINT LOUIS

This year marks the two hundredth anniversary of the French Revolution and lavish celebrations have been laid on to mark the event. The new opera house at Bastille will open its doors, specially commissioned plays will be performed at the Comédie Française, there will be fireworks and dancing on the streets of Paris.

It seems like a good enough excuse for a national bash, but not all the natives are friendly to the idea. There are still six thousand *familles nobles* in France (proof, if you like, that revolutions don't work) and two hundred years have failed to dull their enormous sense of injury.

But whatever the feelings of the French aristocracy, they won't be taking their protest to the streets. History has taught them that keeping their heads down is the best way to avoid getting it in the neck, and in public they seem quietly resigned to republicanism. In private, however, it's as if Marie Antoinette (together with thousands of friends and relations) went to the guillotine yesterday. And bicentenary 'celebrations' are, to put it mildly, in the worst possible taste.

'It's appalling to have this hanging over us,' one very elevated Duchess told me when the Duchess and I met for lunch on the Ile Saint Louis. While I admired her perfectly accessoried Chanel suit (couture M and S, *moi*) and wondered whether to work in or out with the cutlery, she and the Duc relived the horrors of the Reign of Terror. It was a catalogue of suffering and humiliation, spiced with gory detail. Their description of the death of the Mayor of Paris, who had his heart eaten by the *sans culottes*, quite put me off my *saumon en croûte*.

I filled up on cake later. This time I was in the company of a Countess at her sixteenth arrondissement home. 'The Revolution was murder,' the Countess said. (Pause) 'It was murder!' I nodded meekly and ate my gâteau. 'The only thing to do in the face of these ghastly festivities is to stay inside and pray for the souls of the poor innocent victims.' To the Countess, to the Duchess, to all of them it was as if it had happened yesterday.

'In France, there's noble and there's noble,' Monsieur le Duc explained. First division aristos, he said, between twenty and thirty families, date their titles back to the twelfth century. Later ennoblements (or purchases of titles) are not so highly regarded, and cachet decreases in chronological order. Thus a Mortemart (very chic, very *ancien régime*) can look down on a Magenta (not so chic, rather Napoleon Trois). Lower down still come the BCBG (*bon chic bon genre*), the equivalent perhaps of the English Sloanes, the *haute bourgeoisie* anyway.

Such divisions occur in Britain too, but there are significant differences. The French spend less time in gumboots, for one. A circumstance that dates back to the days of Louis XIV. He permanently changed the environs of the French nobility when he opened the gates of Versailles and invited them all over for a bite to eat and a spot of Racine afterwards.

This turned out to be rather a long evening, lasting the whole reign through, and it caused the aristocracy to remove their home bases from the country to Paris, to be near the fun. Here they've remained ever since – city people who occasionally visit rural châteaux, the reverse of their British counterparts, who are countryfolk with places in town.

And there is a certain rigidity, too, that marks out the French from the Brits. No well-bred French home is without a copy of the *Bottin Mondain*, the Gallic equivalent of *Debrett's*. This hefty tome, issued from 28 rue du Docteur Finlay, Paris, lists all the aristocracy and well-respected old families.

Those in the *Bottin* need not bother with telephone directories; everyone they will ever need to know is here. The *Bottin* saves *seizième* hostesses from making an unfortunate choice of dinner guest, and it enables parents to extract daughters swiftly from unsuitable romances. Basically, the rule is, if he's nottin the Bottin, it's not on.

Of course, while being in the book may be a mark of breeding, it does not guarantee sex appeal. And although a class-conscious *maman* would be delighted to welcome a young Quatrebarbes, a Leshideux, or a Bec de Lièvre to her table, the question remains, will such suitors suit her daughter? With names like 'Fourbeards', 'The Hideous One' and 'Harelip', it doesn't seem likely. Perhaps she'll go for a smooth-talking Bastard de Villeneuve instead – and if she does, that's acceptable, he's in the book.

British well-breds like to marry each other too, though they are more prone to messing around with a few ineligibles first. While a French girl is unlikely to permit even the chastest of embraces before a chap's credentials have been thoroughly inspected, a British gel may find disappointment in her *Debrett's* the morning after something very indiscreet. My formidable Countess had recently met two *anglaises* at a country party. 'They were charming girls,' the Countess said, 'from very good families. (Pause) Poor girls, they drank too much.'

No, you don't find young, glamorous, female French aristocrats throwing up outside expensive restaurants. Those are English manners. In France even minor infringements of the noble code, like wearing overlarge earrings at luncheon, or keeping your hat on indoors, are frowned upon. The Brits are a disreputable lot by comparison, but then they've never had the Reign of Terror.

Anglo-Saxon licence owes much to the continued existence of a royal family – reassuring and fairly undemanding role models. The French nobles, still pitifully unsure of their role in a republic, know only that they must stick together and be better behaved than their inferiors. They long for a king to give them back their *raison d'être*, but the main Bourbon contender is fatally flawed. His ancestor was one Philippe '*égalité*' who voted with the Jacobins for the death of Louis XVI, thus tarnishing the name of this family for ever. And indeed, without even saving himself from the guillotine.

Denied a respectable pretender to the throne, French aristocrats cast envious eyes across the Channel, and it's not just the Windsors they want. Since the Revolution, French inheritance law has decreed that estates must be divided equally amongst the children. This has progressively eroded noble legacies, and effectively sent the aristocracy out to work to save their châteaux. In England primogeniture ensures that huge fortunes still exist, and Gloucestershire girls continue to dance in stately homes comfortingly full of priceless possessions.

Meanwhile, French châteaux have become more and more difficult to maintain. Successive divisions have resulted, in the words of the Duchess, in 'furniture without châteaux and châteaux without furniture'. No doubt about it, '*c'est triste*'. The Duchess's eyes were damp.

And now, more and more, you have châteaux *à vendre*. During the past three or four years a huge number of country homes have been sold, often to English buyers. 'And not to anyone of very good family either,' said the Countess. The Countess knew. She was bemoaning the loss of her château, in the family since the 1300s.

Spare a thought, then, for the beleaguered French nobility, as the skies of Paris light up to celebrate the birth of the guillotine. And remember, as you contemplate spending next summer in your new holiday château in Normandy, that hurtful truth, '*Dieu abaisse les superbes*' (God humbles the proud).

January 1989

'We're on a pretty tight schedule, so we won't have time to take in the whole thing. Can you just give us a brief outline?'

Anna Raeburn

LES BOURGEOIS GENTILHOMMES

My first sight of a Frenchman was Jean-Paul Belmondo in an impenetrable film to which I was taken by one of my more enterprising friends. The film was shown in a leaking greenhouse which housed the Foreign Film Society and it was only at the end that I realised that I had water dripping down my neck. I was similarly spellbound by Gérard Philippe a couple of years later. And for the next ten years or so I fell at regular intervals for one or other of the stylish images the French cinema was kind enough to dish up for me.

But I do not remember the face of a single Frenchman on my first trip to Paris, aged 24. I was too busy feeling inept and gaping at the architecture. When I went again with my first husband two years later, his closest friend impressed me when he emerged, diminutive against the *porte cochère* of his apartment in the Marais, and kissed Michael on both cheeks and firmly on the lips. He rejoiced in the name of Proust and he gave me my first calvados. But everybody else we met, with the exception of Proust's wife, became like figures decorating a set. I held my first husband in considerable awe. He could talk to these people, not only in French – which was impressive enough – but in their language. And I could only wonder at them, the intellectuals and activists of '68.

I might have fallen into the trap of thinking that Paris was France had I not been taken to rural Provence a year later by a woman friend who spoke French like a Frenchwoman and impressed upon me the absolute necessity of the courtesies the tourists ignored. These would not make us liked, she added, but they would make us more agreeably tolerated. So we wore bras, our sleeves down, plain clothes, our hair off our faces every time we went into the village. And after we'd had every single pair of pants stolen by a maniac *chasseur* with a gun, who unzipped our tent on the last night to gaze with voyeuristic longing at our sleeping bodies – thus frightening us considerably – the old men of the village unbent sufficiently to tell us that he'd never harmed anybody, and bought us a drink before we left.

In the Paris which I now visit for a long weekend a couple of times a year, I am already with a man, my second husband, and that of necessity colours (for the most part) both my reaction to Frenchmen and theirs to me. However, the Frenchman who made the most impression upon me was not a film star at all. He was a businessman of medium height, balding, with dark twinkling eyes, who accosted me in broad daylight, walking up to me in Mount Street and inviting me to dinner. I explained that I was delighted but unfortunately unable to join him. 'But why?' he enquired. I explained that I had an appointment, that I was a journalist with work to do and that, regretfully, I was married. He was, he said, desolated. I was, I said, charmed. Half a dozen strides past me, he called after me to ask – was I sure? I was, I said. Well then – he thanked me and wished me *au revoir*. On an ordinarily harried morning, an encounter like that with anybody would have been a bonus. To have it conducted in French, which is offered to us as the language of romance, civilisation, chic, was delightful.

Of course, there is a great gap between the Frenchman on the screen and the Frenchman in the street. For a start there is the small matter of class because a working-class Frenchman may cook like an angel and make love like a dream but many of them smell very strongly of *eau de l'aisselle* – sweat imprisoned in synthetic fibres and yesterday's garlic. Admixed with Gauloises, this may be an acquired taste – but it takes some acquiring.

Then there is the fact that you very rarely look up to a Frenchman. He is usually a small man. And his preoccupation with matters of dress can be annoying. A friend of mine who travelled with Jean-Michel Jarre to China to give a concert there recounts her growing fury at the habit of these allegedly sensitive and intelligent people of having endless conversations about which accessories go with which cashmere, and making exclamations of pleasure over matched luggage and complaints about the lack of wine.

In his conscious mind, the Frenchman may be a bandit, laid back, fancy-free, but deeper in his personality he is possessed of a great sense of order and conservatism. Because his way of doing things and what is acceptable are likely to be different from our own, we tend to give them credit they do not always deserve. Sometimes the formalities are charming. Sometimes they are irritating. But many of us were brought up to think that if it is French it must be right. This is often just a continuation of the snobbish idea that if you don't understand it, it must be wonderful. The French add to this with their profound chauvinism. In spite of the increasing inroads into their language by our own, nobody is more chauvinistic about language than the French and men are noticeably more rigid about using it than women.

In England, Frenchmen are famous as lovers. But it would be unfair to portray them as making a pass at just anybody. They choose darned carefully and if you aren't what they're looking for, they'll never look at you. What's more, their pursuit, conducted for the most part in their own language, often adds to the sense of helplessness so many English women seem to need to feel before they can really let go. When you don't understand what the man is saying but the intonation of his voice sounds promising, you can always plead innocence in the cold light of day.

But what mostly appeals to English women about Frenchmen is their talent for flirting, their gift for making anything from a greeting to a farewell sound infinitely promising. It's like finding someone to play a game with, a game you were brought up to play but could never find a partner for. It's all innocent – if you want it to be – but it's enormous fun. That and their genuine emotion and lack of fear about expressing it. They rave about their food, extol their work, annihilate their politicians, adore their children. Well, the typical ones among them do, anyway. And who wants an atypical Frenchman?

April 1986

'All that cheap lamb doesn't seem to be doing the English much good.'

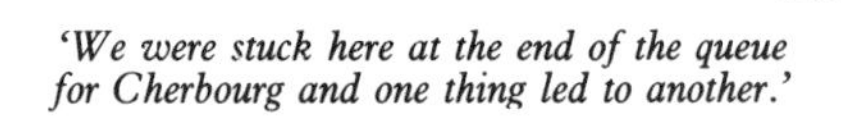

'We were stuck here at the end of the queue for Cherbourg and one thing led to another.'

Geoffrey Dickinson

A PLAGE IN THE SUN

'Are you sure they understood that we wanted the topless beach?'

Miles Kington

THE FRANGLAIS LIEUTENANT'S WOMAN

Un novel complet condensé et traduit de l'original de Jean Fowles

Lyme Regis est un typical village de fishing sur le South Coast d'Angleterre, une de ces petites villes qui, sur la route à nowhere, n'ont pas été totalement ruinées par le progrès et les juggernauts. Pittoresque, mais business-like, Lyme Regis est toujours un beau petit spot, par exemple, comme une refuge pour un auteur comme moi. Depuis 1867 elle n'a pas beaucoup changée. Si un habitant de Lyme en 1867 fut transporté soudain par time travel en 1986, il dirait: 'Pouf! Lyme n'a pas beaucoup changée! Un peu de growth suburbain, peut-être, et ces choses curieuses qu'on appelle saloon cars, mais otherwise c'est pretty much la même.'

C'est ici que j'ai écrit mon novel classique, 'The Franglais Lieutenant's Woman', et c'est aussi ici que les gens de Hollywood ont choisi pour le filming du major movie du même nom. Vous avez jamais vu les gens de Hollywood en action? C'est fantastique. Ils disent: 'Hmm – away avec les pôles de telegraph! Away avec les double lignes jaunes, et les parking meters! Up avec les pseudo-façades Victoriennes! Bring on les stage-coaches et les yokels en smock!' Dans le twinkling d'un oeil, vous avez un fake Lyme Regis. J'aime bien cela. Le mingling de l'illusion et la réalité, c'est mon stock en trade.

Et si vous transporterez l'habitant de 1867 en 1986, il serait quite unaware qu'il était dans un film set. Parce qu'en 1867, il n'y avait pas de film sets. Vous ne savez pas? Eh bien, vous savez maintenant. Parce que mes novels sont pleins de knowledge incidental comme ça. Stick avec moi, et vous allez recevoir quite une éducation.

Où étais-je? Ah, oui. En 1867, à Lyme Regis, Charles et Ernestina prenaient un petit stroll, totalement unaware qu'ils étaient dans un major novel. Charles était un des ces Victorian gents qui ont plenty d'argent et plenty de leisure time. Jeune, prepossessing, un bachelor, avec un joli petit sparkle, il n'avait pas précisément un job. Un job pour un gentleman, ce n'était pas nécessaire en 1867. Maintenant, si vous dites: 'Je n'ai pas un job,' on dit: 'Ah, pauvre petit, vous formez partie de l'army des unemployed, personellement je blâme Mrs Thatcher, je vais avoir un petit mot avec Uncle Fred, peut-être a-t-il un opening dans Allied Drinks, etc.' Mais en 1867, on disait: 'Il n'a pas un job. Il est un gentleman.' Intéressant, eh?

Charles était un fanatique des fossils. Oui, avec son petit hammer et son petit fossilbag, il parcourait le landscape de Lyme Regis et les environs pour chercher les relics jurassiques et dévoniens. Un waste de time? Peut-être. Mais il faut se souvenir qu'en 1867 Charles Darwin était hot news. L'évolution, oui ou non? C'était une burning question. Donc, Charles cherchait les fossils, dans l'espoir de dire: 'Oui! Darwin est sur le ball!* Ce petit fossil est le proof!' Ou bien: 'Darwin est un charlatan, et le Livre de Genesis est le gospel truth.'

Charles était aussi good-looking, pas hunky exactement, mais attractif. Un peu comme Robert Redford, peut-être. Of course, dans le film il était joué par Jeremy Irons qui n'est pas truthfully mon exacte idée de Charles, mais je n'avais pas total control sur le casting. Some vous gagnez, some vous perdez . . .

Et Ernestina était un produit typical de l'époque de Victoria (1837–1901). Sa fiancée Ernestina était jolie, pert, indépendente, bien éduquée, et quite a catch pour un gentleman

* Of course, Charles n'aurait pas dit: 'Sur le ball.' C'est une expression moderne, une phrase de soccer, datant de 1953.

comme Charles. Elle tolérait la passion de Charles pour les fossils, et pourquoi pas? Être jaloux des fossils, c'est stupide. Je ne vais pas donner une pleine description d'Ernestina parce que, si vous voulez vraiment savoir, je ne suis pas un dab hand avec l'analysis des femmes. Elles sont un mystery breed pour moi. Fascinant, mais un mystère. Never mind.

So, Charles et Ernestina prenaient un stroll dans Lyme Regis, en 1867. Vous avez la picture? Up le High Street, down le High Street, et puis along la plage, un stroll ordinaire, quoi. Et ils parlaient des choses dont parlent les fiancés.

'Quand nous nous sommes mariés, il faut que j'aie une chambre spéciale pour mes fossils,' dit Charles.

'D'accord. Et aussi une chambre spéciale pour les enfants.'

'Enfants? Quels enfants? Nous n'avons pas d'enfants . . .'

'Pas encore, Charles. Mais by et by . . .'

'Ça sera chic!' s'écria Charles. 'Des petits enfants, qui vont m'accompagner sur le fossil-hunt! Oui, beaucoup de petits enfants, pour continuer le good work de fossil-hunting.'

Ernestina avait un petit frown sur sa pretty face. Hmm. Fossil-hunting était OK comme un hobby, mais il était un peu obsessionel. La palaeontologie n'est pas nécessairement héréditaire, elle pensa. En quoi, elle était wide du mark, parce que le Leakey family d'East Africa a changé la palaeontologie en un family business. Mais, en 1867, c'était difficile à anticiper.

Meanwhile, Charles et Ernestina continuaient leur stroll jusqu'au Cobb. Vous avez vu le film de 'The Franglais Lieutenant's Woman'? Le Cobb était un landmark dans ce film. C'est un grand breakwater, ou plutôt un quai, ou peut-être un sea-wall – anyway, c'est une grande construction de rocks et boulders qui est un landmark de Lyme Regis, spécialement après le movie. Je ne sais pas pourquoi il s'appelle le Cobb. Je ne peux pas faire le research de tout, vous savez. Je ne suis pas omniscient.

'Regards!' dit Charles. 'Qui est la femme au bout du Cobb?'

Dans la drizzle, ils pouvaient voir une lone figure, dans un cloak, en position au tip du Cobb. Un peu comme la Statue de Liberté, quoi, ou peut-être comme Jean la Baptiste – solitaire, mélancolique, triste, enveloppée dans ce grand cloak.

Ernestina donna un petit shiver. 'C'est the Franglais Lieutenant's Woman.'

'Come again?' dit Charles.

'C'est une triste histoire,' dit Ernestina. 'Elle est une countrywoman qui est tombée amoureuse d'un matelot franglais. Last year, il y avait un shipwreck. Le lieutenant a été rescué. Il a eu une affaire avec une pauvre, simple countrywoman. Puis le lieutenant est rentré en France, en disant: "Attends-moi, honey, je vais revenir avec un ring et une wedding date." Et maintenant, chaque jour, elle est sur le Cobb, avec les yeux fixés sur le coast-line de France.'

En silence, Charles et Ernestina marchaient le long du Cobb. Il était très windy, not to say stormy, not to say tempestueux. La lone figure se tenait là, comme un light-house, ou bien un figure-head, avec le cloak whipping dans le vent. Vous avez vu le film? C'est très dramatique dans le film.

Au bout du Cobb, Charles donna un petit cough. Il ne voulait pas donner un shock à la Franglais Lieutenant's Woman. Heuh, heuh, heuh, fit-il. La lone figure ne se tourna pas.

Heugh, heugh, heugh, fit Charles. Même réaction.

'I say!' dit Charles. 'Etes-vous OK?'

La lone figure se tourna. Consternation! Ce n'était pas une jeune femme. C'était un homme, bearded, avec sun-glasses.

'Mon Dieu!' dit Charles. 'Vous êtes un homme, bearded, avec sun-glasses. Où est Meryl Streep?'

'En California,' dit l'homme. 'Je fais le stand-in pour cette scène. Dans un cloak, from behind, qui sait la différence?'

Charles donna un gasp. L'homme était handsome. 'Qui êtes-vous?'

'Je suis Chuck Yerbonski, 3ème assistant

producteur sur le film. Je suis de la même physique que Meryl Streep, donc un naturel pour le stand-in.' Charles donna un second gasp. Chuck Yerbonski était *très* handsome. Sur le spot, il tomba amoureux de ce chunky 3ème assistant producteur du film.

'Charles!' dit Ernestina. 'Charles? Charles! CHARLES!'

Il était trop tard. Charles, un jeune gentleman de 1867, était madly in love avec Chuck, un assistant producteur de 1980, avec beaucoup de complications sociales. Mais Charles était blind aux implications. Une belle petite histoire, non?

Venant bientôt à votre neighbourhood screen: 'The Franglais Lieutenant's Assistant Producer!' Mind-bobbling, hein? Un blending de réalite et illusion? Well, why not?

'Beats *The French Lieutenant's Woman* dans un cocked hat' (*Barry Norman*). Nominé pour 11 Oscars. Don't miss it.

April 1986

Roy Hattersley

PRESSE GANG

No doubt they all lose in translation. Certainly, *The Chained Duck* is not a title which creates the instant impression of elegant satire or savage lampoon. And last week (at least to the English mind) the cartoons in *Le Canard Enchainé* lacked both bite and wit. Sheriff Ronald Reagan in pursuit of outlaw Colonel Gaddafi is the most hackneyed of ideas. And the *Canard* version did not even make plain whether the drawing illustrated the magazine's opinion of the two men's moral relationship or made a complaint about the President's simplistic view of the world. The escaping convicts, walking to freedom through cracks in the prison walls, were a commentary on either the frequency of recent breakouts or the crumbling condition of French jails. Either way the cartoon was a whimper, not a bang. Jacques Chirac casting behind him somebody else's shadow is not even a new idea; *Punch*, almost one hundred years ago, reported the American triumph of Lillie Langry with a drawing that showed the lady in a spotlight which picked out the silhouette of the Prince of Wales on the stage behind her.

The fascination of royalty persists. *Paris Match* pour 18 Avril publishes the 'album of secret souvenirs which worry the Queen'. The subject is, of course, Miss Sarah Ferguson. The album records 'the pranks of a little English girl when on the loose' – the worst of which seems to be riding into a swimming-pool on a BMX bicycle. She is also shown with an 'unidentified companion' (who is wearing shorts of the respectable length favoured by non-commissioned officers in the pre-war Indian Army), and with 'Paddy McNally, a previous boyfriend aged 48'. These pictures, we are solemnly assured, 'so disquieted Buckingham Palace that MI5, The British Secret Service, were asked to make discreet enquiries' into the previous flirtations of the future Duchess of York.

I think the Queen has real cause for concern on three separate issues. First, Prince Andrew is to marry a commoner who is so impoverished that throughout all her excesses in 'la dolce vita before constrained by the Court', she owned only one sun-hat, which she wore for each separate escapade. Second, she rolls her own. Third, on the evidence of the pictures she is not *une petite Anglaise* at all. She is (or at least was) a rather *Anglaise rebondie* – though I bet that they knew that already and are working on her chubbiness in *le cabinet de la Reine*.

The pictures of 'the future Duchess of York' (*Times* Court and Social – please note) are, with one exception, blurred snaps, taken by anxious amateurs. The rest of the photographs in *Paris Match* – whatever their subject – are simply stunning. Priscilla Presley,

'There is a notice in each compartment which clearly states: "Do not lean out of the window in the tunnel" . . . !'

so bronzed that it is hard to make out the gold bikini; Liza Minnelli, on her fortieth birthday; Anthony Quinn, proclaiming from behind two paint brushes that 'given another twenty years he will be as celebrated as Picasso'; all produce the same immediate emotion as the illustrations to the bomb-in-the-Boeing story and the account of the Mexican plane crash 'with 166 persons including 9 French on board'. Why is there no photojournalism in Britain these days?

It is clearly a weekly art. It is only seen at its best on expensive paper which retails at 10f for 90 pages. And it deals with news stories which are not quite news – an air disaster which took place a fortnight before publication date and life in a tiny African extension of Metropolitan France which is worth writing about because nothing has changed for years. It hurts me to admit it, but sometimes a picture is worth a thousand words – particularly if it is in glorious colour. The photograph of the 'Dallas family' makes them look more tawdry than anything I have seen in any other publication, despite the caption which confides that Priscilla Presley's salary is '700,000f per episode'.

To open *Tours de France* (also 10f, but only 80 pages) is to feel the same sense of deprivation. We need a news magazine. The conversation between Victor Franco and 'Les Enfants de la Guerre' is chilling enough in itself – in a slightly theatrical way.

'Would you like to go from here?'

'Where to?'

'To a country without war.'

'Would I sleep every night in my bed?'

'Yes.'

'And never be afraid again?'

But there is always a suspicion, when the recorded response is too appropriate, that the reporter has ever so slightly polished the replies. The camera can lie. But nobody could doubt the authenticity of the pictures of the lost boys, both Christian and Muslim, who inhabit the ruins of Beirut. Some sit hopelessly amongst rubble and barbed wire. One has made himself a toy machine-gun out of bits of wood. Another, scarcely older, carries a real automatic rifle and gives a Churchillian sign to celebrate a victory that the grown-ups know will never come. A third is pictured 'on the road to school', a satchel on his back. He limps along on crutches. His right foot was blown off by a car bomb.

After that, the pictures of Robert Mitchum at the Cannes (detective) Film Festival; the illustrations for '*Cuisinez avec les grands chefs*', even the photographs taken at the 'inaugural session of the new legislature', are put in their proper moral perspective. But without them – and the fashions from Dior, the story of France's newest film star and even the horoscope – the news stories would never get into the book-stalls. And that would be a pity. In a civilised country, there ought to be a market for photo-journalism – something different from and better than our Sunday colour supplements which are always weeks behind the news and usually too concerned with plugging summer holidays or some other manifestation of the good life.

The French, taking the good life more for granted, snap their lenses at a wider variety of topics and the French public pay good money to see the colours in which the world goes round.

I envy them the opportunity. And I pay my proper respect to pictures. Unlike words (and cartoons) they can withstand the most incompetent translations.

April 1986

Clement Freud

LA GRANDE BOUFFE

When Young Lochinvar reached his 65th birthday, it is said that he had become pretty sick of the prefix to his name; similar feelings have been expressed by generations of Little Billys, Fat Toms and Hairy Jacks who grew, banted or baldened.

So is it with *nouvelle cuisine*, that brilliant innovation which began by eschewing the *cuisine sérieuse* that Carême and then Escoffier had structured upon the main dish and the roux-based sauce, and settled down to provide ever less food on greater expanses of porcelain at increasing prices.

CUISINE MINCEUR, which was the first and most important sub-culture of the new movement, has similarly run its course and there is currently a burst of enthusiasm for

CUISINE NATURELLE, which is greatly feared by manufacturers of food additives. Under this banner you are served a slice of lamb, simmered in its own bouillon, garnished with a forcemeat of lamb's brains spread on lamb's tongue, served on a lamb's-wool platter. They also go for bread sandwiches.

CUISINE TOURISTIQUE remains strong; the serving staff listen for foreign accents, tell the chef – and old, stale, burnt and leftover food is brought forth with a flourish as a waiter writes '*non*' between '*taxes et service*' and '*compris*'. This means, 'We will not understand what you say unless you cough up the VAT and tip a lot.'

CUISINE TARD is gaining in popularity: you order your dinner and nothing much happens for a long time; then hardly anything happens and then you get food. It has spawned the CUISINE FERMÉE where you order and wait and when you have had a second bottle of wine the waiter comes along and explains that the chef has gone home. '*Alors, qu'est-ce qu'on peut faire . . . hein?*'

CUISINE GRÈCE is either Greek or greasy food; if you are terribly unlucky, it is both, on a skewer.

CUISINE SALE came about as a result of the French belief that chefs who spend time cleaning the kitchen neglect the more important aspects of the culinary arts. Their battle-cry is 'The dirtier the kitchen, the better the food.' It is not necessarily true.

CUISINE OUBLIEUSE is practised in provincial towns, traditionally by catering *arrivistes*. You order and they forget; then you complain and they serve what you ordered to someone else. You get the wrong bill and when you leave the chef greets you and asks whether you have booked a table. They lose your coat, too.

CUISINE NOIRE means that the chef is black.

CUISINE TRAGIQUE is practised by the '*Quelle horreur!*' school of cookery. All that you want is impossible to give you; voices are lowered, meaningful glances exchanged, the waiter has one leg, the blind cashier knits and in the background you can hear children screaming.

CUISINE SOMBRE – the chef is gloomy.

CUISINE BLONDE – the chef drinks pale ale.

CUISINE OBLONGUE is a new and interesting concept: sod the ingredients, grab the shape. Dishes are rectangular with adjacent sides unequal. The cuisine was introduced by a one-star *cafetier* from Limoges who burnt a Spanish omelette, cut off the unacceptable parts and served it with a flourish to a food-writer. Lesson to be learned here.

CUISINE AIGUË came soon after; it is another positional cuisine, in which everything is sharp except the taste. Asparagus, spare ribs, *alumettes* potatoes and angelica is a popular *aiguë* bill of fare.

CUISINE COÛTEUSE is catching on. Dishes on the menu are marked with the letters SG instead of a price – SG meaning 'dependent on size'; they know that no one entertaining guests is going to ask the price of pigeon, consequently they can chortle all the way to the bank. *Cuisine coûteuse* also practises *menu surprise*, the main surprise being how little you get for the amount that you pay.

CUISINE VIVANTE is actually non-cuisine. The gorilla in the kitchen arranged the oysters and other livestock on suitable dishes. Sprouting beanshoots are *de rigueur*. Gives new meaning to the term 'movable feast'.

CUISINE RHYTHMIQUE – another concept where the food is secondary, this time to presentation. The chef prances around the room making you wonder who is minding the stove. The maître d'hôtel pirouettes (French: *faire la pirouette*) between tables and at a signal from him the amalgam of waiters approach tables and all snatch off the silver covers at the same time; then they prance off again.

CUISINE OPTIMISTIQUE – chef who believes that people making notes on pads work for *Le Guide Michelin*; also known as CUISINE NAIVE.

April 1986

David Taylor

EN VOITURES!

Far-sighted Frenchmen were in at the start of the dream of self-propulsion, whatever Mercedes-Benz may claim. Not cars, *au début*, but just a thing which over *two* centuries ago had wheels (three) and lumbered along without horses. They have it stashed at the Paris *Conservatoire des Arts et Métiers*. Capitaine Joseph Cugnot (a steam buff and contemporary of Watt) caused consternation and I dare say cries of *Ptfui!* when in the summer of 1769 he trundled out and fired up his five-ton, timber-framed gun carriage – a Brobdingnagian trike with a whopping, kettle-shaped boiler up front. This contraption was good for 6mph or so, full steam ahead, but by no means easy to handle. Watched in awe by its sponsor, the Duc de Choiseul, it chugged triumphantly for the best part of a quarter of an hour before demolishing a brick wall and slumping into the ditch. Cugnot promptly built another he called *fardier*, for which the haulage of heavy loads was *pas de problème*, and really the French have been hard at it making *véhicules extraordinaires* ever since.

Their first shot at a petrol-driven car came together in the late 1880s, at the heady time when in Germany Carl Benz and Gottlieb Daimler were feverishly engaged in their separate pursuit of the horseless carriage. Edouard Sarazin, a Parisian lawyer, was at the time French representative for Daimler's pioneering engines and to maintain the patents he was obliged to manufacture locally. So Sarazin persuaded his friend Emile Levassor (who with René Panhard ran a factory making power saws) to knock out a few Daimler-type engines under licence. Sarazin, *malheureusement*, then passed away but his widow was plainly of the right stuff and concluded the arrangement with Levassor. She married him, too, *entre nous*. Panhard & Levassor, with La Veuve Sarazin now at his side, made a formidable trio: determined to manufacture from scratch a vehicle purpose-designed to exploit their Daimler engine. After nearly two years of tinkering, *voilà!* They had got something we'd still recognise as a car, with a familiar front-to-back layout – radiator, engine, friction clutch, gearbox and final drive to rear wheels – which they called *le système Panhard*. Cue *La Marseillaise*.

Now Levassor had a mate called Armand Peugeot. Armand had never made power saws, but Peugeots had for ages made farm implements and coffee-grinders and designer corsets, or anything else they reckoned might sell through the family's hardware business. By the late 1880s, Messrs Peugeot were concentrating their energies on the new-fangled fashion for bikes. Armand's bright idea was to stick an engine on. His not-so-bright idea was to choose Serpollet's 2hp steam job, a dead loss if ever there was one, although Armand got the *Légion d'honneur* for his efforts just the same. Tell you what, Armand, then whispered Levassor, try one of Daimler's engines instead, lovely little motor, stick on a few more wheels, we could have a nice little runner. Very soon France had its first commercial car factory. Cue second verse of *La Marseillaise*.

Enter Count Albert de Dion, a gent, a sportsman, also rich as Croesus despite his passion for gambling. One wished to make a whatsit, motor-car, declared the count. Like Benz, he'd always liked clockwork and mechanical toys. Righty-ho, said he, it shall have a small but efficient steam engine. *Hélas*, it was not so hot. Righty-ho, said le comte de Dion, *encore une fois*, I shall develop with my hands a petrol one instead, very light you know, and with some foresightful touches like an ignition with a battery, coil and contacts. This I shall mount into a little tricycle, such as Peugeot can make, and the ladies of fashion can thus tour the Bois de Boulogne in some style. Very soon we shall have some bigger and more powerful machines, we can race them maybe against some Levassor ones – a Paris to Rouen trial for *la gloire*. It was the start of motor sport. Cue verse three.

Come the start of this century France was making more cars than anyone and had invented the waiting-list. Months were

'Do you remember darlings? We saw it on the Bayeux tapestry.'

quoted for delivery of a Peugeot, Darracq or Dalahaye, years for a Panhard. Louis Renault re-worked a De Dion for fun, sold it to his lawyer, and decided to team up with his brother Marcel to make a few more. Within twelve months they had 100 employees and couldn't make Renaults fast enough. It was le boom. The war came, but immediately after it another French pioneer risked ridicule with the bold assertion that, noting what was happening in America, he planned to turn out 100 cars *per day*. His name was André Citröen and he was no fool. With a cheap and cheerful 1.3 tourer built on Europe's first assembly line, he was soon up to 250 units a day and making his fortune. He set trends all his life, did Citröen, none more startling than the 1934 *Traction Avant*, pioneering front-wheel-drive, not to mention unitary body construction, all-round independent suspension, even aerodynamics. And it looked terrific – Maigret's car-to-be.

Post-war Citroën built the quirky car which is still *the* quintessentially mad French design: the legendary 2CV. The original brief was quite specific: a car to transport four citizens and 50kg of belongings at a speed of 50kph without them getting too hot, *s'il faisait beau*, or too wet if it rained. Suspension had to be so supple that a farmer might transport a basket of eggs across a ploughed field without breakages. And should a 2CV owner want to drive to church, the headroom had to be sufficient for him to wear a decent hat. *Alors.* Most of the integral virtues still remain in the time-warped austerity of the 2CV today. But we'd better not talk about today. For French cars, times is currently hard, even harder than elsewhere in Europe. The French market is broadly a three-way split between Renault, the Peugeot group, PSA (which includes Citroën and Talbot) and foreign importers. Only the importers seem happy.

Still France might claim an edge for mass-production of quirky cars: the versatile Renault Espace, the indefatigable Citroën CX and now BXs, or an advantage with fashionably OK small cars like unstoppable Peugeot 205s or re-vamped R5s. For the moment the French industry has the jitters. The last verse of *La Marseillaise* had better hang on for a bit.

April 1986

Stanley Reynolds

AN AMERICAN IN PARIS: A MEMOIR

'Hullo, Kebs,' Papa said as I came up to his table at the Dôme.

It was April and I was in Paris for the first time and actually talking to Ernest Hemingway, with Hem sitting at his favourite table whittling a sentence with a kraut dagger he captured off Marlene Dietrich. 'Swell to see you, Mouse,' Papa said to me, 'pull up a cognac. You know Scott? Scott Fitzgerald, says he's a writer.'

'Scott Fitzgerald,' I said. 'I thought he was dead.'

'No,' Papa said, 'he just smells bad.'

Well, you know how it was in Paris in those days, with James Joyce tapping his way down the street with his white cane, with Zelda and Isadora doing the Black Bottom on the top of the bar at the Ritz Hotel, and with, of course, from the Avenue Huysman each morning the terrible sound of Marcel Proust coughing.

Papa said: 'Proust is coughing with a great seriousness this morning, Wedge.' Papa always called me Wedge in those days when he wasn't calling me Mouse or Kebs. 'He coughs with a great seriousness,' Papa said. 'But not with the truly great seriousness of Kafka.'

'If Kafka did not have that cough,' Scott said, 'he would have made the varsity at Princeton.'

POPULAR MISCONCEPTIONS – PARIS (1939)

'Franz Kafka's father did the catering at my first communion,' Zelda said. 'You know a lot of things, but I'll bet you never knew that.'

'Never mind her, she's crazy, Wombat,' Papa said to me. Papa was now calling me Wombat when he was not calling me Kebs, Mouse or Wedge. 'Zelda is crazy, but it is not a craziness of the great, serious craziness of a Rimbaud or a Verlaine. It is only a small craziness which is of no great moment, like the craziness of T. S. Eliot's wife.'

'We were all a little crazy,' Morley Callaghan said. 'That summer in Paris, we were always a little crazy.'

'No,' Papa said, 'you were always a little welterweight that summer in Paris.'

'I think, actually,' Scott said, 'that it wasn't Kafka after all, but Marcel Proust who could have made the varsity at Princeton; if, of course, things had been different.'

'Not Marcel,' Papa said, 'Moose. Moose Proust. But let's talk about the war. Let's go to a good zinc bar and have a marc and talk of the war. Then, later, we can go to the dancing.'

'Let's talk about the horses,' Gertrude Stein said. 'Alice likes it best about the horses.' Alice B. Toklas was sitting there looking very stoned and very, very ugly. She was a very flat-chested woman, which, as Hemingway said, may have been okay for a lesbian, we really didn't know. Gertrude Stein had big tits, but then, as John Dos Passos said, you had to take the rest of her into consideration as well. So we were all pretty happy about Gertrude and Alice being lesbians that April in Paris.

'March,' T. S. Eliot said. 'March is the cruellest month.'

'April, ass-hole, April,' Ezra Pound said.

Many people do not realise about the free-and-easy-going banter that existed between T. S. Eliot and Ezra Pound. Neither Peter Ackroyd nor Richard Ellmann has fully realised the nature of the relationship between Pound and Eliot, but then neither of them was there in Paris to see it for themselves like I was. I ask Ellmann and Ackroyd only one thing: How else could these two really big men have collaborated so closely together?

'London is a man's town,' Eliot said, 'with power in the air, but Paris is a woman with a flower in her ear.'

'Jesus H. Christ,' Ezra Pound said, 'pencil that out, will you, A-hole.' I wish I had kept more extensive notes on this because I'm sure it would be of great interest to students of literary Paris. But I was young.

'Paris is beautiful,' T. S. Eliot said.

'Except for the French,' Scott said. He was drunk. Bad drunk, mean drunk.

'Yes,' Hem said, 'you have noticed that, have you? Truly, there are a lot of French here.'

'And Parisians, too,' Scott said. He was trying to stuff flowers down Alice B. Toklas's blouse. It was all terribly embarrassing. We were all terribly embarrassed for him.

'It goes without saying,' Papa said. 'It goes without saying about the Parisians. You do not have to mention the Parisians.'

'Picasso is a Parisian, but he is not French,' Gertrude Stein said.

'Truly,' Papa said.

'And you, Papa,' Gertrude said, 'you are truly a Parisian without being French.'

'All Parisians are French in their own way, but some Parisians are Parisians in their own special way,' Leo Tolstoy said.

'Put the pencil through that one,' Pound said. 'Give that one a miss.'

'Paris is the capital of the world,' Zelda said, 'and Bismarck is the capital of North Dakota, but what is the capital of Florida?'

'When good Americans die,' Gene Kelly said, 'they go to Paris.'

'We bombed in New Haven,' Abe North said, 'but we died in Philadelphia.'

'Have a marc,' Papa said. 'Have a demi-blond, have a whisky and soda, have a bourbon on the rocks, have a grappa. Waiter,

'Who ordered the large Pernod?'

eighteen pints and a bag of crisps. He is a good waiter,' Papa said of the waiter. 'Yes, he is a good, clean boy, with a beautiful left hand. He has a left hand like a sword, for a waiter that is.'

'Tallahassee,' James Joyce said; he knew the exact word for everything. 'Tallahassee is the capital of Florida.'

That summer in Paris the French were always with us but we did not talk with them. We stayed at the Dôme or at the Ritz. Gertrude Stein arm-wrestled with Papa. They were locked elbow-to-elbow for 38 hours, silent, relentless, remorseless, with a great seriousness which was truly relentless and remorseless in the great meaning of those things, sustained only by Alice B. Toklas's marijuana cookies and Zelda's chicken noodle soup. Zelda was actually a great cook. Not fancy. Basic, but a great cook. She was also almost as flat-chested as Alice B. Toklas. Scott did not seem to mind. Hemingway took Scott to the Louvre and showed him all the statues of the women with big tits but still Scott did not mind.

That was Paris for me. It will always be thus. No matter how many times I have revisited her over the years, I will always remember her that way. The rattle of her taxi cabs was music to my ears. Paris, city of light, of Sartre and his beautiful young wife, Brigitte Bardot, another great cook.

The memories of Paris keep flooding back, of my Paris in what I like to call 'The Crazy Years'. Goodbye, Paris. No, not goodbye, *auf wiedersehen*.

April 1986

Richard Gordon

CARTESIAN CO-ORDINATES

The cultured Englishman abroad stops in France.

Only readers of our cultured Sunday papers can appreciate *le Muscadet, les escargots, le Massif Central* and *le bidet*, in which uncultured people wash their feet or the lettuce for their picnic. (Dropping *mots* into the *oeuvre* makes you instantly a cultured writer.)

The French are of course cultured; they have a radio station called *France Culture*. They are a nation more polite than affable, impatient rather than bad-tempered, less formidably Cartesian than admirably rational. Food, drink and sex are bodily needs to be satisfied seriously and as enjoyably as possible. They *faire l'amour* mainly in the mornings, which accounts for the skimpiness of the French breakfast.

They are a grubby lot: the men shower sporadically, the girls attend to *les petits soins de la personne* but refuse to treat their armpits like operation sites. They eat strawberries without cream, and cheese with a knife and fork. They ride bicycles as earnestly as we play cricket. They are careful about money, to the extent of hammering it as gold Napoleons behind their door jambs.

Like everyone else, the French watch TV and munch McDonald's, to the despair of cultured Englishmen who never adjusted to displacement of *la vespasienne* – in which you could see the gentlemen's feet while they did it – by the plastic computer-operated *Europissoir* as embellishes Leicester Square.

Le Midi! A mythical land created by cultured Englishmen before advice that 'the best novels are written in cheap hotel bedrooms in the South of France' became economically

THE BRITISH CHARACTER
FONDNESS FOR EVERYTHING FRENCH

laughable. 'Sizzling down the long black liquid reaches of Nationale Sept, the plane trees going sha-sha-sha through the open window, the windscreen yellowing with crushed midges, she with the Michelin beside me, a handkerchief binding her hair . . .' Cyril Connolly was pseuding along nostalgically when the N7 was *rue barrée* by the Wehrmacht.

Provence in the 1930s offered at reasonable prices the inspiration of the wine-dark Mediterranean with all mod cons, unlike the skimpy menus and mattresses of Calabria or Greece. Grey rocks and ochre walls, the February mimosa, the *Nice Matin* and fresh *croissants* on the station trolleys, greeted bleary eyes on the overnight Blue Train and provided the literary mileage of daffodils for Wordsworth.

The carnation has faded in Europe's buttonhole, the hotels resemble those in LA and Cincinnati to prevent the Americans feeling away from home, the *Côte d'Azur* is a sunsoaked traffic jam, but the mirage of those wine-dark writers still flickers. Collins's latest *Guide to France* says of Cannes' La Croisette, 'Here the *beau monde* takes its evening stroll,' when like Eastbourne prom it airs mostly the local geriatics, well-muffled against the sun or *le mistral* (any wind blowing down there).

Gay Paree was founded by Thomas Cook. The strip-shows are cultural, all those ostrich feathers (the management spares tourists being mugged by *apaches* by locking the doors during intervals to prevent nipping out for a café drink instead of suffering their own extortionate prices). You can still take the Metro via *art nouveau*. The Louvre is the repository of past centuries' culture, ours is in the Pompidou Centre, a building with its life-supporting entrails festooned outside its carcase, appropriate among the lurid *boucheries* of les Halles. Gay Paree enjoys a rich heritage from Ernest Hemingway and other refugees it spared from Prohibition.

La nouvelle cuisine is the greatest French culinary disaster since ergot in the rye bread begat the Devils of Loudun. A gourmet's dinner arriving slopped all over one plate is a conception only in transport caff nightmares. He smacks his lips over a decorative dishful of brightly coloured bits and pieces presented under a dome as once kept the flies off British Rail sandwiches. Gastronomic quality has been ousted by artistic. You might as well tuck in your napkin and bite into a Picasso.

La nouvelle cuisine was created only through the expense of training and employing competent waiters. Any white-jacketed *commis* can introduce you to your food as though it were a distinguished fellow-diner and whip off the dome with the air of a conjuror discovering a *lapin sauté* under a top-hat – it takes experience to load a hot clean plate with skilful servings of the delicious meat and two lovely veg sizzling on the meths.

'At the age of thirty-five one needs to go to the moon, or some such place, to recapture the excitement with which one first landed at Calais,' Evelyn Waugh was writing when the alternative was a safe hyperbole. It is no longer necessary to land at or even see Calais,

'Three billion light years just to try out his French.'

en route for the Auchan supermarket on the St Omer road.

Travellers can quit their coach in the car park and load their wire-mesh *chariot* with plastic bales of tinned beer, washing-powder, wine, chocks, cooking oil, loo paper and other items which come so much cheaper in France, climb aboard and watch the videos until unloading in Birmingham. These persons are not cultured, but they have the right idea.

We are two nations who can never love each other. We think they are proud. They think we are quaint. We respect each other's institutions. They have the Eiffel Tower. We have *La Dame de Fer*.

April 1986

Miles Kington

LET'S PARLER FRANGLAIS!

Lesson Vingt-Neuf
Dans le Travel Agency

AGENT: Bonjour, monsieur! Vous désirz une no-trouble, sun-blanched, soleil 'n' sable vacance?

MONSIEUR: Non, merci. Je désire un fortnight historique et culture-riche en Yugoslavie.

AGENT: J'ai la very thing! Un 14-jour monument 'n' mausoleum package avec Yugorelic.

MONSIEUR: Non, merci. Je veux loger au Hôtel Adriatik, 9 rue Tito, Splenk.

AGENT: Splenk, eh? Jolie petite resorte, avec ses ikons, ses cafés et son twice-daily train . . .

MONSIEUR: A la chambre 128.

AGENT: Ah. Je suis désolé, monsieur. Chambre 128 est totalement mass-booked. C'est une bloque-réservation pour Swedohols. Je peux vous donner Chambre 127 . . . ?

MONSIEUR: Non, merci. C'est exactement au-dessus des cuisines. Je déteste la fragrance de Yugochips. En ce cas, je fais ma seconde option: une there-et-back ocean outing.

AGENT: J'ai la very thing! 14 jours de sparkling, sec, vintage sunshine avec Medcruise.

MONSIEUR: Non, merci. Je désire 14 jours de ciel gris à la Mer du Nord avec Durham Ferries, sur la SS *Visibility Nil*, dans la cabine No. 46. Top bunk.

AGENT: Oui, c'est libre! En effet, c'est le premier booking de 1979 pour Durham Ferries.

MONSIEUR: Bon. J'aime les no-passenger boats. Et les services du vieux Harry Palmer, le steward fidèle avec ses yarns et sa tendance à refuser les tips.

AGENT: Hélas, Harry Palmer est maintenant dans le retirement. Il a été remplacé par le jeune Vic Pitt, qui contrôle aussi le night-time disco.

MONSIEUR: Quelle horreur! Cancellez le Durham Ferries booking. J'arrive à l'option dernière: un day return à Peking pour afternoon thé.

AGENT: Rien de plus facile. Du lait?

MONSIEUR: Un soupçon.

AGENT: Combien de lumps?

MONSIEUR: Deux, s'il vous plaît.

AGENT: Bon. Voilà votre ticket. Day return à Peking, £450. Tea, gratuit. Shortbread, £3.50 extra.

MONSIEUR: Bon. Voilà mon chèque.

AGENT: Bon.

July 1990

Merrily Harpur

AUX ARMES, CITOYENS

'Well, at least there's a corner of a foreign field that is forever England.'

'What worries me is that by the time we get to the front of the queue the Morley St Denis 1972 may be past its best.'

'Fantastic! The fields are just one mass of orange Day-Glo nylon, as far as the eye can see . . .'

'This is just like the EEC – the only thing it's worth staying in for is to annoy the French.'

'These are dummies! The Johnsons have escaped!'

Miles Kington

ANGLO-FRENCH RELATIONS

A Punch *Inquiry on Cross-Channel Attitudes*

The English Said That the French . . .

talk too fast . . .

do not love animals, unless cooked . . .

are agriculturally retarded . . .

live in controlled tipsiness from the age of five, induced by vin ordinaire . . .

employ laughably small policemen, with the exception of Maigret who is really English . . .

have something called haute cuisine, which is a system of disguising flavour with garlic and sauces . . .

provide superb excuses for poor performances . . .

are demon lovers, not that they need to be with all the easy virtue lying around . . .

have a tendency to leave dismembered waitresses in luggage lockers in the Gare de Lyon . . .

drive their cars with deliberate intention to cause accidents . . .

are money-grubbing twisters . . .

have based their cultural supremacy entirely on a few Impressionists, a backlog of unreadable poetry and Racine's school-texts . . .

have based the myth of their fighting forces entirely on Napoleon (a Corsican), lost all their battles since then and always called in the British to rescue them . . .

are Catholics and not really to be trusted . . .

are parental tyrants . . .

only stop waving their arms to go to sleep . . .

shoot nightingales . . .

The French Said That the English . . .

are broke . . .

are arrogant (who else calls it the English Channel?) . . .

have an obsession with dogs . . .

make poor racing cyclists . . .

are blundering lovers (when not queer) but have to break through the defences of those frigid horsewomen somehow . . .

think they are still masters of the world, which is absurd; the top nation is, of course, France . . .

speak 'O' Level French, a language unknown across the Channel . . .

are exploiters of au pair girls . . .

are calm at all times, not so much because of a stiff upper lip as an inability to become enthusiastic . . .

love processions . . .

live on ketchup . . .

never talk in railway carriages, in the street or even at home – they only burst into speech when giving away confidential conversations . . .

have no artistic talent; their only geniuses are a few writers who have been hailed in France and ignored in England . . .

are parentally permissive . . .

hunt what they cannot eat . . .

expect all foreigners to speak English English, and not American English . . .

will gamble on anything (even the mortality of de Gaulle) . . .

have humour but no wit . . .

March 1969

Fenton Bresler

ACROSS THE CHANNEL AND INTO THE DOCK

The fundamental principle of French law is never to use one word where two – or preferably three – will do. No doubt this is a characteristic of all lawyers. But the French really do carry it to a pinnacle of achievement.

An English juror, for instance, takes the Bible in his left hand and swears 'by Almighty God that I will faithfully try the several issues joined between our Sovereign Lady the Queen and the prisoner at the bar and give a true verdict according to the evidence'. Clear, neatly expressed – and to the point. A French juror has to stand there embarrassed and silent in the jury box while the presiding judge puts to him this formula (in an unauthorised Bresler translation):

'You swear and promise before God and before men to examine with the most scrupulous attention the charges which will be brought against the accused, to betray neither the interests of the accused nor those of the society that accuses him; not to communicate with anyone until after your decision; to listen without hatred or wickedness, without fear or affection; to decide after hearing the charges and the methods of defence according to your conscience and your intimate conviction with the impartiality and the firmness which are appropriate to a proper and free man, and to preserve the secret of your deliberations even after the cessation of your functions.'

Quite a mouthful. If any one of the nine jurors then refuses to say, 'I swear it,' the whole trial has to be put off to another session. And started all over again.

No French lawyer or judge is ever at a loss for words. Next time you are in Paris, or any other large French town, pop in for a few moments to the local Palais de Justice, and you will at once see – and hear – what I mean. The French Bar is dedicated to the Marshall Hall school of advocacy. It went out of vogue in England at least forty years ago, but in France it is still very much 'à la mode'.

Recently, in Paris, I wandered into one of the courtrooms of the Chambre Correctionelle at the Palais de Justice near Notre Dame and saw an avocat, his left hand raised, index finger pointing urgently to the ceiling, assuring the three judges that his bored-looking young motorist client who had screeched round a busy street corner in the heart of the city at a speed of one hundred and twenty kilometres an hour was 'of extremely good faith' and 'conscious in the intimacy of his heart' of the wrong he had done in nearly flattening an old lady to the ground. The look of distrust in the eyes of the two judges who were actually listening to him expressed all the malaise and resentment between two branches of a legal profession that are kept more rigorously separate than black and white in an apartheid state.

It isn't that French judges disapprove of French lawyers talking too much. The judges themselves are far from silent. In the Cour d'Assise, for instance, on the same visit the presiding judge put about five minutes of questioning to each thirty seconds of answer from the accused man. Recently, an English High Court Judge's decision was over-ruled by the Court of Appeal because the appeal judges said that he had talked too much and intervened too much in the proceedings: no such complaint would ever stand a chance of success in a French appeal court.

French judges accept French courtroom lawyers' right to be long-winded. They simply tend not to believe a word that they say. Unlike English judges, they have never themselves practised at the Bar. They have been civil servants from the moment that they have entered into gainful employment. There

"Poor devil. He was hopelessly outnumbered."

is little camaraderie of spirit between Bench and Bar, as in England. They are not members of the same club. They are suspicious of the – often, better paid – free-lance, private enterprise lawyers arguing vehemently in front of them.

As Maître Jacques Hamelin, a distinguished Parisian barrister, has written, 'The judge is inserted in a hierarchy. The contacts between judges and barristers are made up of nuances and embrace a diversity, if not difficulties, that practice alone reveals.'

It is not only French lawyers who tend to think of judges as little more than State functionaries. When a lower court judge commented adversely on the fact that a petty criminal was before him for the same kind of offence for the sixth time in four years, he got the reply: 'It's not my fault that you haven't got promotion.'

In one respect alone, French judges are remarkably like their English brethren: in their capacity for talking nonsense. Like the assize judge who, when a man sentenced to death for murder struggled and shouted in the dock, warned him: 'Don't make your case any worse.' Or the judge who, when a poor slum girl confessed tearfully to submitting herself to the attentions of a back-street abortionist, commented: 'Why didn't you go to a clinic in Sweden? It's legal there.'

One somehow feels that a French judge would have a fellow-feeling with the English judge I saw some years ago who said to a homosexual pleading guilty to an offence with another man in a public urinal: 'Next time you're feeling lonely – find a woman!'

Close contact with reality is not an ever-present feature of the Bench: on either side of the Channel.

Yet at least English judges do try and stay awake in court. There is the famous story told in Paris of the elderly French appeal judge who confided to his clerk that he thought he had reached his decline. 'Why?' asked the clerk, concerned for the old man's health. 'I can no longer sleep during the arguments of counsel,' said the judge.

'Above all, gentlemen,' once counselled a presiding judge to his two new junior colleagues, 'never take coffee after lunch. It prevents you sleeping in the afternoon.'

Of course, there are things the French legal system does better than ours. Every free French citizen over the age of thirty can be called for jury service – there is no antiquated property-qualification dating from the 1820s as in this country. After every criminal trial, there is procedure for a convicted criminal at once to be ordered to pay compensation to his victim. The legal mechanics of buying and selling a house in France are far simpler and cheaper than ours.

Nor is it true to say – as most Britishers still believe – that in France a man is presumed guilty until his innocence is proved. 'That is a canard,' a French presiding magistrate told me many years ago. 'Here, it is as much for the prosecution to prove a man's guilt as in your country.' In fact, probably more villains are acquitted in France than in England.

This basic truth was well appreciated by the Parisian judge who, when a man charged with murdering his father was inexplicably acquitted by the jury, asked him if his mother was still living. 'But, yes!' replied the newly freed prisoner. 'In that case, until the next time!' said the judge.

'Our men of justice: are they men of the circus, at the same time clowns and acrobats, or are they high-priests and sometimes even sorcerers?' asked French lawyer Maître Jean-Marc Varaut in a magazine article last year. It is a difficult question to answer.

December 1970

ffolkes

EN FRANÇAIS

'Well, Monsieur Robespierre, you've certainly given politics a shot in the arm.'

'They're auditioning at Notre Dame.'

'It stood for Rest In Pernod.'

*'No, I'm Alexandre de Toulouse-Lautrec.
My brother couldn't come.'*

OUR COUNTRYMEN ABROAD (1870)
SKETCH OF A BENCH ON THE BOULEVARDS, OCCUPIED BY FOUR ENGLISH PEOPLE WHO ONLY KNOW EACH OTHER BY SIGHT.

George Mikes

THEM AND US

France and England (later Britain) have been tied to each other with the strongest of bonds: mutual mistrust and dislike. Their warm and intimate dislike has survived centuries of wars (which is easy) but also decades of alliance (which is much more difficult). The New Zealanders love the British more than any other nation in the world. It is easy for the New Zealanders. They are as far away from us as possible; if they were farther away still, they would be nearer. Love over 10,000 miles away from the beloved is child's play. To love thy neighbour, that's the really difficult exercise. The Scots find it considerably more difficult to love the English than the New Zealanders. And the Tahitians find it easier to love the French than the British do.

The French are placed somewhere halfway between Scotland and New Zealand. It seems to superficial geographers, who go by appearances, that the Channel, at its narrowest, is about twenty miles wide. Wiser people know that this is nonsense. According to my own calculations the Channel, at its narrowest, is 6,500 miles wide; which is about 1,000 miles narrower than a few years ago.

Because – everyone says it and I know it to be true – Anglo-French relations have not been so good as they are now for generations. The merit for improving them (and this is no false patriotic pride in me) belongs to us British. We did what we could to endear ourselves to the French. Some low types suggest that we did it because we want to join the Six; if the French wanted to join the British Commonwealth, they add, the merit for improving relations would belong to them.

I have a book in front of me, *The Myth of France* (by Raymond Rudorff). The primary aim of the author could not have been to improve Anglo-French relations further. He takes the so-called myths of France and, one by one, knocks them. He knocks some more convincingly than others. But what about the Myth of Britain? And what about, especially, the latest and most up-to-date myths of Britain?

A miraculous metamorphosis has occurred lately about British food: it has become definitely eatable. In many restaurants and clubs it has become very good indeed and it is becoming better. A welcome development; but Britain's food-guide authors are waxing lyrical and over-enthusiastic and keep telling us that one can eat and drink as well in London as in Paris today. That *Beaujolais Anglais* is just as enjoyable as *Beaujolais Français*. There was tremendous scope for improvement and the Gastronomic Gap between the two countries has been successfully narrowed; today it is not wider than the Channel (6,500 miles). The Americans know how to send people to the moon; the British know how to create a civilised and tolerant atmosphere; but it is the French who know how to eat and drink. You cannot call that 'a matter of taste' any more than you can say that Ian Fleming was a greater novelist than Balzac. Loos, admittedly, are incomparably better in this country. With loos we win hands down. The solution seems to be clear: eat in France and use the loo in Britain.

Then we have the Myth of Swinging Britain. *Paris Match* keeps sending photographers to King's Road, Chelsea, on Saturday afternoons. English youths and foreign au pair girls know that *Paris Match* will be there on Saturdays, between two and four, so they go to King's Road and swing. Perhaps I frequent the wrong places. Admittedly, I dance

'Looks as though the bread's stale again.'

and shake and listen to pop music less than I ought to; I chase women just a shade less arduously than I did, say, twenty-five years ago. I love London as much as the next man but, thank Heavens, it just does not swing. What happened is that the English have discovered sex and since the end of the war they have multiplied in the same way as other nations. On the other hand the French – prim, puritanic and old-auntish – used to be regarded as a sexy nation. French prostitutes used to give Paris the reputation of being the sex capital of the world; today British strip-tease girls claim the same glorious title for London. British businessmen used to go over to Paris for naughty weekends; today French businessmen come to London. I have been told that some of the so-called orgies arranged would pass as respectable family entertainment in the eyes of the Borgias. The gist of the matter is this: Britain has realised that she must decimalise her currency, must go metric and must become sexy if she wants to join the Common Market. At least as sexy as Luxembourg. So Britain has become a sexy country; not an erotic country, by any means, but a sexy country.

Then we have the myth that the French are logical and the British empirical. That the French love clarity and reason while the British learn from experience. Gaullist France, the Land of Cool Reason, was the most emotional and chauvinistic country in the West; a kind of old-fashioned, emotional, bombastic rhetoric prevailed which would have made German politicians blush and English ones laugh. On the other hand, look at British empiricism. We had – to take one example – the stop-go type of economic crisis under the Tories while Labour were laughing their heads off about Tory clumsiness; then we had Labour stop-goes and the Tories castigated Labour's inefficiency; now Labour is amused once again and the Tories seem to be getting ready to start the old game all over again. Something of the same happened between France and Britain. France smiled coolly and smugly and was watching with Latin clarity while Britain was devaluing her currency; then it was Britain's turn to sit pretty, most empirically, while France devalued.

One of the ancient myths is that the French are much ruder than the English. British rudeness perhaps is not quite so apparent as French. When a Frenchman shouts, snarls and sneers at you you know that he is being rude. But when an Englishman asks you quietly, 'Oh, is that so?' or says, 'You don't say,' you may believe that he is courteous although he is actually calling you a bloody liar in his own, polite way.

There is no doubt, however, that this one myth is still valid: the British *do* have better manners than the French. They envy the French for their rudeness: they have always regarded rudeness as one of the virile vices and they always tried to look a shade ruder than they could manage. A few so-called tele-

'Dad's a farmer, he burnt my French homework Miss.'

'I think it must have changed hands.'

vision personalities became famous and rich just because they are ill-mannered and the British admire rudeness. The French, on the other hand, envy the British and try to improve *their* manners. Periodically, courtesy campaigns are initiated and on one occasion even *smile vouchers* were given to foreign tourists to be distributed by them among Frenchmen whose heartwarming courtesy made them smile. The smile vouchers were quickly forgotten; the smiles even more quickly.

I am a fake Englishman today but I could be a fake Frenchman. In 1938, when I was sent to London from Budapest, as a correspondent, I could have, with a little effort, chosen Paris. France was spared from me but it was a near miss. I love the French but have no regrets whatsoever. Today I might be speaking an accented French instead of my accented English. But in France the language is taboo and sacrosanct, like gloire, the tricolor or the Marseillaise. Speaking French badly is something approaching high treason while here, among the tolerant English, my Central European drawl has become one of the accepted, legitimate dialects of the language, rather like a Yorkshire accent. It is better than Yorkshire because it is completely classless.

But once I told a French colleague that I might have preferred to become a French *writer*. In France a writer, irrespective of what he writes, is somebody; in Britain he is lost in the crowd, far behind business executives and property speculators. Then there are all those lovely prizes in France. Four major prizes and hundreds of minor ones. I always wanted a prize and never got one. In France, I am sure, I would have been chosen by at least two obscure societies. True, my French colleague agreed, but there is one argument to be said in favour of Britain. In France there are more writers than readers; in Britain there are still more readers than writers. So I leave the gloire to the French and will have to be satisfied by mere cash. An arrangement both nations were quite happy to accept in the nineteenth century.

December 1970

'Now they'd like to take one of you consulting your phrase-book.'

Quentin Blake

TOURIST IN FRANCE

'Well, this place certainly gives the lie to the myth of the lethargic southerner.'

'He's right you know: a field amputation of a nether limb takes precedence over an eight-month unwanted pregnancy.'

'According to this it's either a traditional fruit-festival or a seasonal demonstration against the government's farming subsidies.'

"Such a change, yer know, from alwis torkin' yer own Langwidge!"

Alan Coren

UN COTTAGE DE WEEKEND

'. . . so when Gilbert had such a *succès fou* with his *Trotsky And Hancock: Parameters Of Caring*, twelve impressions and the Prix Chomsky, we thought, well *I* thought – you know Gilbert, give him a few weeks on a narrow boat each year and his Sunday soccer on Primrose Hill and he's perfectly happy with Highgate – I thought it would be rather nice to splash the Canadian rights on a little place in France, *un chaumière*, or is it *une*, a small farmhouse, perhaps, a *pied-à-terre*.

For weekends, short trips, half-terms, all that kind of thing.

Somewhere in the centre, somewhere *tout rural*, away from, well, English cyclists in Halford anoraks, if you know what I mean, and those terrible people in white Rovers who always leave the *Guide* on the table, even in the most fearful hamburger places. Did you see *Une Partie de Campagne*, by the way, all those wonderful vests, those forearms, you could smell the earth. That's what we were after. Not the Dordogne, of course, it's become so common, you see louvred doors being delivered to even the tiniest villages, we passed through one once and Gilbert spotted five different faces from telly commercials, and they were all wearing new berets and waving *baguettes* terribly ostentatiously, I'm sure none of them ever opened a book in his life.

Their children had T-shirts with pictures of Wagner on them.

Lot-et-Garonne is really the only place to be, you know. The naturalness of it. *Le sans-souci*, as we say down there. Our little *ferme* used to be the village pesthouse, you know; you can still see where sufferers from scrofula banged holes in the foundations with their heads, because Gilbert chipped away all the plaster and exposed the original cell walls, he's truly wonderful with rough tools, once he's out of an academic environment. Man is naturally a maker, after all, and none more so than Gilbert; he treats reason as a livelihood, no more than that.

He is both Rousseau *et rousseauisme*, if you follow me.

I'm the same. I make a rough *terrine* when I'm down there exactly as it has been made for eleven centuries, you steam the live rabbits then jump on them in clogs just before they're completely asphyxiated, and then dice them with a *sauve-pichet*, it's a kind of single-headed axe. I bake my own bread, too, and Gilbert has an arrangement with a local vineyard, he pays five francs a cask for a wonderful black wine, the locals use it for shrivelling head-lice, I believe it may have something to do with their religion, their observances are quite medieval at times.

We encourage it, where we can. There's a terrible danger of their wonderful primitive spirit being overtaken by *le super-marketisme*, I have seen young women carrying frozen *haricots*; many of the houses have central heating, although Gilbert is doing something about it, he got together with a few close friends in the village and they tarred and feathered the heating engineer, I don't think he'll come back. It was quite a victory. Gilbert can be very dominant, you know, he's very different down there from the way he is in lectures, he wears studded wristbands. We never take deodorants down there. I let my armpits flourish, too; it puts us in touch. *C'est très engagé.*

April is our favourite time of year, the children can help with the slaughtering. Little Cordelia has been butchering lambs ever since she was old enough to wield; it's one of the things missing in progressive boarding-schools, I sometimes feel one can have too much Idries Shah and Jerome Robbins, don't you? The twins have neck-wringing races with the chickens, they're such enthusiastic boys! They dance the *pisanne* nude, well we all do, it's a wonderfully stimulating local dance celebrating the sexual energies of the hog. Pig-farming is so important down there, sow-fertility is never far from one's thoughts. We introduced the *pisanne*, as a matter of fact, we thought it was about time the region had its own dance, the locals took it very well, they don't all join in, of course, at least not yet, but they all come along and clap and hoot when we dance it for them.

It may be the rhythm of the *pisanne* that's behind the awakening of sexual experiment down there. That and the fact that we've been distributing the Pill, and holding seminars on Oriental concepts; well, Gilbert felt that the Roman Catholic church was repressing natural peasant instinct, strangling it, even. I think they're happier, now.

We are, certainly. It's marvellous to have this completely alternative world to escape to, away from professional responsibilities, and agents, and accountants, and TV interviews, and dinner parties, all the well-dressed chatty dreariness of the whole London bit . . .

France is so civilised, I find.'

March 1976

'It's a doddle you said – we'll sell up, move down here and do a Peter Mayle you said!'

5

THE OTHER EUROPEANS

'I just know I'll never get used to these new EEC directives.'

THE WALL GAME

Germany

Humphrey Lyttelton

YOU'LL NEVER SING ALONE

Ah, yes, I remember them well! Johanna, Rosi, Hannelore and Eva, four diminutive blondes in pillar-box red whose singing act, under the collective name of Geschwister Jacob, was a sort of augmented Teutonic version of Geschwister Beverley. Their pert faces, barely distinguishable one from the other, grin out at me from one sleeve of an LP which they gave me and which has hung about the house ever since, a constant reminder to me that I am no rival, either now or in the foreseeable future, to Sir Lew Grade.

Geschwister Jacob and I were on the same bill at a concert for the British Forces in Germany a few years ago. Afterwards, in the Officers' Mess, I rather rashly accepted a massive Churchillian cigar from the mess orderly and lit up. Combined with the information, imparted by some careless talker, that I had a radio programme in Britain, the formidable torpedo clearly gave the girls the impression that I was an important impresario, and within seconds they were all over me. As if by magic, one of them managed to produce a hefty cuttings book from the depths of her doll-like decolletage, and I was shown page after page of press notices, biographies and write-ups, all of them in, to me, inscrutable German.

Someone with sharper predatory instincts might have used the cigar as a prop in some Groucho Marxian by-play. I've always been a bit slow on the draw when it comes to the 'I can make you a big star' routine. Furthermore it was quite apparent that in all matters affecting their professional advancement, they came as an indivisible package. So what might have been the start of four beautiful friendships petered out in vague promises about mentioning their names in the right places and letting them know. I see that their address is hopefully scrawled on the LP sleeve.

I didn't, of course, do a thing about it, not only through laziness but for the much better reason that German entertainment doesn't travel and the product was clearly unsaleable. In recent years, Britain has taken kindly to French, Italian, American, Spanish, Greek, Israeli, African, Indian, West Indian, Australian, Brazilian and even Russian popular music. But when did you last hear a German popular song in our Hit Parade? In wartime, you will answer, nonchalantly humming a few bars of *Lili Marlene* or *Auf Wierdersehen* and at the same time putting a finger on the very hub of the matter.

Being mercifully free of any hint of prejudice, insularity or jingo-ism, I am the last man to subscribe to popular myth regarding national characteristics. Indeed, nothing annoys me more than to see a performance in which I have manifestly flipped my lid referred to in some Frog or Jerry newspaper as 'phlegmatic'. But we have to admit that whenever the Germans burst into song, it's no more than a few bars before the arms are swinging in line with the shoulders, the knees are going like pistons and the heels are digging fiercely into the tarmac. You have only to read the titles on the Jacob girls' LP to be in your neighbour's garden in a jiffy, swinging a hoe and demanding *Lebensraum*. 'Ein Cowboy der braucht Liebe,' 'Durch lisenburg die lise raucht,' 'Am blauen See im grünen Tal', 'Sitzt a klaans Vogert im Tannenwald', 'Liebe muss kein Märchen sein' – I don't know what they mean, but they've got me going before the cymbals and the big bass drum have had a chance to get off the mark.

It would never go down here. For one thing, this sort of German popular music is deeply rooted in the sing-along, and the German and British approach to spontaneous communal vocalising is fundamentally different. For the British style, whether it be *You'll never walk alone* on the terraces, *Tears* in a Ken Dodd show or *Nellie Dean* at turning-out time on a Saturday night, the word is not 'phlegmatic' but 'maudlin'. Not to put too fine a point on it, we drone. Listen to us in church, mooing away in unison and endowing even *Onward Christian Soldiers* with a sort of lugubrious sentimentality, and you have to admit that, if World War II had been fought on the basis of a Eurovision Song Contest, with enthusiasm, verve and aggression as the criteria, it would have been all over in a night and we would have learned by now that they have ways of making us sing.

The strong element of audience participation saves German radio from total saturation by Pop. Having travelled all over Germany many times in a band coach with the radio at full blast, I can say with some confidence that German radio has no equivalent to Jimmy Young. The language helps, of course. With all those consonants swishing and clashing away like combatant swordblades, it just doesn't lend itself to the diarrhoeic verbal flow of a British-type DJ and it's impossible to conceive a German equivalent to 'orft we jolly well go!'. For this reason they go in for musical friezes rather than musical wallpaper, with Pop songs, trad jazz and sing-along music à la Geschwister Jacob following each other in an endless procession. And when the German songs come along, the coach-driver invariably joins in.

In many respects, the German language is responsible for isolating German entertainment. If we are ignorant about German popu-

'Wild boar? No, Countess, this is the Black Forest!'

lar songs, we know even less about German comics. It's not just that we don't know the lingo. It's possible to pick up a French or Italian comedian on the radio and to know, just by the way he is speaking, that he is being funny. German comics all sound like Jimmy Edwards with a mouthful of cornflakes, and if it weren't for the gusts of laughter from the audience we might be listening to a live broadcast from the local council chamber, with an irate bürgermeister on his feet.

This handicap spreads to quite unexpected areas of German entertainment. Hamburg has long prided itself on being the erotic capital of the world, with the notorious Reeperbahn providing frank spectacles for the voyeur long before Lord Longford ever knew they existed. Alas, Germanic rompings, usually accompanied by guttural and Wagnerian running commentary, have always been played by the British visitor strictly for laughs.

It is impossible to sound lascivious in German. When I tell you that one naughty entertainment, in which topless ladies wrestled in mud, was called 'Damen in Schlamm', you'll agree.

Long since superseded, first by Mersey Beat and more lately by hard porn, the mud wrestling used to be quite a feature of our band visits to Hamburg. Few entertainments could rival it for sustained hilarity. It was a continuous performance punctuated by dancing and other acts. The appearance of the band on stage held faint echoes of Isherwood and the Weimar Republic in that its musicians had, to a man, the cadaverous, decadent look of extras from *Dr Caligari*. At regular intervals a plump and elderly tenor, made up as if for a silent movie and held into some sort of human shape by a huge cummerbund, minced on and sang *Granada*. Then there was a striptease of sorts, undertaken with amateurish amiability by what looked like a housewives' guild doing fund-raising theatricals, and hardly likely to arouse the passions of anyone save, perhaps, a fanatical student of abdominal surgery.

One knew that the main event of the evening was about to take place when the usherettes went round wrapping protective sheets round the customers at the tables near the front. From under the stage an extension emerged with much rumbling and clanking, shown by a strategically slanted mirror above to be a huge box partially filled with grey mud. Two vast ladies then came onstage, candidates for an Olympic hormone test if ever I saw one and quenching any residual allure with a totally unbecoming line in bathing caps and bum-bags.

Into the mud they leapt and joined combat, sending great gobbets of the stuff arching away into the auditorium, spattering the swathed customers and plopping into their drinks. The inevitable climax of the act came when, after a few noisy and spectacular throws, one contestant applied a hold on her opponent which enabled her to shove fistfuls of mud into the lady's drawers, while the victim, in true wrestling tradition, uttered outraged cries of fear and indignation. When gravity took its inevitable course, the band played a triumphant chord and the performance was over.

It was all good clean fun, but it would never go down here. Or would it? 'Hello, is that you, Morrie? Listen, Morrie, I've got this fantastic wrestling act, boy . . . it's called Geschwister Jacob in Schlamm . . .'

February 1973

'Excuse me, mein Herr, but if you recall, you only held the bridge for three hours and we took it back!'

A. P. Herbert

THOUGHTS IN A BEER-GARDEN

I am sitting on a small portion of that large wicked place, 'the Continent'. I am sitting in one of those corners of Hell, a German, or rather an Austrian, beer-garden. The day is that dreadful day, 'the Continental Sunday'. And I am surrounded by members of those pagan and dissolute races, the Germans and the Austrians.

I have my revolver handy; for at any moment, I imagine, an orgy may break loose and one of these pagans stick me with a knife.

At the moment, it is true, they do not look like rough stuff, like pagans, libertines or drunkards. They look more like respectable bourgeois patresfamiliarum with their wives and families – yes, families. Indeed, except that they wear more amusing clothes, they look strangely like the patresfamiliarum of Wimbledon or Winchester.

They sit under the chestnut-trees and talk and watch their fellow-citizens stroll down the ancient street. So far, not one of them has burst into Dionysian song, no woman has been struck, no child has fled before his reeling father's blows. Nay, I strongly suspect that all these people have been to church.

Yet this is a Continental 'beer-garden', a garden, that is, where beer may be sold all day and, if the proprietor likes to keep it open, nearly all night. The licensing system of this town is delightfully simple – there is no licensing system. True, the manager of this café or beer-garden has to have a licence to sell beer; but, if he were a bookseller or milliner or theatrical manager, he would have to have a licence to sell books or women's clothes or seats. Whatever you sell you must have a licence to sell, to ensure that you are a man of substance and can and will treat your employees properly. But nobody supposes that beer is more dangerous than shirts or stalls; and once you have your licence to sell beer you may sell it when and how you will; and the amazing thing is that, in deciding when you will sell it, you are governed by the views of a lot of people who want it and not by the views of a few people who don't.

Another odd thing about this crowded beer-garden is that only a small proportion of the people in it are drinking beer. By far the greater number are drinking coffee or water, or eating rolls-and-butter, sausages, chocolate-cakes and other perilous foods. That, indeed, is the secret of a beer-garden – it is a place where you can get not beer only but everything including music and fresh air.

But suppose some fool of an authority said (as they say in England very often), 'You shall not provide music and you shall not sell beer in the open air, because this will make beer more attractive and more people will drink beer.' The result would be (as it is in England) that fewer people would have music and fresh air and more people would have nothing but beer. And if the State said (which is inconceivable), 'You shall not drink beer in this beer-garden after 10 or before 7,' everybody in this place would want beer and nothing else. The people now drinking coffee would drink beer instead; and at a quarter to ten everyone would look at the clock and begin drinking beer as fast as they could *till they were stopped* (as they do in England). And it is possible that then you might see a citizen or two who had had too much, which in this old cathedral town, as things are, you never do.

But in England, of course, we are too virtuous – or too vicious? – for this sort of thing. Which is it? Are we too good to drink beer in the open air or are we so lacking in self-control that we cannot be trusted to do as the Germans do? Considering how much our statesmen dislike the German civilisation, it is really rather odd that they are so keen on preserving it. We must all be international nowadays, they tell us; we must get together with the Germans and the French, because they are jolly good chaps. But suggest to the same statesmen that we might perhaps benefit by imitating the social arrangements of the jolly Germans and the French, and they can only splutter insults about the nations mentioned. 'Beer-gardens' and 'the Continental Sunday' are definitely terms of abuse and moral condemnation. And yet we are expected to lend our money to these debauched peoples, who drink beer in their parks and go to plays on Sundays! Odd. Very odd.

How our statesmen must suffer when they go to Paris or Berlin!

Odd. Very odd. The only thing, I suppose, is to shut my eyes to the horrid scenes about me and think with proper pride of the English Sunday now so beautifully drawing to a close. In the old cathedral towns of England there are many who might be glad to sit under an awning or a tree with their families, drink coffee or beer, eat sausages or chocolates, and watch their fellow-citizens stroll down the ancient street. But no – thank God our country is too good for that! Pious paterfamilias makes a rush for the pub at six or seven and his family see him no more. How much more wholesome and godly an arrangement! As for the young of our worthy cities, spared from the corrupting horrors of the Continental Sunday, from the beer-garden and the café and the wicked theatre, they slouch up and down the main streets, 'clicking' or making a noise, or, entering one of the temples of Hollywood, hold hands in the dark. How much more wholesome than the beastly beer-garden! And all of them, of course, unlike the godless youths of the Continent, have been to church. Let us give thanks indeed that we are English, a virtuous nation in a bestial world.

August 1931

'It's always the same – every oasis is full of bloody Germans!'

POPULAR MISCONCEPTIONS IN GERMANY – THE GERMANS
(1940)

F. F. Gillespie

SCOTLAND ÜBER ALLES

A Tartonic union proposal

Considerable public interest has been aroused by my proposal that Scotland be incorporated into the new, united Germany, along with the *Länder* of the now defunct German Democratic Republic. Among the more interesting responses my suggestion elicited came from Bonn itself, in the form of a most kind letter from Chancellor Kohl:

'Dear Herr Gillespie (wrote the Chancellor, that embodiment of all that is *Gross* about Deutschland):

'Your proposal for a German-Scottish *Anschluss* came as a welcome reminder to us. It is not only the question of Germany's eastern border which must be decided by a future united German parliament, but also its *western* border. For who can deny that Germany has as much of a right to Troon and Cumbernauld as it has to Danzig and Stettin?'

Who indeed?

A still more gratifying reply came from the *Bund der Heimatvertriebenen und Entrechteten*,

'But what if it should fall into the wrong hands?'

the Association of Expellees and Disenfranchised, which represents the interests of those ethnic Germans expelled from their traditional homelands at the end of World War II. After praising my column to the skies, the BHE generously invited me to visit West Germany, to address representatives of perhaps the least-known expelled group: the Clyde Germans.

The fate of the Clyde Germans is surely one of the darkest secrets of modern times. Indeed, to read most British history books, you would think the thriving German-speaking community in the West of Scotland had simply never existed. Yet, as I discovered when I spoke to Hans-Dieter Farquharson and Hamish McKrupp, President and Secretary respectively of the *Bund der Clydedeutschen*, the memory of German Clydeside is still alive and well in the German heartland, despite nearly half a century of exile.

'People forget that there was a time when you could walk from one end of Glasgow (or "Glasgau", as the Germans prefer) to the other without hearing a word of English spoken,' says Hamish McKrupp, son of the legendary Celtic goalkeeper 'King Kruppie' McKrupp. 'Nearly half the population of Parkhead – or Parkkopf as it then was – was German. And as for the Gorbals; why, you would have thought you were in Hamburg or Bremen. Of course, we still prefer to call it by its old name, the Goebbels.'

Today, almost every trace of the Clyde Germans' once-thriving culture has been obliterated in Glasgau. The old Sauchiehall Ratskeller, where Kohlquhouns and Rommelsons once toasted the Kaiser with pints of Tartan Pilsner, is now Big Rabbie's Saloon Bar. The vast estates on the outskirts of Glasgow which once belonged to the old Laird, the Maczollern von dem Ilk, were long ago carved up and turned into bleak council housing-estates. All that remains to remind us of the Clyde Germans' sufferings is the cruel song – still to be heard on the football terraces today – which rang in their ears as they were turned out of their *Heimat*: 'Go home, you Huns. Go home, you Krauts; back where you belong.'

In the small Bavarian town of Auldvolksheim, however, the old days have not been forgotten. Here the Clyde Germans gather every year for their annual Hochland Games – to toss *der Kaber*, dance the Gay Gudruns and drink a few wee *Dramen* for the sake of *Alt Lang Sein*. And, as the day draws to an emotional close, who can resist joining in the moving chorus of '*Wir gehören zu Glasgau/ Und Glasgau gehört uns*'?

'You know, we have never given up dreaming that one day we would be able to return to our homes,' says Korag von Prestwicz zu Flughafen, daughter of the present Laird of Maczollern. 'But now suddenly it seems that our dream could actually come true.' The reopening of the German Question since the collapse of the East German regime last November has given the Clyde Germans a new sense of hope, and contingency plans are already underway for a goodwill exchange of sauerkraut and haggis. 'At this rate, Glasgau could belong to me by Christmas,' smiles a kilted Adolf Hitlerson, leader of the radical Tartan Vehrmacht.

But what do the Scots make of this sudden echo of their Teutonic past? Here in Troon, I must say, there is surprisingly strong support for the idea of *Anschluss* across the North Sea. Of course, many of us still treasure our memories of 'Oor Adolf' in the days when he and Eva Broon used to spend every Glasgau Fair weekend out on the links. But, nostalgia apart, there are sound practical reasons for Schottland to accept the German embrace. For example, it really is our only chance of winning the World Cup, an issue of no small importance in a land where *Einig Footerland* has always taken precedence over *Einig Vaterland*. And, more important still, what better way of escaping the Poll Tax?

I might add that I have been given a clear undertaking by Chancellor Kohl on this question. He has assured me that one of the first actions of a future German administration in Scotland would be to abolish the said tax. 'There will be no Poll Tax in a united Germany,' his letter clearly states. 'Only the traditional German Pole Tax.'

How reassuring dear Dr Kohl can be.

March 1990

David Williams

A TO Z GERMAN COURSE

A is for Achtung.

Pronounce as if you were getting up deep phlegm successfully: a word of warning = 'Watch it' or 'Look out'. Striking a querulous note, 'I say; look here.'

B is for Bekommen.

The same as 'Become'? Not a chance. It means to get, and foxes the German-in-England as much as den Engländer in Deutschland. 'I am sitting here since half an hour,' one of them said, drumming on his café table, 'and when shall I become a poached egg?' A monoglot psychiatrist opposite took out his notebook.

C is for Cologne (Eau de).

Only they call it Kölnischwasser (Curlnishvasser) which lacks allure I always think.

D is for Der, Die and Das.

They all mean The. But German needs 3 words, having 3 genders: – Masculine, Feminine and Neuter. Sensible? Yes, but wait. Gender has nothing to do with sex – the Mary Whitehouse language in fact. Das Mädchen (Mairdshen – Girl) is neuter. Der Mond (Moaned – the moon) is masculine. Die Sonne (Zonner) feminine, which never sounds right to me however it may sound to Germaine Greer.

E is for Eigentlich (Eye guntlish).

A fill-up word to be popped in while thoughts are composed. The German ecktually in fact.

F is for Frühstück,

which means early piece, or breakfast. The ü is half way between oo and ee. Pull faces at yourself while shaving. The meal consists in Germany of coffee, rolls and chem. When taking the order they'll sometimes say questioningly 'mit?'. Say Ja (Ya) to this. You get a boiled egg thrown in without extra charge (Zuschlag – Tsooshlarg).

G is for Grenze (Grentser),

the place where you fish for your passport. A Die (feminine) word. 'An der Grenze' = 'At the frontier.' Why **Der**? Listen: Die becomes der in the dative case. And **an** requires any noun controlled by it to be in the Dative, provided the sense is 'at rest', not 'motion towards'. 'I am at the frontier' (resting) = 'Ich bin an der Grenze.' 'Wir marschieren an die Grenze' = 'We march to the frontier.' Bring this up with Ted (Comprehensive) Short who dislikes the word 'grammar'.

H is for Halb (pron: halp).

It means 'half'. But when Lufthansa tells you: 'Ihr Flugzeug fährt um halb elf (eleven) ab' they mean it goes at half *ten*. Get this clear or get stranded.

I is for Ihr (pron: 'ere, as in ''ere you!').

This has as many meanings as the small print in a guarantee certificate. So Achtung. Ihre Seidenstrümpfe (Zydenstrumpfay) = **Her** silk stockings or **Their** silk stockings. You also use it when you want to be familiar or insulting to more than one person. ('Hunde! Wollt Ihr ewig leben?' 'Dogs! Do you want to live for ever?' – Frederick the Great to his everloving soldiers.) Also 'To her' i.e. 'She likes it' = 'Es gefällt ihr' – 'it is pleasing to her.' Cheer up. You get into the way of it.

J is for Jeder (yayder),

meaning every. The 'er' part comes and goes. 'In every fat man there's a thin man trying to get out' = 'In jed**em** dicken Mann steckt ein Dünner der gerne herausmöchte (murshty).' It's that Dative business again.

K is for Kraftwagen (a Der word).

Literally Powerwagon, a better word than our bleating monosyllable, 'car'. Shortened into Pkw = Personenkraftwagen = car, and Lkw (Elkavay) = Lastkraftwagen = burden-powerwagon = lorry = juggernaut. Note German love for portmanteau words. For example (steady now): Rheindampfschiffahrt – not as disgusting as it looks: – a Rhine steamboat trip.

L is for Lokal (Lo, Karl!).

Where you eat and drink. The English pub word 'local' comes from it. 'Herr Ober, bringen Sie mir, bitte, ein Gläschen Wacholder.' Write it out and stick it under the waiter's nose if you can't pronounce it, and want gin.

M is for Morgen (pron. like Welsh Morgan).

Guten Morgen = Good morning. But note that with a small m it means tomorrow – 'morgen werde ich eine letzte Steuermahnung bekommen' – I'll be getting a final demand from the Revenue tomorrow. (Shtoyermarnoong.)

N is for Nach.

It means after, but is hideously idiomatic.

'Schlagen Sie diesen Satz im Woŕterbuch nach' – Look this sentence up in a dictionary. Nach is like marriage: you discover the awful complications as you go along.

O is for Order of words.

In German strict. Verb takes second position in main sentence and brings up the rear, like Marshal Ney, in a subordinate clause. Are you with me? Literally a German would say: Although I ninety am, play I in goal for Manchester United when Sir Matt not looking is. Tortuous? Well, it gives a wonderfully suspenseful quality to German oratory: the crowd hangs on in electric silence waiting for the verb.

P is for Postamt = Post Office.

A word here about the glottal stop. You mustn't say 'Poss Tamt'. Say 'Post' – then momentarily shut the air off to stop vocal cords vibrating (glottal stop), then on to 'amt'. The English keep their vocal cords vibrating all the time like a bagpipe drone. Practise, remembering that over-indulgence can give you hiccups.

Q is for Quatsch (kvatch).

A riposte, meaning balderdash or balls.

R is for Rathaus = Town Hall.

Important not because you're a ratepayer but because Rathäuser (Rahrhoyser – plural) have Ratskeller – basements used as restaurants where you can have Schnapps, Schinken and Fun while upstairs they're deep in sewage and minutes.

S is for Selbst (zelbst),

which means 'self' coming after – 'Ich tät' es lieber selbst' – the Sinatra motto, 'I'd rather do it my way.' Coming in front though, it means 'even'. Even Howard Hughes was there – 'Selbst H.H. war da.'

T is for Treffen.

Basically this means 'to meet'. Tread warily though. Like the Stock Exchange, it never stays put for long . . . 'Agreed!' a German might say. 'You're bang on there, mate!' – 'Topp! Du triffst' – e to i, you see how the thing plays you up – 'auf den I-punkt zu.' (Owff deign ee-poonkt tsoo.)

U is for Umgebung.

All ung-words are Die words, and there are thousands, which is a comfort. Resist the temptation to pronounce this **Oom**gyboong. It's Oom **gay**boong, and it means surroundings (personal or geographical). 'Er hat schlechte Umgebung' means 'He keeps bad company'. But you could say: 'Has your apartment nice surroundings?' – 'Befindet sich Ihre Wohnung in einer schönen Umbegung?'. And you reply: 'No. I live behind the gasworks.' – 'Nein, leider wohn' ich hinter den Gasanstalten.' – 'Nine, lyder vohnish hinter deign Gasanshtalten.'

V is for Verstehen (Fershtayen).

It means 'to understand', which is what you'll be straining every nerve to do, I hope (hoffentlich). A confusing word for us because it resembles our 'understand', but not by any means exactly. A brazen remark like 'I understand what you say' would be 'Ich verstehe was du sagst'. But the equally brazen one, 'I understood what you said' would be 'Ich verstand was du sagtest'.

W is for Werden (Verrden).

An absolute must of a word, never off the scene, in one disguise or another, for long. Basically it means 'to become' (see the poached egg business above). But you also make futures with it. Thus 'I'll be through with this by tomorrow' would be 'Ich werde mit der Arbeit morgen fertig sein (fertish zyne)'. Remember to gargle those r-sounds, not tongue them. If instead of doing things, the subject **has things done to it**, Werden is recalled for duty. Nixon has been re-elected President – 'Nixon ist wieder zum (tsoom) Präsidenten erwählt (errvairlt) **worden**.'

X is for X-Beine (eex-Byner) = knock-knees.

'Der Onkel hat O-Beine und die Tante hat X-Beine' – Uncle has bandy-legs and Auntie has knock-knees. Two cases for the NHS.

Y is for Yauen,

which describes the noise donkeys make (useful!). The absolutely sole initial Y I can think of. Hellish to pronounce. Easier simply to make the donkey's noise.

Z is for Zahnartzt = toothdoctor = Dentist.

'Im Wartesaal des Zahnarztes (dess tsarnarstess – God, how menacing it sounds) lese ich Punch. (Guess that.) Drin heult (hoylt) ein Mann aus vollem Halse (Inside a bloke is yelling his head off). Ich lese immer weiter entzückt' – I read on entranced (advt.).

February 1973

Spain

Dillie Keane

HYSTERIA IN IBERIA

It was my first visit to Spain. The arctic cold was blasting down from the stars, and the frost was severe. We were heading eastwards out of Malaga, away from the Costa Del Boy, into the heart of Andalusia. It's one of the last of the hippie trails. No hotels, señoras in black, men hanging round bars and lots of mules. You almost expect Robert Mitchum to fire at you from the church bell tower.

My companion bought a small house last year in a remote village and I went with her for her first sight of the renovation. She'd met the architect in London at a party: for plastic food boxes, read orange groves. You chat, he says he's moved to Spain, you say you dream of buying there. He says, 'I just happen to sell and renovate properties in unspoilt Andalusia.' Two months later, you're on what could be your very own roof terrace, oohing over the view. You visualise ceramic plates piled high with *gambas*, barbecues sizzling with *chorizo*. Dreamily, you hand over a cheque.

It was night when we arrived. 'I hope I can remember how to find the village,' said my friend, as we left the main road. I hoped so too. I didn't fancy getting lost and hypothermia in a rented Spanish car.

After some confusion, we found the village. 'I hope I can remember how to find the house,' said my friend, as we drew up in the square. I didn't care for the litany effect she was creating. A chorus of mongrels bayed dismally as we lugged our bags and bedding through the labyrinth of irregular streets. Suddenly, there was the house, transformed from the collapsing byre she'd last seen. A vision.

Inside, it was a dream. And if you like sleeping in a wine cellar, the temperature was fine. At 1.05 a.m., after we'd inspected everything, there was a loud noise outside. Through the shutter, I saw a figure in the dark. I waved. Seconds later, the place was full of señoras wearing black and kissing us fondly on both cheeks. Upstairs they went, inspecting everything, yammering loudly, offering us blankets and feeling the tog on the duvets to check we wouldn't freeze. I've never felt so welcome anywhere.

We were at an ex-pat beano drinking musto sans gusto. 'Do you know the architect too?' said the mealy-looking man at the New Year's Eve do. 'He's the one reason why we all met and he's the one person nobody's talking to. Our balcony nearly killed our neighbour when it fell into her garden! So what's wrong with your friend's house?'

'Nothing,' I said, 'it's lovely.'

'Just wait and see,' said his smirk.

'We get on ever so well with the villagers,' said the mealy man's partner. 'We just say "Hola!", "Buenas Dias", "gracias" and "por favor". It's enough. We don't let our neighbour put her pots on our patio though, as a matter of principle.'

I was hijacked by a loud woman who'd been a sunbed too far. 'Take 12 grapes, one to be eaten on each chime of the clock! Old español custom!' I backed away. 'I'm not normally this loud!' she honked.

A tired woman in a kaftan looked depressed as she clutched her grapes. 'I'm recovering from breast cancer,' she said.

The chimney started on television. A large man who seemed to be about to give birth to a bouncing beer barrel called the bongs wrongly, so we were all left with a redundant grape at the end. My friend and I prepared to leave. 'You can't go now!' said the beer barrel. 'We've got British New Year at one on the World Service.'

'Our house costs us £67,000 to do up!' cried the noisy suntan after battering the cancer victim in an energetic rendition of 'Auld Lang Syne'. '£50,000 over the estimate! So what's wrong with yours?'

'Nothing,' we said. She sniggered.

'Come over tomorrow. Everyone knows us – the mad English. Just ask for *los ingleses locos*.'

The next day, the shower cascaded into the kitchen below. We lit the wood-burning stove in the top room and the wall cracked. We nearly lit the fire in the kitchen and were rescued from immediate incineration by the señoras, who said the fireplace was a fake. The water heater sounded terrifying, like the exorcism of a soul in torment. I could hear the ex-pats' sniggers echo round the valley.

Later, we met the Irish wife of the valley's

'Our new Spanish colleagues haven't quite got the hang of the EEC yet.'

best builder. 'You don't need an architect,' she said, after hearing our woes. 'You just need a decent builder. Mind you,' she said, 'these English expect miracles for buttons. And the Spanish think they're bonkers. They say, why do these English say "por favor" and "gracias" all the time? It drives them crazy.'

Back in the house, the old señora dropped in. Picking up a supermarket lemon, she shook it furiously, as if to say, 'Don't you insult me with your shop-bought lemons! I'll show you lemons!' Later she was back with a bagful from her own grove. I've never smelt anything like it. It was a perfume so lovely as to make you weep. And I couldn't help saying 'gracias, gracias', but not too fulsomely. And the sniggering of the ex-pats seemed to recede away down the valley.

January 1992

Basil Boothroyd

CAPRICES ESPAGNOLES

it was just like the basque separatists to blow up the Madrid telephone exchange the day I'd planned to call Señor Don Pedro on the Costa Granadina. These people don't give a damn what trouble they cause in places like Sussex.

As I said to my wife, what had we ever done to them? She said I should have called a month earlier, as soon as the cheap flight offer came up. She was right, and I hate to say it. I didn't say it. I said that owning foreign property was no joke. You have other things to worry about besides checking that it's ready to move into for a week: such as were you out of your mind to buy the place, and does Spanish voltage explode imported electric kettles.

They don't have kettles in Spain.

So it meant the international postal service, not the acme of dependability, as all know who keep getting back home before the gloating postcards they banged off on their first day away. Write and hope, was all.

The Costa Granadina is really a bit of the Costa del Sol. I think. But at the best end. It's what Don Pedro puts on his official stationery, and why not. A señor who slices a million tons off a mountain and plants a high-class development in there (what the Spaniards dismally call an *urbanización*) wants it to be clear that he isn't after the sausage, beans and fried bread trade. We feel the same, and have agreed that when we come to draft the ad for prospective clients, dawn to dusk sun, balcony commands breathtaking panorama, sparkling bay, etc., we ought to get in, '50m Torremolinos', and they can read it as good or bad according to taste.

It isn't that we feel lofty, you understand, towards sharers of our cheap flights in their erotically inscribed T-shirts. Far from it. They could be clients the next time out. Not only that. We envy their loud Spanish banter with the Iberian hostesses, in the cadences of Liverpool and Leeds. We are strangers to the Peninsular. I was once stuck in Barcelona for an afternoon during an air-traffic dispute, and learned, by trial and error, that *Caballeros* was Spanish for Gents, which gave me an air of swagger, but no great grasp of the language. This lot have been roaming the low sierras for years. When it comes to fronting up the resident in his native tongue they leave us standing at the phrase book.

What a pity, it later struck me, or *Qué lástima!* if preferred, that the phrase-book joke has passed. Or passed into disrepute. It threatened an honoured comeback when concierge Pepe, as distinct from taximan Pepe – they're peppered with Pepes round there – finally came up with the right key and threw open our door. One glance inside and my book fell open at sight-seeing. 'Why is this place in ruins? What happened?' I'd give you the Spanish if I had an upside-down question-mark to kick it off. (Anyone tell me how that works with the spoken word?)

It wasn't strictly in ruins. Curtains on the floor, a tile or two strewing the balcony, only one dining chair and no table. It wasn't, in any case, a question to put to concierge Pepe: not even in Spanish, which he was using freely to explain the dead light-switches, or perhaps the dry plumbing, or why the cooker was hanging out of the kitchen wall and contained an empty crisp-packet labelled BUM. These were matters, he indicated, in the intervals of melodious whistling, with trills, for Señor Don Pedro. We could follow this. He kept repeating 'Don Pedro', and pointing from the balcony up the dusk-dimmed mountains towards the Señor's administrative headquarters, which were closed until Monday. This was Saturday evening.

I don't mean he said they were closed until Monday. Well, he may have. We had our own premonitions, though, and deemed it better to walk up the mountain and check without delay. Not far, but steep. Say half an hour, with gasping pauses, ostensibly to admire the panoramic bay on which night had now fallen, and ponder emptily on the airline's lamb stew, of which we had been pettishly critical at the time of serving, which hadn't been recent.

The office was closed all right. It was always hard to tell, as we knew from our first and only visit, hesitantly peering through the heavily tinted windows. Where the sun-king rules, and pallid aliens cast off their garments and prostrate themselves, the subject on the spot shuns his awful face, wears wool, seeks caves. Even when open, it had a closed air. From the fine, broad counter, demurely decked with chunky empty ashtrays and a prop-up calendar with a saint for every day, sometimes two, nobody was to be seen, some sort of jut-out in design concealing any outer-office personnel. Silence. The faintest scrape of paper. Sometimes, after patience long exercised, a dazzling señorita would silently break cover, glide towards the Señor's private door.

If you were quick enough with an arrestive throat-clearing she would turn, surprised to find other people in the world, and approach with dark eyes of enquiry, many perfect teeth and no English.

'Señor Don Pedro?' one would ask. In Spanish.

Melting with regret she would shake her head.

'When?'

A radiant blank.

'Quando returno?' H'm.

Comprehension, but the shake again. Like a beautiful, intelligent horse, she would have spoken if she could, but only sketched her helplessness in the air with delicate fingers, and slipped through the door of power. It puffed to, on a snatch of her master's voice, in German, Swedish, France, English, Croat, tribal dialects of the Australian aborigines . . .

He was not, I should have explained, a Señor at all, more of a Mynheer, a small, domed Dutchman, pale from evading the ultra-violet. In his holy place everything would be happening. Muted, alchemistic. Wondrous changes wrought before his very calculator. Dollars, francs, kroner, Deutschmarks, even the captious pound sterling, magically transformed into these glittering white pads by the sea. Piccolo Pete – our pet name for Mynheer Pieter Pronk, for the time being in abeyance – had moved mountains and filled the hole with haciendas or smaller, multi-levelled in terraces of shaved Bermuda grass, neither neighbour nor prudently spaced palm tree blocking the gaze: though the hibiscus and jacaranda could have been a nuisance, but for the watchful gardening peons, bending everywhere to the earth in protective hats and cardigans.

But that was last time. Last time, back in sunny March, we penetrated the heart of the action, and parted with our five million. What's money, I always say? Not always, perhaps, but then. If you've sold your house and married into a free one, the stuff's only wandering miserably about looking for a home. It had been common kindness to fix it up. And if I have said harsh things in my time about fat cat plutocrats with Mediterranean villas, I don't retract. It's just that we're different.

Besides, it wasn't a villa that we got, in the end. One thing about dealing with the Dutch, it puts even me on my business mettle. I was firm when he offered a villa. Nine and a half million? Don't go mad. Even in pesetas.

However. Closed till Monday. We tried a last unhopeful rattle of the great glass entrance doors with scrolled dolphin handles in fool's gold. Our mail, we deduced from one thing and another, hadn't got through them.

At least it was downhill all the way back to the ruin, or *apartamento, si?* It gave us a margin of breath for comment.

'So much for Piccolo Pete.'

'Can't blame him for the Basques,' I said, as a gapped string of fairylights popped out at the beach café far below. 'What's the Spanish for sausage, beans and fried bread?'

She'd tell me one thing, she said. We should have looked in the other rooms to see if there were any beds in there.

(Continuado)

June 1982

Holte

AMONG MY SOUVENIRS

'You press this little button here – and he sings "O Sole Mio" and makes a grab for your cornetto.'

'Right, the scene is set . . . release the mosquitos, Bernard.'

Alan Coren

IN A LITTLE SPANISH TOWN

Although the ETA threat must not be minimised, it is our experience that the British holidaymaker in particular takes such things very stoically. And, of course, our hoteliers are going out of their way to reassure guests by every possible means. Most people will notice nothing out of the ordinary at all.

Spanish Tourist Authority
spokesman, on BBC

Hotel Perdicion,
Las Ruinas,
Costa Brava.
Wednesday

Dear Auntie Doreen,

Well, here we are in viva espana as we say down here, olay, olay, and the sun coming down a treat, Kevin's head is already wrinkled like pork crackling and unable to wear free hat but never mind, it will come in useful as an oven glove, not his head, the hat, thank God he had Bakofoil round his conk is all I can say, he's a sullen bugger when he's peeling, I remember last year in, I think it was Crete, the place where they have sardine dances anyway, I remember last year when flakes kept falling off his nose into the soup, there was no living with him, all them long silences, I can see him now sitting up in bed all night, glowing like that thing on the bottom of the freezer, pilot light is it?

I thought he was going to get upset on our first day, mind, when there was this big bang and our balcony blew off, he'd hung his Aertex shirt on it to dry the armpits out on account of us having to stay four hours in the airport bus due to mines being dug out of the road in front, but it wasn't as bad as it sounds, they give us free oranges and a colouring book for the kids which Kevin said would have cost he reckoned over a pound in the shops, only trouble was little Darryl drew on the woman in front with his felt-tip and there was a bit of a row, her going on about sitting down to dinner with PIS OFF ARSNEL on her back. They come and told us the mines had been put in the road due to clerical error and Kevin said typical.

Anyway, he went out on the balcony, or where the balcony would have been, and naturally said where's my bleeding leisurewear etc., but the manager come up and said he was terribly sorry, they were celebrating the forty-second anniversary of nearly the end of the Spanish Civil War and a firework had fallen off the roof, and Kevin replied quick as a flash, no wonder he's popular up Standard Telephone & Cables, Kevin replied first I've heard of celebrating anything by blowing up somebody's shirt!

Well, the manager took his point, that is what they're paid for after all, and he was back in two minutes with a brand new floral shirt, very sheek, it's sort of a yellow, I suppose you'd call it, with these cocktail glasses all over it, Kevin looks like Ryan O'Neal in it except for his head of course.

Lucky he was not wearing it for dinner that night, is all I can say! He had fortunately changed into an old white one you can drip dry over the bath because you know what foreign food is like with sauces and so forth, I remember one year we went to Italy or somewhere, anyway you have to go by coach, and they give us this big plate of spaghetti absolutely *swimming* in tomato sauce and within ten minutes Kevin had to take his No-Glu Hairpiece off, in front of everybody, because, as he went to some length to point out, they do not make them from real human hair so you have to get them dry-cleaned, and it probably cost a fortune in Italy and suppose they lost it? He got most of the meat out with his serviette, but it smelt of garlic all that

'I claim this land for the Fraud Squad and Scotland Yard.'

winter, people kept moving away up the bingo.

So he was wearing his old white shirt as a precaution, and he must be physic, because one minute he was looking at his paella and next minute it had exploded, there was bits of prawn everywhere. Naturally, he called the waiter across and said Oy, I never bloody ordered this, did I, and the head waiter came over and apologised and said there had been a mix-up in the kitchen and brought him double egg chips and beans, and Kevin said that's a bit more bloody like it. He doesn't like making a fuss, but you have to show these people who's boss, after all, it's not as if you weren't paying for it.

Darryl and Tracy and Sharon all had the fish finger special and were sick all over the lift afterwards, which was particularly embarrassing for Sharon, being fourteen and with a big bust due to being on the pill, girls are sensitive at that age, and the manager calling the doctor only made matters worse, his hands were all over her, I don't think they have the same medical ethics in Spain, if he done it at home he'd have been in the *Sun*, anyway he said whatever it was it was definitely not rat poison in the batter, any talk of rat poison was idle gossip, he would personally stake his reputation on the fact that none of it was due to rat poison. After he'd gone Kevin said typical, they probably want us to think it's rat poison to disguise the fact that it was their lousy cooking, he would ask for a refund at the earliest opportunity, he did not call haute cuisine something that ended up on the floor of a lift. Not much gets past Kevin!

They brought us breakfast in bed next morning, and I said that's nice, Kevin, and Kevin said hang about, we never asked for this, I bet there's a room service charge, and then the waiter pulled a knife out, and Kevin said what did I tell you, he only wants a bloody tip on top of it! But the waiter said no he didn't, he was a free Basque and we were his hostages, and Kevin said sod that, this holiday was costing £159 a head not to men-

tion deckchairs also six hours in Gatwick due to baggage-handlers' strike and would the waiter care to step out on the balcony and discuss it, so the waiter stepped out onto where the balcony was before the firework blew it off and he fell fifteen floors into the car park, and Kevin said next year it's Clacton, definitely.

But he cheered up on the beach. He's never been one for the beach, nothing to do he says except keep washing stuff off your feet, but there was some sort of local folk thing on like the time we were in, is Morocco the one I brought you back the clock from, where the cuckoo falls out, anyway it was sort of like that, Kevin and me and everybody else had to sit behind this barbed wire they've got, and there was people with Napoleon type hats on at one end in holes in the sand and a lot of other people in overalls at the other end, and they all had machine-guns. The manager came out with a tin hat on and a megaphone and said it was all being done for a film, and Kevin said stone me, it's bloody realistic, that bloke's head's just come off, but the kids liked it, except Darryl, who had a hole shot through his Mickey Mouse bucket and his crab got out, and Kevin said bloody kids, typical, always complaining about something, a hundred-and-fifty-nine quid, but he smacked Darryl's head and felt better.

Due to the kitchen burning down unexpected we had to have cold meat and Kevin said sometimes this bloody country amazes me, they do everything here with bloody onions except pickle them, typical. If I was Sarsons I'd open a factory here, you could clean up. He's always been full of good commercial ideas, as you know, but his view is, what's the point of making a million, they don't let you keep it, don't talk to me about bloody governments. The way Kevin sees right through things is uncanny sometimes.

Like the business with Sharon after lunch. This little Spaniard come up while we was having what they call a siesta by the Watney's stand and he shoved this note in Kevin's hand and ran off. Kevin looked at it and informed yours truly what it said: we have got your daughter, signed ETA. So I said who's ETA and Kevin informed me that he did not bloody know, but he was going to ask the manager, and when he came back he said the manager had told him it stood for English Tourist Authority and they often came and took girls off for a bit and gave them a good time, it was all part of Anglo-Spanish relations etcetera and he'd tell Kevin more about it sometime when he wasn't quite so busy, he had to go now and see about repairing the telephone wires, they had all been cut due to gulls pecking through them.

So Kevin went back to sleep, and next thing we knew there was Sharon waking us up saying could she have a hundred pesetas for a coke, she had just been raped and it made her thirsty. And I said raped? raped? what do you mean raped? and Sharon said it was something they did in Spain, it was like Charlie Matthews next door, only quicker. So Kevin gave her the money, and after she'd gone he said all I seem to do is bloody shell out, if she's in pod I'll sue that bloody pill company, I'm not spending a fortune on prams etcetera at my age. If that's what the English Tourist Authority calls entertainment, it's a bloody disgrace, she can get all that at home, why they didn't they take her on a pedalo?

July 1980

Larry

COSTA LIVING

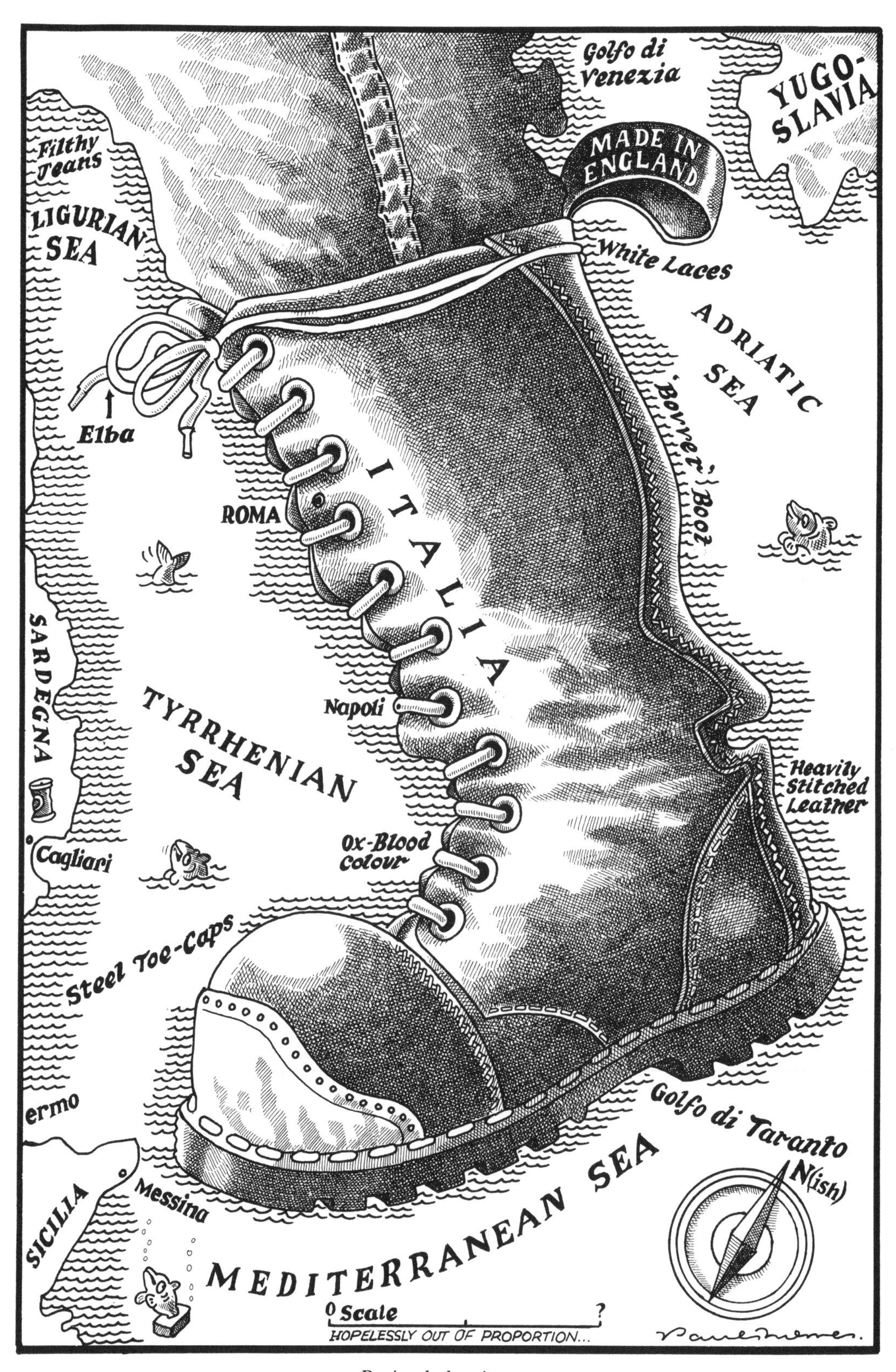

Putting the boot in . . .

Italy

William Davis

SPAGHETTI ALLA MAFIA

He looked like a worn-out Anthony Quinn – dark-skinned, unshaven, pot-bellied, sad. His eyes were bloodshot, and the hand that raised the half-filled glass of wine was shaky. His jacket was stained with the remnants of countless forgettable meals. His name was Rosario Terrasi, and he was the chief of his local Mafia. Or so the judge in Palermo had said.

'They took me from my eighteen grand-children,' Rosario wailed. 'I never even had a chance to say goodbye.'

We were on the tiny island of Filicudi, a respectable distance from the east coast of Sicily. Few people had ever heard of the place until Terrasi and fourteen other alleged Mafia chiefs arrived there some weeks ago. They were arrested in a dramatic swoop, and dispatched to Filicudi under an Italian law which permits the banishment of 'undesirables' even if they have still to be tried and found guilty. The one hundred and ninety-seven islanders promptly abandoned Filicudi in protest, and returned only when Rome promised to send the Mafiosi men elsewhere. They are now in Sardinia; I was there when the islanders waved them goodbye.

On this hot afternoon, a few days before they left, Terrasi was sitting outside the Hotel Sirena. The Sirena has seen better days, but that isn't saying much. As we talked, the other Mafiosi joined us one by one. They were bored, and we offered a break in a dreary routine.

To understand the Sicilian Mafia (whose influence is almost entirely confined to the western part of the island) one has to accept several basic facts: the long history of corruption, the widespread distrust of officialdom, the poverty of much of the population, the superstitions of ignorant peasants, the Sicilian's devoted pursuit of power through fear, and the deep-rooted belief that real strength lies in loyalty to family and friends. Sicilian pride is often absurd, and violence lies close to the surface, but the Mafia continues to exist because it is based on a way of life. Mario Puzo's best-seller, *The Godfather*, is set in America, and the America of several decades ago at that. But Don Corleone is impressively real. 'Does this man have real balls?' he asks his *Consigliori* before tackling a rival, and Puzo explains what he means: does he have the courage to risk everything, to take a chance on losing all on a matter of principle, on a matter of honour; for revenge? The *Consigliori* is made to put it another way: 'You're asking if he is a Sicilian.'

I did not find it difficult to visualise the fifteen Mafia men of Filicudi as the entire cast of *The Godfather*. Even Terrasi, despite his unimpressive appearance, fitted in. He was less smooth than his city colleagues, but one could see him oozing sentimentality one minute and being utterly callous the next. If someone got hurt, he would smile sweetly and explain that it was entirely the victim's fault: he shouldn't have got in the way. The others looked even more convincing. There was Calogero Sinatra (yes!), a sly, intelligent-looking man who looked capable of anything. And Giacomo Coppola, a thick-set, aggressive type proudly displaying an immensely hairy chest. And Antonio Buccelato – a short, powerfully built Sicilian who shouted every word and underlined his arguments with swift karate chops that made the heavy table tremble. And a quiet, white-haired man who wouldn't give his name, but told me in excellent English that he despised the communists but adored the late Winston Churchill 'because he knew what he wanted, and got it'. And a slim George Raft type who, despite the heat, was immaculately dressed. And an old man with a limp who appeared harmless until my companion, a photographer from Milan, suggested that he was lucky to be in Filicudi because the sun was shining and the sea was wonderfully blue. The old man suddenly turned violent and lashed out with his walking stick. For fully ten minutes he heaped abuse on the world, and the Italian Government in particular. He had been arrested by mistake, he hated the place, they wouldn't let him see a doctor, there was no justice, and all journalists were swine. He would make everyone pay for it as soon as he got home.

It was all very convincing. But, of course, appearances can be deceptive. I always thought that Humphrey Bogart and Jack Palance made utterly convincing villains – more so than, say, Al Capone. And the head of the police force guarding the Mafiosi confessed, with a grin, that when a foreign television crew had found it difficult to get enough Mafia men together for an interview, he had stepped into the breach. Who, after all, would know the difference?

Coppola and Buccelato invited us inside the hotel for a beer, and for the next two hours we had a heated discussion. There wasn't a policeman in sight, except for the obliging commandant, dressed in sweat shirt and an old pair of trousers. 'We can't,' he explained, 'have policemen walking up and down in the sun.' Buccelato nodded agreement. 'We and the police,' he said, 'understand each other.' He went on to claim that he'd been arrested because he was making a lot of money, and people were jealous. He was a nice chap really, a family man whose brother was a Monsignore. How could anyone possibly think that he was a Mafioso? 'There is no Mafia in Sicily,' he declared. 'They only use it as an excuse.' He was 'like a little stone thrown into a well'. He couldn't claim to be an angel, but if he and the others were really Mafiosi they wouldn't be in Filicudi. 'The real Mafia is sitting behind beautiful desks, with servants opening their doors for them,' he said. 'If you want to find the true Mafia bosses, look at the closest friends of politicians.'

Coppola (accused of being involved in an American drug ring) also claimed that they were being offered up as a sacrifice. 'If they make a show of arresting people like us from time to time,' he said, 'they can leave the real villains alone.' He was bitter about the islanders who, he said, had been 'very insulting'. They were treating them like monsters. 'Children run away from us,' he said. 'I tried to offer one some money and his mother pulled him away. One small boy even asked me if it was true that we eat children. My God, we have children of our own!'

Buccelato said it was high time that the Government formed a body which could establish what a Mafioso is. Was a man who took bribes, in return for awarding someone a profitable contract, a Mafioso or just a clever businessman? Was a fellow who got into a fight, in order to defend the family honour, a Mafioso or merely a decent, upright Sicilian? Was a corrupt politician who used his office to advance his own interests a Mafioso, or simply a man who recognised that if you don't look after yourself in this harsh world, no one else would do it for you? 'If Jesus had been born in Palermo,' he added, 'he would have been a Mafioso too.' He hit the table to emphasise his point, and ordered another round of beer. We could see that they were really quite decent fellows, couldn't we? Did we think they were capable of killing people? They loved their little children, and missed their homes. They had been unfairly treated, because Italy wasn't a civilised country. It couldn't happen anywhere else in the world.

We finished our beer (the eager hotel

We never put a foot wrong in Sardinia.
We were friendly, we were polite, we got on well with the natives....
Didn't puke at the local food, Didn't ever get drunk Didn't get into any fights...
Then Melvin started to chat up the local talent....
...Silly sod!...
McLACHLAN

'That's what I love about Italians. They breed before your very eyes.'

proprietor insisted that it was 'on the house') and said goodbye. Eight of the Mafiosi insisted on accompanying us to our boat. 'Come again tomorrow night,' they said. 'We'll get some fish and cook dinner.' The commandant nodded agreement, and they all waved until our boat was out of sight.

Around the corner, on the other side of the island, some of the local tradesmen confessed that they would miss the Mafiosi. There had been a lot of talk about Filicudi losing tourist trade, but the truth was that there had never been much of it anyway. They had put up a sign 'Tourism is our bread' for the benefit of television crews. The Mafiosi had done for Filicudi what Ingrid Bergman had done for Stromboli. Millions of people around the world had heard of Filicudi for the first time. They would come to see where the Mafia chiefs had stayed. And they would eat spaghetti alla Mafia – a new dish just invented by the best cook in Filicudi (garlic, parsley, oil and red pepper). Who knows, one might even be able to sell some Mafia souvenirs.

The Mafia chiefs, they went on, were not really such bad fellows. Some of the islanders actually regarded them as heroes – though, of course, it didn't pay to say so. Look how many policemen it had taken to bring them to Filicudi!

We tasted the spaghetti alla Mafia, and decided that the tradesmen were right. The protests had been unnecessary; Filicudi had collected a fortune's worth of publicity. We also decided that, if Mafia meant corruption, the world was full of Mafiosi. The Mafia was, in Barzini's phrase, a 'many-headed dragon' and bigger heads than Terrasi's and Buccellato's were going free. Not least, we reflected that the most effective weapon against secret organisations like the Mafia is ridicule. The Mafia's power depends on fear. Make them look big, and you enhance their prestige. Laugh at them, and people will laugh with you.

July 1971

THE PUNCH ITALIAN PHRASE BOOK

Barbirolli

mussolini: a kind of small shellfish.

cellini: several small cellos.

risorgimento: a cheap peasant dish made from the leftovers of several risorgimentos.

colombo: a dove, hence a member of the Mafia who is anti-shooting.

cosi fan tutte: a kind of Neapolitan ice cream with five different colours.

Cognoscenti: a very ancient Roman family who own most of the props used in Kenneth Clark's 'Civilisation'.

ciao

autostrade: racetrack.

Borgia: a top make of Italian racing car.

fellini: several small films.

perry como: a cheap kind of Italian wine made from pears.

basso profondo: after thirty, most Italian women develop a basso profondo.

il miglior fabbro: T. S. Eliot's favourite Italian proverb, which meant 'It's better at Faber's'.

e pericoloso sporgersi: a delicious Genoese speciality made from eggs, spinach and cuttlefish.

tedeschi

garibaldi: disparaging term for an ageing American film star.

Sotto Voce: Tony Bennett's real name.

Uomo Universale: highly successful Italian film company specialising in multilingual westerns.

andante cantabile: term applied to a slow but cheerful waiter.

pasta: basic commodity which can be shaped into different products such as stucco, fresco, baldacchino or terra cotta.

Gnocchi: the most famous of all Italian clowns.

pianissimo

Concerto Grosso: Tony Bennett's real name.

la donna e mobile: Italian garageman's phrase – literally, 'the thing that connects the engine is working loose.'

Sal Volatile: one of a number of legendary Italian art thieves (others include Ben Trovato, Al Fresco and Tony Bennett).

papa: derisive comment on the supposed celibacy of the Pope.

allegro ma non troppo: kind of Italian male who will pinch bottoms but go no further; also, basso continuo.

mario e franco: sundry items on a restaurant bill.

oggi

mazzini: small kind of tasty biscuit.

chianti: the art of guessing how much wine is left in the bottle behind the straw.

lamborghini: delicious kind of sparking-plug.

tempo giusto: weather forecast.

scampi: Italian journalists.

Tempo Rubato: Tony Bennett's real name.

con amore: service not included.

e pur si muove: 'if it moves, pinch it.'

antonioni: the state of not being able to grasp that a film has just finished.

commedia dell'arte: film festival.

October 1971

Jill Tweedie

NO! NO! A THOUSAND TIMES NO!

I number among my acquaintances a busy executive femme d'un certain age who keeps a large lilo among her summer effects. As the holiday season approaches she may be found testing it for punctures on the sitting-room floor, bouncing energetically up and down in a haunting *déjà vu* sort of way. She demands only two things of her annual fortnight off – sunshine and sex and as much of both as possible – so she always goes to Italy. Italian men, she says, do not scorn her merely because her dolly days are over, nor do they waste her highly paid time with preliminaries. The lilo is provided, she explains, to take the crunch out of sex al fresco, no point at all in sunshine or sex when you can get a package deal. Thoughtfully, she also throws in a bicycle pump for the lilo so the wind is not taken untimely from her partner's sails.

Ladies who share this full frontal approach to carnal knowledge may well find Italian men God's gift, in quantity if not necessarily in quality. Almost touchingly indiscriminate, they come on like circus barkers, flogging their often high-class wares *con brio*. I have sometimes wondered why they don't get round to crashing even the language barrier with neatly Xeroxed press releases on the merits of their very public parts in German, French and English, for distribution at likely street corners or beauty spots. I remember, once, lying day after day upon an Italian beach, being endlessly harangued by the resident beachcomber on his unique fitness for my bed. My fitness for his bed never seemed to enter his mind, I could have been an elderly midget without, I think, in any way deflecting his aim. Unhampered by any sexual Trades Descriptions, he kept on hour after hour as the sun moved his shadow full circle round his feet and I found out that 'basta' is a spurious word invented by foreigners. Inside the borders of Italy it is quite meaningless.

Of course, Italian men would hardly continue these tactics without the feedback of some occasional triumph, so I can only imagine that now and then some female, weakened by the incessant chat, pulverised by this Italian version of the water torture or, more likely, fast asleep, plummets like an unripe chestnut ripped from its branch by dedicated schoolboy proddings. Ripe chestnuts, like my lilo'd friend, are already lying about on the ground, talked down these many years ago.

Nevertheless, so constant and catholic is the onslaught that no woman with anything at all up her jumper can hope to escape its rigours. I passed one entire week in *bella Roma* without glimpsing anything more ravishing than my own feet, so intent was I on avoiding Roman eyes. My downfall came at a zebra – as I shuffled across, more crone than girl by now, I gave the faintest possible nod in the general direction of the motorist who had stopped for me. Immediately, mayhem broke out. To a crash of brakes, a squawk of gears, a salvo of hoots, the car lifted itself off the ground, twisted in the air and dumped itself down over the road beside me, all set to follow where'er, from then on, I walked. Its driver addressed my stony profile for block after block after block, evidently convinced (as are they all) that some magic combination of phrases would suddenly click into place and my knickers would fall down. I discovered, eventually, that only the word 'finocchio', hissed through clenched teeth,

THE BRITISH CHARACTER
TENDENCY TO KEEP OUT OF FOREIGN POLITICS (1938)

scattered such marauders – Freud knows why, since it means 'homosexual' and seems an odd weapon against men so patently committed to heterosexual activity.

Though, on second thoughts, Freud obviously did know why. The Italian man is hag-ridden by virility fears, condemned by a matriarchy thinly disguised as a patriarchy to rush after anything in skirts that crosses his path, whether he will or no. Dancing, once, with an Italian friend of a friend – a man doubly doomed to ceaseless activity by his sea-green eyes and alarming good looks – I felt the inevitable beginnings of the ritual grope, the steely pressure of a manly chest, the swimming look designed to pierce clean through my Horrocks cotton to the eternal Eve below. Breaking his sinewy hold I stepped back and gave him an open English gaze. Vittorio, I said, afire with all the throbbing sexuality of a hockey stick, let's talk about your car. For the first time, then, those perfect features melted into a face as relief came down like rain on the desert and he talked and talked about his car. I had released him from that exhausting never-ending challenge. I had made it clear that I didn't think he thought I thought he thought I thought he ought.

It is, of course, only the female tourist in Italy who takes Italian men even half seriously. Italian women mostly treat him as a cosmic joke, a tiresome small boy committing ruderies behind the school lavatories. In my naivety I used to feel stabs of pity for Italian wives left behind at home to scrub floors and feed babies while their menfolk tarted themselves up for the tourist trade. But then I realised that Italian wives had no need of my pity. As the doors close behind Piero and Giuseppe and Carlo, great feminine sighs of relief breeze gently out with them. At last we are alone. At last we can get on with the important things of life, rid of these males, these *uomi non respetati*. I suspect they actually egg their husbands on: go on, boy, get the tourists, get out from under my feet. Women in Italy do not have Women's Lib but what they do have, on a far greater scale than in England, is a strong Alternative Society in which man is the second-class citizen, the weaker sex, the peacock, the buffoon.

Mind you, I shouldn't like to underestimate the Italian man, either. What about that young capitano during World War I, facing the enemy in the trenches? Drawing out his sword, beckoning his men, he leads the charge over the top with a great cry of 'Avanti!' Back in the trenches, firmly back in the trenches, his men cheer and clap: 'bravo, Capitano, bravo.' Men like that can't be all bad.

October 1971

'I wish someone would tell that bloody woman to clear off!'

THE STEAM-LAUNCH IN VENICE (1882)
('SIC TRANSIT GLORIA MUNDI.')
'Andsome 'Arriet. 'OW MY! IF IT 'YN'T THAT BLOOMIN' OLD TEMPLE BAR, AS THEY DID AW'Y WITH OUT O' FLEET STREET!'
Mr Belleville (referring to Guide-book). 'NOW, IT 'YN'T! IT'S THE FYMOUS BRIDGE O' *SIGHS*, AS *BYRON* WENT AND STOOD ON; 'IM AS WROTE *OUR BOYS*, YER KNOW!'
'Andsome 'Arriet. 'WELL, I NEVER! IT 'YN'T *MUCH* OF A *SIZE*, ANY'OW!'
Mr Belleville. ''EAR! 'EAR! FUSTRYTE!'

Bill Tidy

WILL THE ITALIANS CIVILISE THE ENGLISH?

Many years ago, Soho, a famous eating district of Naples, was secretly brought to England, stone by stone, in the pockets of emigrants.

Italians enjoy eating. It is illegal to eat in Italy in groups of less than twenty. Italians noticed that English visitors ate secretly and soundlessly in secluded corners.

Missionaries were sent to England disguised as waiters. Many gave up promising opera careers to teach the English about eating.

Normal Saxon reaction against foreign interference was typified by tinned spaghetti. This is a popular Mafia torture. The Mafia is a restaurant gone wrong.

Many problems remain to be solved. The Italian hair council hopes to do something about bald English football referees . . .

. . . the incredible practice of sending English children to bed before 11 o'clock . . .

. . . and gloomy English weddings in co-operative rooms . . .

. . . but in time Latin ingenuity will overcome. The one disquieting note is that when our Italian advisors return to the mother country, they all seem to remark on what a peculiar crowd the Italians are.

'My God! It's the Belgian Inquisition!'

Belgium, Switzerland and Holland

À Beckett

AN IDYLLIC ISLAND

When we came to Amsterdam, we determined, PASHLEY, SHIRTLIFF and I, that we would take the earliest opportunity of seeing Marken. Wonderful place, by all accounts. Little island, only two miles from mainland, full of absolutely unsophisticated inhabitants. Most of them have never left Marken – no idea of the world beyond it! Everybody contented and equal; costumes quaint; manners simple and dignified. Sort of Arcadia, with dash of Utopia.

And here we are – actually at Marken, just landed by sailing boat from Monnickendam.

All is peaceful and picturesque. Scattered groups of little black cottages with scarlet roofs, on mounds. Fishermen strolling about in baggy black knickerbockers, woollen stockings, and wooden shoes.

Women and girls all dressed alike, in crimson bodice and embroidered skirt; little cap with one long brown curl dangling coquettishly in front of each ear. Small children – miniature replicas of their elders – wander lovingly, hand in hand. A few urchins dart off at our approach, like startled fawns, and disappear amongst the cottages. Otherwise, our arrival attracts no attention.

The women go on with their outdoor work, cleaning their brilliant brass and copper, washing and hanging out their bright-hued cotton and linen garments, with no more than an occasional shy side-glance at us from under their tow-coloured fringes. 'Perfectly unconscious,' as SHIRTLIFF observes, enthusi-

astically, 'of how unique and picturesque and idyllic they are!'

All the more wonderful, because excursion steamers run every day during the season from Amsterdam.

We walk up and down rough steps and along narrow, winding alleys. SHIRTLIFF says he 'feels such a bounder, going about staring at everything as if he was at Earl's Court'. Thinks the Markeners must hate being treated like a show. *We* shouldn't like it ourselves!

That may be, but, as PASHLEY retorts, it's the Markeners' own fault. They shouldn't be so beastly picturesque.

Fine buxom girl approaches, carrying pail. On closer view, not precisely a girl – in fact, a matron of mature years. These long, brown side-curls deceptive at a distance, impression, as she passes, of a kind of Dutch 'Little Toddlekins'; view of broad back and extensive tract of fat, bare neck under small cap. She turns round and intimates by expressive pantomime that her cottage is close by, and if we would care to inspect the interior, we are heartily welcome. Uncommonly friendly of her. PASHLEY and I are inclined to accept, but SHIRTLIFF dubious – we may have misunderstood her. We really can't go crowding in like a parcel of trippers!

Little Toddlekins, however, quite keen about it; sees us hesitate, puts down pail and beckons us on round corner with crooked forefinger, like an elderly Siren. How different this simple, hearty hospitality from the sort of reception foreigners would get from an English fishwife! We can't refuse, or we shall hurt her feelings. 'But whatever we do,' urges SHIRTLIFF, 'we mustn't dream of offering her money. She'd be most tremendously insulted.'

Of course, we quite understand *that*. It would be simply an outrage. We uncover, and enter, apologetically. Inside, an elderly fisherman is sitting by the hearth mending a net; a girl is leaning in graceful, negligent attitude against table by window. Neither of them takes the slightest notice of us, which is embarrassing. Afraid we really *are* intruding. However, our hostess – good old soul – has a natural tact and kindliness that soon put us at our ease. Shows us everything. Curtained recesses in wall, where they go to bed. 'Very curious – so comfortable!' Delft plates and painted shelves and cupboards. 'Most decorative!' Caps and bodices worn by females of the family. 'Charming; such artistic colour!' School copybooks with children's exercises. 'Capital; so neatly written!' What is she trying to make us understand? Oh, in winter, the sea comes in above the level of the wainscot. 'Really? How very convenient!' We don't mean this, but we are so anxious to please and be pleased, that our enthusiasm is degenerating into drivel. Girl by the window contemplates us with growing contempt; and no wonder. High time we went.

Little Toddlekins at the end of her tether; looks at us as if to imply that she has done *her* part. Next move must come from us. PASHLEY consults us in an undertone. 'Perhaps, after all, she *does* expect, eh? What do *we* think? Would half a gulden – What?'

Personally, I think it *might*, but SHIRTLIFF won't hear of it. 'Certainly not. On no account! At all events, *he*'ll be no party to it. He will simply thank her, shake hands, and walk out.' Which he does. I do the same. He may be right, and anyhow, if one of us is to run the risk of offending this matron's delicacy by the offer of a gratuity, PASHLEY will do it better than I. PASHLEY overtakes us presently, looking distinctly uncomfortable. 'Did he tip her?' 'Yes, he *tipped* her.' 'And she flung it after you!' cries SHIRTLIFF, in triumph. 'I knew she would! *Now* I hope you're satisfied!'

'If I am, it's more than *she* was,' says PASHLEY. 'She stuck to it all right, but she let me see it was nothing like what she'd expected for the three of us.'

SHIRTLIFF silent but unconvinced. However, as we go on, we see a beckoning forefinger at almost every door and window. Every Markener anxious that we should walk into his little parlour – and pay for the privilege. All of them, as PASHLEY disgustedly observes, 'On the make'; got some treasured heirloom that has been in the family without intermission for six months, and that they would be willing to part with, if pressed, for a consideration. We don't press them; in fact, we are obliged at last to decline their artless invitations – to their unconcealed disgust. Nice people, very, but can't afford to know too many of them.

'At least the *children* are unspoilt,' says SHIRTLIFF, as we come upon a couple of chubby infants, walking solemnly hand in hand as usual. He protests, when PASHLEY insists on presenting them with a cent, or one fifth of an English penny, apiece. 'Why demoralise them, why instil the love of money into their innocent minds?' SHIRTLIFF wants to know.

He is delighted when they exhibit no sort of emotion on being thus enriched. It shows, he says, that, as yet, they have no conception what money means.

The pair have toddled off towards a gathering of older children, and PASHLEY, who has brought a Kodak, wonders if he can induce them to stay as they are while he takes a snapshot. SHIRTLIFF protests again. Only spoil them, make them conceited and self-conscious, he maintains.

But the children have seen the Kodak, and are eager to be taken. One of them produces a baby from neighbouring cottage, and they arrange themselves instinctively in effective group by a fence.

PASHLEY delighted. 'Awfully intelligent little beggars!' he says. 'They seem to know exactly what I want.'

They also know exactly what *they* want, for the moment they hear the camera click, they make a rush at us, sternly demanding five cents a head for their services.

SHIRTLIFF very severe with them; not one copper shall they have from *him*, not a matter of pence, but principle, and they had better go away at once. They don't; they hustle him, and some of the taller girls nudge him viciously in the ribs with sharp elbows, as a hint that 'an immediate settlement is requested'. PASHLEY and I do the best we can, but we soon come to the end of our Dutch coins. However, no doubt English pennies will – Not a bit of it! Even the chubby infants don't consider them legal tender here, and reject them with open scorn.

Fancy we have compromised all claims at last. No; Marken infantry still harassing our rear. What *more* do they want? It appears that we have not paid the baby, which is an important extra on these occasions, and which they carry after us in state as an unsatisfied creditor and a powerful appeal to our consciences. Adult Markeners come out, and seem to be exchanging remarks (with especial reference to SHIRTLIFF, who is regarded as the chief culprit) on the meanness that is capable of bilking an innocent baby.

'What I like about Marken,' says PASHLEY, when we are safely on board our sailing boat, to which we have effected a rather ignominious retreat, 'what I like about Marken is the beautiful simplicity and unworldliness of the natives. Didn't that strike *you*, SHIRTLIFF?'

We gather from SHIRTLIFF'S reply that he failed to observe these characteristics.

August 1898

Eastern Europe

'Do you take Czechs?'

'It'll take time before they're sophisticated enough to field Monster Raving Loony candidates . . .'

AT HOME
CENTRAL EUROPE (1938)